The Second Afghan War 1878 – 1880

CASUALTY ROLL

Compiled by
Anthony Farrington

1,000 copies of this book
have been printed and bound in this style
of which this is number:

Published by

The London Stamp Exchange Ltd. EST 1890

5 Buckingham Street, Strand, London WC2N 6BS
Telephone 01-839 4684
The Military Book & Medal Specialist

ISBN 0 948130 70 9

P R E F A C E

In placing yet another casualty roll before the medal world I am all too conscious that there must be some omissions, for which I can only apologise in advance. However, I hope that I have at least achieved my primary aim of producing a properly referenced compilation.

Sources are indicated throughout, either at the head of each regiment etc or after each individual, and are noted according to my numbering of the despatches, by Proceedings number or by other conventions (see the SOURCES section for details). Casualties who received gallantry awards or who are mentioned in the citations for other men's awards are cross-referenced to the GALLANTRY AWARDS section.

The main despatches for the six actions which earned clasps, plus the defeat at Maiwand and the expensive Deh Khojah sortie from Kandahar, are reproduced in a slightly edited form.

Whenever the precise details of a casualty are given they are included here in full. I have also listed all the Indian officers and men I could trace, for two reasons: firstly, from a conviction that it would have been invidious to omit them; secondly, in the belief that the information now made available will stimulate collecting interest in the often neglected 'medals to natives'. A glance at the Indian Order of Merit citations alone will reveal how rewarding the Indian Army can be.

I have, however, omitted Indian followers although they appear in the returns for some actions - after Maiwand, for instance, nearly 600 followers were reported as killed or missing, compared to 900-odd regulars killed or wounded. Regrettably, it also proved impossible to list comprehensively the indirect casualties of the war, from cholera, typhoid, heat-stroke, pneumonia or sheer exhaustion, and my initial attempts had to be abandoned.

A J F
March 1986

CONTENTS

ABBREVIATIONS

actg	acting
attchd	attached
Bgde	Brigade
Bmdr	Bombardier
Bty	Battery
Cav	Cavalry
cmdg	commanding
Cmdt	Commandant
Col-Sgt	Colour-Sergeant
Corp	Corporal
Cpt	Captain
D	Despatch
d	dead/died
dang	dangerously
dow	died of wounds
Drm	Drummer
Dvr	Driver
FF	Field Force
Fus	Fusiliers
GGO	Government of India General Order
Gnr	Gunner
gs	gunshot
Hldrs	Highlanders
Inf	Infantry
IOM	Indian Order of Merit
k	killed
Lce	Lance
Lcrs	Lancers
LG	London Gazette
Lt	Lieutenant
miss	missing
mort	mortally

MR	Medal Roll
Mtn	Mountain
NI	Native Infantry
offic	officiating
PFF	Punjab Frontier Force
Pte	Private
QM	Quarter Master
Regt	Regiment
sev	severely
Sgt	Sergeant
Sgt-Maj	Sergeant-Major
sl	slightly
S&M	Sappers & Miners
Tmptr	Trumpeter
2-i-c	second-in-command
w	wounded

SOURCES

DESPATCHES

Published in Government of India General Orders and the London Gazette

21-22 Nov 1878 Ali Musjid

1 Lt-Gen Sir S J Browne 29 Nov 1878
GGO 10a/18 Dec 1878
LG 28 Jan 1879 pp.409-11

2 Lt-Gen Sir S J Browne 17 Mar 1879
GGO 610/11 Jul 1879 pp.126-27
LG 7 Nov 1879 pp.6286-87

2 Dec 1878 Peiwar Kotal

3 Maj-Gen F S Roberts 5 Dec 1878
GGO 1226/31 Dec 1878
LG 4 Feb 1879 pp.525-30

4 Maj-Gen F S Roberts 24 Jan 1879
GGOs 210/8 Mar 1879 & 610/11 Jul 1879 pp.127-28
LG 13 May 1879 pp.3310-11 & 7 Nov 1879 pp.6287-88

6-10 Dec 1878 reconnaissance to Shutar Gardan pass

5 Maj-Gen F S Roberts 16 Dec 1878
LG 21 Feb 1879 pp.864-65

12-14 Dec 1878 march from Ali Kheyl to Fort Kuram (Sapari pass)

6 Maj-Gen F S Roberts 18 Dec 1878
GGO 610/11 Jul 1879 pp.128-30
LG 21 Feb 1879 pp.865-66

19-23 Dec 1878 first expedition to Bazar Valley

7 Lt-Gen F F Maude 26 Dec 1878
GGO 610/11 Jul 1879 pp.130-34

4 Jan 1879 Saif-u-Din

8 Brig-Gen C H Palliser 5 Jan 1879
GGO 610/11 Jul 1879 pp.135-37
LG 7 Nov 1879 pp.6292-95

7 Jan 1879 Matun, and occupation of Khost District

9 Brig-Gen H Gough 9 Jan 1879
LG 21 Mar 1879 pp.2305-07

10 Maj-Gen F S Roberts 10 Jan 1879
GGO 610/11 Jul 1879 pp.137-40
LG 21 Mar 1879 pp.2303-05 & 7 Nov 1879 pp.6295-97

11 Jan 1879 Fort Shergash

11 Brig-Gen F H Jenkins 13 Jan 1879
LG 28 Mar 1879 p.2473

24 Jan-4 Feb 1879 second expedition to Bazar Valley

12 Lt-Gen F F Maude 13 Feb 1879
GGO 610/11 Jul 1879 pp.140-44
LG 7 Nov 1879 pp.6297-301

20 Feb 1879

13 Secretary of State for India's congratulations for Ali Musjid and the Peiwar Kotal
GGO 2a/28 Mar 1879

26 Feb 1879 Kushki-Nakhud

14 Lt-Col J H P Malcolmson 1 Mar 1879
GGO 610/11 Jul 1879 pp.144-46
LG 7 Nov 1879 pp.6301-03

24 Mar 1879 Deh Sarak

15 Brig-Gen J A Tytler 30 Mar 1879
GGO 610/11 Jul 1879 pp.146-48
LG 7 Nov 1879 pp.6303-05

24 Mar 1879 Baghao

16 Maj F J Keen 25 Mar 1879
GGO 610/11 Jul 1879 pp.149-51
LG 7 Nov 1879 pp.6305-07

27 Mar 1879 Saiad-Bud

17 Maj F T Humfrey 28 Mar 1879
GGO 610/11 Jul 1879 pp.151-52
LG 7 Nov 1879 pp.6307-08

2 Apr 1879 Fatehabad

18 Brig-Gen C J S Gough 2 Apr 1879
GGO 610/11 Jul 1879 pp.152-54
LG 7 Nov 1879 pp.6308-10

4 Aug 1879

19 Resolutions of both Houses of Parliament, thanking the commanders in Afghanistan
GGO 1085/31 Oct 1879

10 Sep-13 Oct 1879 operations from Thal to the entry into Kabul

20 Maj-Gen F S Roberts 15 Oct 1879
GGO 1136/21 Nov 1879 pp.1-7
LG 16 Jan 1880 pp.209-13

2 Oct 1879 Shutar Gardan

21 Lt-Col G M Money 3 Oct 1879
GGO 1136/21 Nov 1879 pp.7-9
LG 16 Jan 1880 p.213

2-13 Oct 1879 from Shutar Gardan to the entry into Kabul (Charasiah)

22 Maj-Gen F S Roberts 20 Oct 1879
GGO 1136/21 Nov 1879 pp.10-18
LG 16 Jan 1880 pp.213-18

6 Oct 1879 Charasiah

23 Brig-Gen T D Baker 10 Oct 1879
LG 16 Jan 1880 pp.221-24

24 Casualty list
GGO 1136/21 Nov 1879 pp.18-21
LG 16 Jan 1880 pp.219-20

7 Oct 1879 hills around Charasiah

25 Brig-Gen H T Macpherson 10 Oct 1879
LG 16 Jan 1880 pp.226-27

8 Oct 1879 Asmai heights

26 Brig-Gen T D Baker 11 Oct 1879
LG 16 Jan 1880 pp.224-25

8 Oct 1879 Deh-i-Mozund

27 Brig-Gen W G Dunham Massy 11 Oct 1879
LG 16 Jan 1880 pp.225-26

12 Oct 1879

28 Proclamation at Kabul by Maj-Gen Sir F S Roberts
GGO 1136/21 Nov 1879 pp.21-22
LG 16 Jan 1880 p.227

13 & 18-19 Oct 1879 entry into Kabul and disturbances at Shutar Gardan

29 Maj-Gen Sir F S Roberts 30 Oct 1879
GGO 1136/21 Nov 1879 pp.24-29

30 Lt-Col G N Money 19 & 20 Oct 1879
GGO 1136/21 Nov 1879 pp.29-33

Oct 1879

31 Officers mentioned by Maj-Gen Roberts 22 & 30 Oct 1879
GGO 1136/21 Nov 1879 pp.23-24

1878-1879

32 General return of casualties in Afghanistan Nov 1878-Jul 1879
GGO 136/5 Mar 1880

8-24 Dec 1879 operations around Kabul

33 Lt-Gen Sir F S Roberts 23 Jan 1880
GGO 137/5 Mar 1880
LG 27 Jan 1880 p.391 & 4 May 1880 pp.2836-58

17-24 Dec 1879 advance of Gough's Brigade from Gandamak to Kabul

34 Lt-Gen Sir F S Roberts 2 Feb 1880
GGO 177/19 Mar 1880 pp.98-104
LG 4 May 1880 pp.2858-62

35 Brig-Gen C J S Gough 26 Dec 1879
GGO 177/19 Mar 1880 pp.105-07
LG 4 May 1880 pp.2862-64

19 Apr 1880 Ahmed Khel

36 Lt-Gen Sir D M Stewart 5 May 1880
GGO 326/4 Jun 1880 pp.145-50
LG 30 Jul 1880 pp.4197-202

23 Apr 1880 Arzu

37 Lt-Gen Sir D M Stewart 11 May 1880
GGO 326/4 Jun 1880 pp.150-51
LG 30 Jul 1880 p.4202

24-25 Apr 1880 Shekabad

38 Maj-Gen J Ross 26 & 27 Apr 1880
GGO 327/4 Jun 1880
LG 30 Jul 1880 pp.4202-04

25 Apr 1880 Charasiah

39 Col F H Jenkins 28 Apr 1880; Brig-Gen H T Macpherson 30 Apr 1880; Lt-Gen Sir F S Roberts 11 May 1880
GGO 328/4 Jun 1880
LG 30 Jul 1880 pp.4204-09

18-23 May 1880 Mazina Valley

40 Brig-Gen W A Gib 27 May 1880
GGO 479/17 Aug 1880

19 May 1880 Besud

41 Brig-Gen J Doran 27 May 1880
GGO 383/2 Jul 1880

1 Jul 1880 Patkao Shana

42 Brig-Gen C H Palliser 2 Jul 1880; Maj-Gen J Hills 12 Jul 1880
GGOs 493/27 Aug 1880 & 670/10 Dec 1880
LG 22 Oct 1880 pp.5377-82

14 Jul 1880 Girishk

43 Lt-Gen J M Primrose 23 Jul 1880
GGO 480/17 Aug 1880
LG 15 Oct 1880 pp.5283-85

27 Jul 1880 Maiwand

44 Brig-Gen T Nuttall 3 Aug 1880; Brig-Gen G R S Burrows 30 Aug 1880; Lt-Gen J M Primrose 6 Sep 1880; Maj-Gen G R Greaves 25 Sep 1880
GGO 551/27 Sep 1880
LG 19 Nov 1880 pp.5799-824

45 Lt-Gen J M Primrose 1 Oct 1880
GGO 598/27 Oct 1880
LG 31 Dec 1880 pp.7003-04

28 Jul 1880 march to meet Maiwand stragglers (Konekar)

46 Brig-Gen H F Brooke 8 Aug 1880
GGO 589/22 Oct 1880
LG 3 Dec 1880 pp.6545-47

29-30 Jul 1880 retirement to Chaman

47 Maj W Jacob 31 Jul 1880
GGO 514/10 Sep 1880

Aug 1880 siege of Kandahar and Deh Khojah sortie

48 Lt-Gen J M Primrose 26 & 30 Aug 1880
GGO 566/8 Oct 1880
LG 3 Dec 1880 pp.6519-30

16 Aug 1880 defence of Kach

49 Col T W W Pierce 16 Aug 1880
GGO 590/22 Oct 1880

Aug-Sep 1880 march of Bombay Division to relief of Kandahar

50 Maj-Gen R Phayre 16 Oct 1880
GGO 693/24 Dec 1880
LG 25 Jan 1881 pp.336-39

Aug-Sep 1880 Kabul-Kandahar march and battle of Kandahar

51 Lt-Gen Sir F S Roberts 26 Sep 1880
GGOs 582/12 Oct 1880 & 600/27 Oct 1880
LG 3 Dec 1880 pp.6530-45 & 31 Dec 1880 p.7005

52 Lt-Gen J M Primrose 27 Sep 1880
GGO 599/27 Oct 1880
LG 31 Dec 1880 pp.7004-05

6 Jan 1881

53 Secretary of State for India's thanks for the Kabul-Kandahar march
GGO 80/11 Feb 1881

17 Feb 1881

54 Secretary of State for India's thanks for the Bombay Division's march
GGO 183/25 Mar 1881

5 May 1881

55 Secretary of State for India's acknowledgment of the Viceroy's minute on the services of officers
GGO 315/10 Jun 1881

5 May 1881

56 Thanks of both Houses of Parliament to the commanders in Afghanistan
GGOs 399-400/15 Jul 1881

19 May 1881

57 Secretary of State for India's acknowledgment of the Viceroy's minute on the services of Lt-Gen Sir D M Stewart and Lt-Gen Sir F S Roberts
GGO 352/24 Jun 1881

21 Jul 1881

58 Secretary of State for India's thanks to Lt-Gen Sir D M Stewart for the evacuation of Afghanistan
GGO 479/26 Aug 1881

24 Nov 1881

59 Additional mentions for services in Afghanistan
GGO 709/23 Dec 1881

GOVERNMENT OF INDIA MILITARY PROCEEDINGS

The proceedings consist of matters considered by the Commander-in-Chief in India and the members of his Military Committee. Those relating to the Second Afghan War were placed in a separate sequence, numbered 1-21227, and the more important (called Part A) were printed in full (but not published) for circulation within the government in India and for the information of the India Office in London. Routine papers (Part B) were summarised in printed appendices. About 85% of the papers produced by the war were classified as 'A' and the length of particular items varied from a few paragraphs to fifty or more pages. The proceedings include a mass of information which does not appear in the published despatches, for instance: details of single casualties and minor actions; maps, plans and survey reports; field diaries; and the organisational measures which lay behind actually getting troops into Afghanistan and supplying them once they were there.

India Office Records

P/1186	Nov-Dec 1878	Nos 1-584
P/1370	Jan-Apr 1879	Nos 585-3007
P/1371	May-Aug 1879	Nos 3008-5074
P/1372	Sep-Dec 1879	Nos 5075-6654
P/1534	Jan-Mar 1880	Nos 6655-8002

P/1535	Apr-May 1880	
P/1536	Jun-Jul 1880	Nos 9849-11179
P/1537	Aug-Sep 1880	Nos 11180-12813
P/1538	Oct-Dec 1880	Nos 12814-15023
P/1721	Jan 1881	Nos 15024-15749
P/1722	Feb 1881	Nos 15750-17045
P/1723	Mar-May 1881	Nos 17046-18452
P/1724	Jun-Sep 1881	Nos 18453-20290
P/1725	Oct-Dec 1881	Nos 20291-21227

MEDAL ROLLS

The India Office Records holds the rolls from which the medals were actually issued; as a result, they contain frequent annotations for late issues, forfeits and replacements. Detail varies according to the standards of each regiment's orderly room, but they have provided useful cross-checks for first names and regimental numbers. Unfortunately, there are no rolls in the UK for Indian officers and soldiers, merely a record of how many medals and clasps were despatched for issue in India.

The British Army rolls are duplicated (but without all the later annotation) in Public Record Office: **WO 100/51-54.**

India Office Records

L/MIL/5/110
British Cavalry: 6th Dragoons, 8th Hussars, 9th Lancers, 10th Hussars, 15th Hussars
detachments or singles - 11th Hussars, 12th Lancers, 13th Hussars, 14th Hussars

L/MIL/5/111
Royal Engineers

L/MIL/5/112
Royal Horse Artillery: D/A, F/A, I/A, A/B, D/B, E/B, H/C, I/C
Royal Artillery: H/1, I/1, C/2, D/2, F/2, C/3, E/3, G/3, A/4, C/4, E/4, G/4, L/5, 1/8, 5/8, 6/8, 13/8, 11/9,

13/9, 14/9, 15/9, 5/11, 6/11, 10/11, 11/11
1st-4th Mtn Btys, Ordnance Dept, Staff officers
detachments or singles - RHA: G/A, B/B, C/B
RA: J/2, A/3, B/3, D/4, K/5, 16/8, 8/11, 9/11

L/MIL/5/113
British Infantry: 1/5th, 2/7th, 2/8th, 2/9th, 2/11th, 1/12th, 2/14th
detachments or singles - 2/1st, 2nd, 3rd, 1/6th, 2/6th, 1/14th

L/MIL/5/114
British Infantry: 2/15th, 1/17th, 1/18th, 1/25th, 51st, 59th, 2/60th, 63rd
detachments or singles - 2/16th, 2/17th, 21st, 22nd, 26th, 29th, 33rd, 39th, 40th, 43rd, 54th, 4/60th, 61st, 62nd, 65th

L/MIL/5/115
British Infantry: 66th, 67th, 70th, 72nd, 78th, 81st, 85th, 92nd, 4th Btn Rifle Bgde
detachments or singles - 68th, 73rd, 83rd, 88th, 90th, 100th

L/MIL/5/116
Staff
British Army: Army Medical Dept, Army Veterinary Dept, Transport, Signallers

L/MIL/5/117-120
Bengal and Bombay Armies: Europeans only, each volume indexed

L/MIL/5/121
Madras Army: Europeans only, index

L/MIL/5/122
British Army: Kabul-Kandahar Star

L/MIL/5/123
Bengal Army: Kabul-Kandahar Star

L/MIL/5/124
Miscellaneous papers on the issue of the medal and the star

MUSTER ROLLS

The British Army regimental muster rolls and pay lists in the Public Record Office (**WO 16**) are of only limited use. The class, which comprises a continuation of **WO 12**, begins in 1877 and gives far less detail than in earlier years. First names rarely appear in full and the sections for casualties are not normally specific enough for this present compilation.

There are no muster rolls in the UK for Indian units.

PUBLISHED WORKS

The literature of the war is largely official and may not be generally available outside the major libraries. The most useful is Shadbolt's second volume, which gives biographies (and photographs) of all officer casualties by death. There are few modern works.

Ashe, Waller ed
Personal records of the Kandahar campaign by officers engaged therein (London, 1881)

Baring, Thomas George [Ist Earl of Northbrook]
A brief account of recent transactions in Afghanistan (no imprint, 1880)

Cardew, Francis Gordon
The Second Afghan War (Calcutta: Govt of India, 1897)

Chapman, Edward Francis
Two years under Field-Marshal Sir Donald Stewart in Afghanistan 1878-80 (Edinburgh, 1902)

Colquhoun, James Andrew Sutherland
With the Kurram Field Force 1878-79 (London, 1881)

Cooper, H.
What the Fusiliers did: an account of the part taken by the 1st Battalion 5th Northumberland Fusiliers in the Afghan campaigns of 1878-79 and 1879-80 (Lahore, 1880)

Diver, Katherine Helen Maud
Kabul to Kandahar (London, 1935)

Duke, Joshua
Recollections of the Kabul campaign 1879 and 1880 (London, 1883)

Eastwick, William Joseph
Lord Lytton and the Afghan War (London, 1879)

Ellis, William Verner
Kandahar Field Force, Afghanistan, 1878-80 (Bristol, 1912)

Gillham-Thomsett, Richard
Kohat, Kuram and Khost; or experiences and adventures in the late Afghan war (London, 1884)

Hanna, Henry Bathurst
The Second Afghan War 1878-80; its causes, its conduct and its consequences (London, 1889) 3 vols

Heathcote, Thomas Anthony
The Afghan Wars 1839-1919 (London, 1980)

Hensman, Howard
The Afghan War of 1879-80 (London, 1881)

Le Messurier, Augustus
Kandahar in 1879 (London, 1880)

Male, Arthur H.
Through two campaigns (London, 1914)

Maxwell, Leigh
My God, Maiwand!: operations of the South Afghanistan Field Force 1878-80 (London, 1979)

Milner, Ferdinand Henry & Savile, Albany Robert
The Anglo-Afghan War of 1878 (London: War Office, 1878-79)

Milner, Ferdinand Henry
The Anglo-Afghan War of 1879-80 (London: War Office, 1881)

Mitford, Reginald Colville William Reveley
To Caubul with the Cavalry Brigade: a narrative of personal experiences with the Force under General Sir F.S.Roberts (London, 1881)

Parliamentary Papers - House of Commons

Session 1878/9	Vol LVI	Nos 10-11,72,100,234, C.2190-91, C.2250-51,C.2293,C.2362,C.2401-02
Session 1880	Vol LIII	Nos C.2457,C.2690
Session 1881	Vol LXX	Nos C.2776,C.2811,C.2852,C.2865,C.3090

Causes of the Afghan War: being a selection of papers laid before Parliament, with a connecting narrative and comment (London, 1879)

Robertson, Charles Gray
Kurum, Kabul and Kandahar: being a brief record of impressions in three campaigns under General Roberts (Edinburgh, 1881)

Shadbolt, Sydney Henry
The Afghan campaigns of 1878-80 (London, 1882) 2 vols

Swynnerton, Charles
The Afghan War: Gough's action at Futtehabad (London, 1880=

Wilson, Thomas Fourness
Afghan campaign 1879-80 (London; India Office, 1881)

SELECTED DESPATCHES

ALI MUSJID 21-22 November 1878

From Lt-Gen Sir S J Browne, KCSI, Commanding 1st Division Peshawar Valley Field Force, dated Dhaka, 29 November 1878

On the receipt at Jamrúd of orders to advance the force under my command, it moved in the following order:—

The 2nd Brigade under Brigadier-General Tytler, C. B., V.C., consisting of Her Majesty's 17th Foot, the Guide Infantry and the 1st Sikhs, at 6 P. M. on the 20th instant; followed at 2-30 A. M. of the 21st by the 1st Brigade, under Brigadier-General MacPherson, C. B., V. C., consisting of the 4th Battalion Rifle Brigade, the 4th Goorkhas, the 20th Regiment Punjab Infantry, and No. 4 (Hazára) Mountain Battery. Both these brigades took the same route, *viâ* Gudur Lashora to Sapri, the 1st Brigade being ordered to detach a party of 400 men under Major Gordon from Torbai for the Rotas ridge.

Brigadier-General Tytler was directed to diverge from Sapri to Kata Koosta, a spot two miles behind Ali Masjid, where the defile begins to open, and which is here about 100 yards wide.

The 1st Brigade was ordered from Sapri to make for the continuation of the Rotas ridge and crown the heights above, and a little in rear of, Ali Masjid.

The route as far as Sapri, which lies through a glen separating the Rotas Mountain from the main Tatara Range, had been reconnoitred previously by the Corps of Guides; but beyond that I was altogether guided by native information. It was a trying and most fatiguing march to Sapri, and the ground beyond proved to be more difficult still.

In my direct attack on Ali Masjid by the ordinary pass road I relied on the co-operation of the 1st Brigade by about 1 P. M. of the 21st, but as it turned out it could not reach its destination by the appointed time, owing to the very difficult nature of the hill it had to traverse. The Guides and 1st Sikh Infantry, however, occupied Kata Koosta about 4 o'clock in the afternoon.

Counting on the co-operation above alluded to, I marched from Jamrúd at 7 A. M. on the 21st with the remainder of the force in the following order:—

The advanced guard under Brigadier-General Appleyard, C. B.—

250	14th Sikhs.
250	81st Foot.
2nd and 3rd Companies	Sappers and Miners.
40 Sabres	11th Bengal Lancers.
I Battery C Brigade, Royal Horse Artillery.	
No. 11 Battery 9th Brigade, Royal Artillery.	

and remainder of the 14th Sikhs, followed by the Engineer Park; and at half-a-mile distant the remainder of the 81st Foot, the 27th Regiment Punjab Infantry, E-3rd and 13-9th Royal Artillery. Lastly, the 4th Infantry Brigade, with the Cavalry Brigade bringing up the rear.

No baggage was to leave Jamrúd until the following day.

Three days' rations were taken by the troops.

On arrival at the commencement of the road which was made by us in the Afghán War of 1839-42, and which is known as the Mackeson Road, the Mountain Battery (11-9th Royal Artillery) with 200 Infantry diverged to the right, taking a course parallel to the column between it and the high Rotas Range.

Some little delay was occasioned owing to the bad state of the road just beyond Mackeson Bridge; and here a picket of the enemy's Cavalry was seen on the low hills in front of us. This picket gradually retired as we advanced.

At 11 A. M., the head of the advanced guard reached the Shagai Ridge; and as a large body of the enemy were now visible on the Rotas Ridge to my right, a part of the 4th Brigade was detached to occupy the intervening ridges.

The advanced guard threw out parties to its right and left, and one of 100 rifles was sent on in advance to occupy a rocky ridge some 200 yards in front, and to cover the working party employed in making passable for guns, the descent between it and the Shagai Ridge into the Khaibar stream.

We had occupied the Shagai Ridge half-an-hour or more, and had made our dispositions without opposition, when the enemy opened fire simultaneously from the fort, from a gun on a peak to the right of Ali Masjid and overlooking it, and from three other guns below the fort, but invisible to us.

The practice was excellent, shot after shot hitting the ridge; but our little force in the front was well sheltered, and only suffered slightly. The fire continued about an hour without our replying to it.

In the meantime I-C., Royal Horse Artillery, had come up and taken up a position to our right, out of the line of fire; and shortly after, I ordered up two guns from that battery on to the ridge and opened fire. The other four guns subsequently came into action; and the fire was continued till the Heavy Battery came up at 1-30 P. M., and opened fire at 2,800 yards. Our firing was good, and was kept up all day.

The fire from the 40-pounders seemed at first to cause the enemy's fire to slacken; but after a short respite it recommenced as warmly as ever.

Hoping that my detached brigades might be nearing their destination, I, at 2-30 P. M., ordered an advance. Brigadier-General Appleyard was to descend and cross the Khaibar stream at Lalla China, and, under shelter of a spur, to work round towards the line of the enemy's intrenchments to our left; our right to advance on to the ridge in front of Shagai; 11-9th Royal Artillery (Mountain Battery) to take up a position there also and open fire; and I-C., Royal Horse Artillery, with the escort of the 10th Hussars, to descend into the Khaibar stream and take up the most suitable position to aid in silencing the enemy's fire.

About 3-30 P. M. my right was in sharp conflict with the enemy's left, which occupied an inaccessible position along the face of a precipitous cliff, and on one point of which they had a gun in position. No further advance could be made on this side, beyond pushing on a small party in the right centre, which, from the nature of the ground, was well protected.

In the meantime the Heavy Battery and E-3rd Royal Artillery, taking the place of the Horse Artillery, kept up a constant fire on the enemy's position, and I.-C., Royal Horse Artillery, having descended and advanced to the bend of the stream came into action there at 1,000 yards.

As the day was closing in, I sent word to Brigadier-General Appleyard not to advance beyond an indicated ridge; but before my orderly officer could reach him to deliver the order, his skirmishers had advanced and had arrived close on the enemy's position, when a sharp fire was exchanged within a very short distance. At this point Major Birch and Lieutenant FitzGerald, of the 27th Punjab Infantry, met their death whilst gallantly leading their men. Here also Captain Maclean was wounded, and many casualties took place in the 14th Sikhs and 27th Punjab Infantry.

Darkness now stopped further operations; and Brigadier-General Appleyard withdrew his men to the ridge I had previously selected for him to hold.

In these positions we bivouacked for the night: and up to this time I had failed to receive any intelligence of the movements of my two brigades which, as has been previously indicated, had been detached to turn the enemy's flank.

During the night I decided to reinforce Brigadier-General Appleyard with the Mountain Battery and some infantry from my right, so as to attack the enemy's right defences the following morning, after the Artillery had shelled the position well for half-an-hour.

When it was daylight, I observed the Mountain Battery, which was on its way to join Brigadier-General Appleyard, crossing the stream unmolested, where, on the previous evening, I-C. Royal Horse Artillery had been under a sharp fire; and there being also no reply to the three guns which then opened on the fort, I concluded it was abandoned. Further firing was therefore stopped; an advance was ordered; and, as supposed, the fort and entrenchments were found to be abandoned. The camp was standing, and there was evidence of a hurried flight, nothing whatever having been carried away. Twenty-four guns and large quantities of ammunition, both ordnance and rifle, fell into our possession.

The prisoners, of whom a number were captured by the turning brigade, stated that the cavalry, at about 5 P. M., first attempted to escape, but were checked at Kota Koosta by the Guides and the 1st Sikhs, and that they were followed by a portion of the infantry, who laid down their arms after receiving a volley. The main body of the garrison, finding the direct line of retreat cut off, fled by the Pesh Bolak track, which lay through their right entrenchments. The flight appears to have commenced when it became dark, but the Pass Afridis, who had been watching the combat during the day from the neighbouring heights, were soon in pursuit, and robbed the enemy of all they possessed, securing a great number of rifles.

The Mir Akhor and other Sardars, it is stated, escaped by this route.

I remained during the 22nd at Ali Masjid, and opened communication with my two advanced brigades. On the 23rd I marched for Lundi Khana with I-C. Royal Horse Artillery, the 10th Hussars, the Guide Cavalry, and the 14th Sikhs, arriving there at 3-30 P. M. The Guide Cavalry, accompanied by Major Cavagnari, C. S. I., I ordered on to Dhaka, ten miles further on, and which place they reached and occupied at 6 P. M.

Brigadier-General Appleyard followed the next day with the 3rd Brigade and 11-9th Royal Artillery to Lundi Khana Kotal, where they have remained. The 1st and 2nd Brigade came on to Dhaka.

The 4th Brigade under Brigadier-General Browne, with 3rd Royal Artillery and the Heavy Battery, I left at Ali Masjid, the 11th Bengal Lancers remaining also in the vicinity, in view to keeping open my communication at the lower end of the Pass.

The above is a general report of the proceedings of the force under my command from the time of leaving Jamrúd to the occupation of Dhaka. Subsidiary reports will be submitted when I am in receipt of them from the officers commanding brigades.

I trust the result of the operations will be deemed satisfactory.

I can now only further add that the whole of the troops, officers and men, did their duty in a manner meriting the warmest approval of Government, and upheld the character of the British and Native Army of Her Majesty.

PEIWAR KOTAL 2 December 1878

From Maj-Gen F S Roberts, CB, VC, RA, Commanding the Kurum Column, dated Camp Zabardast Kila, 5 December 1878

Right Column.

Brigadier-General Thelwall, C. B.
Squadron 12th Bengal Cavalry.
2 Guns No. 1 Mountain Battery.
5th Goorkhas.
72nd Highlanders (Wing.)
2nd Punjab Infantry.
2 Guns F-A, Royal Horse Artillery, on elephants.

Left Column.

Brigadier-General Cobbe.
Squadron 12th Bengal Cavalry.
2 Guns No. 1 Mountain Battery.
2-8th Foot.
5th Punjab Infantry.
23rd Pioneers.
29th Punjab Native Infantry.
2 Guns F-A, Royal Horse Artillery, on elephants.

* No. 1 Mountain Battery.
2-8th Foot.
29th Punjab Native Infantry.
5th Punjab Infantry.
23rd Pioneers.
Subsequently reinforced by 5th Goorkhas.

IN continuation of my telegram of the 3rd instant, I have now the honor to submit, for the information of His Excellency the Commander-in-Chief and of the Government of India, a detailed account of the military operations which have led to the capture of the Peiwar Pass by the troops under my command.

2. The force detailed in the margin, marching by separate roads in two brigades, arrived at Habib-kila about 10 A. M. on the 28th instant. Here I received information that the enemy was flying in confusion up the eastern side of the Peiwar Kotal, and that, owing to the difficulties of the road, they had already abandoned twelve guns.

3. I therefore pushed a reconnaissance* in force up the south-eastern flanks of the Peiwar, which elicited the fact that, so far from the enemy having abandoned any guns, they had taken up an extremely strong position on the Pass, and that they were well provided with artillery judiciously placed. I had ordered the camp to be marked out on some dry rice fields, about 2,500 yards from the enemy's position, but as they pitched some shells into the middle of this ground, it was abandoned and the camp removed to a more secure site.

4. This reconnaissance was not accomplished without loss; and I have to regret the occurrence of the following casualties—

29th Punjab Native Infantry—One officer (Lieutenant Reid) severely wounded.
Four sepoys wounded (one severely.)

5th Punjab Infantry—Subadar-Major Aziz Khan severely wounded.
Three sepoys slightly wounded.

No. 1 Mountain Battery—One driver killed.
One mule wounded.

5th Goorkhas— One sepoy dangerously wounded.

5. By the evening of this day I had seen sufficient of the enemy's position to convince me that it could not be carried by an attack in front without incurring very heavy loss.

6. I resolved therefore to halt for a few days; first, with the view of recruiting the men's strength, which had been severely taxed by several days' continuous marching over extremely difficult roads; and secondly, to gain time to ascertain by reconnoitring whether the position could not be turned, or failing that, in what manner it could be most easily attacked in front.

7. It will be convenient for me here to give a short and necessarily imperfect description of the Peiwar Kotal position. I have issued instructions for detailed topographical reports to be prepared; but as these will necessarily take some time to complete, a written description will be better than none.

8. The enemy's position extended from the Spin Gawai Kotal, on their left, to some commanding heights about a mile south of the Peiwar Kotal. It thus had a front of about four miles facing due east, the Peiwar Kotal being about the enemy's right centre. From right to left the position ran along a lofty and rugged range of mountains, mostly covered with dense pine forests. The range was precipitous towards the eastern side, but was known to descend on the western by a succession of upland meadows towards the valley of the Hariab.

9. The position, as thus described, was crossed by only two regular roads, *viz.*, the Peiwar and Spin Gawai Kotals or *cols*. At two or three other points the range was crossed by paths, but these were too narrow and precipitous for the passage of troops.

10. An important military feature in the position was that the successive ridges or peaks, into which it was broken, dominated each other from the left to the right: that is, a force placed on the height to the south of the Spin Gawai *col* would have a command over each succeeding eminence as it advanced along the ridge towards the Peiwar Kotal.

11. The Peiwar Kotal is a narrow depression in the ridge commanded on each side by high pine-clad mountains. The approach to it from the Kurum Valley, or east, is up a steep narrow zig-zag path, entirely commanded throughout its length from the adjacent heights, and difficult to ascend by reason of the extreme roughness of the road, which was covered with large fragments of rock and boulders. Every point of the ascent was exposed to fire from both guns and rifles, securely placed behind breastworks constructed of pine logs and stones. At the top of the pass was a narrow plateau, which was again commanded from the thickly wooded heights, which rose to an elevation of 500 feet on each side of the valley. On the western side the road passed by a gentle descent through a narrow valley with pine-clad sides for about one and a half miles, when it reached the open valley of the Hariab near the hamlet of Zabardast Kila.

12. The Spin Gawai Kotal, which formed the extreme left of the enemy's line, is a position far less capable of defence, and of an altogether different character from that of the Peiwar. The approach to it is through a comparatively open valley; the ascent is not steep except when close to the summit; and the valley is of sufficient width to admit of the movement of troops. The position does not, in short, possess the natural military advantages which are so remarkable at the Peiwar Kotal.

13. On the 29th November, the approaches to the Peiwar Kotal from both the north and south sides were thoroughly reconnoitred, and plans were drawn up for a direct assault on the enemy's position. A reconnaissance was also pushed through the hills to obtain a view of the Spin Gawai Kotal, and of the upper part of the road leading thereto.

14. The result of these reconnaissances convinced me that a front attack, though it might be successful, would certainly entail great loss, and I formed a design for a secret night march on the Spin Gawai, by which I hoped the enemy's position in our front might be turned.

15. On the 30th I ordered the three guns of G-3rd, Royal Artillery, and two guns of F-A, Royal Horse Artillery, to move up to my camp from the Kurum fort. The 12th Bengal Cavalry were also ordered up from Habib-kila. On this day reconnoitring parties were again employed at the Peiwar Kotal, and every means adopted to induce the enemy to believe that we intended to attack him in front,

and to withdraw his attention from his left. A secret reconnaissance, unaccompanied by troops, was also made from the village of Peiwar up the regular road to the Spin Gawai, and the two officers making it (Major Collett, Assistant Quartermaster-General, and Captain Carr, Deputy Assistant Quartermaster-General) succeeded in reaching a point about one and a half miles distant from the Kotal, and getting a fairly good view of the approaches thereto. On the evening of the 30th I made up my mind to abandon any attempt at attacking the Peiwar Kotal in front, and to undertake the flank turning movement by the Spin Gawai.

16. To render the success of this enterprise possible, it was necessary to maintain the utmost secrecy, and to adopt every means to divert the enemy's attention from my intended attack on his left.

17. On the 1st December ostentatious reconnoitring parties were sent to both flanks of the Peiwar Kotal, and batteries were marked out on the small plain near the hamlet of Turri. These proceedings seemed to have the desired effect; the enemy shelled the working party employed at the battery; placed fresh guns in position on the south side of the pass; and paraded their troops and showed every sign of expecting an attack. In the evening of this day, the half battery G-3rd, Royal Artillery, and the 12th Bengal Cavalry arrived from the rear. I had them marched up in full view of the enemy, and made as great a parade as possible of their arrival. At this time every officer and soldier in camp, and certainly all the natives, were fully persuaded that I intended to attack the Peiwar Kotal the next morning.

18. The general plan of the intended operations, which was explained to Commanding Officers at 4 P. M. on Sunday, the 1st instant, was briefly as follows :—

The following troops were detailed to form the turning force under my immediate command, and were instructed to march at 10 P. M. that night, without noise or bugle sound, in the order mentioned below. No orders of any sort for the march to be given before 9 P. M.—

29th Punjab Native Infantry 5th Goorkhas ... No. 1 Mountain Battery ...	Under Colonel J. J. H. Gordon, 29th Punjab Native Infantry.
72nd Highlanders ... 2nd Punjab Infantry ... 23rd Pioneers ...	Under Brigadier-General Thelwall, C. B.

4 guns F-A, R. H. A., on elephants, with two companies of Pioneers as escort.

Each of the above corps was directed to leave their camp standing, with a party of 30 men as a camp guard.

The following troops under the command of Brigadier-General Cobbe were directed to remain in camp:—

2-8th Foot.
5th Punjab Infantry.
12th Bengal Cavalry.
2 Guns F-A, Royal Horse Artillery.
3 Guns G-3rd, Royal Artillery.
The Turi and other levies, under command of Major Palmer, 9th Bengal Cavalry.

Brigadier-General Cobbe received general instructions to open fire upon the enemy about 6 A. M.; to get his troops into position in front of the Peiwar Kotal by half past eight, and to storm the place when the flank attack should have become sufficiently developed to shake the enemy's defence.

19. The troops marched at 10 P. M. on Sunday night to the village of Peiwar, where they entered the bed of the *nullah* which forms the road to the Spin Gawai. This was extremely difficult marching for infantry, as the *nullah* was nothing but a mass of stones, heaped into ridges and furrowed into deep hollows by the action of the water. The night was fine, but bitterly cold; and we did not get the advantage of the moon after midnight. While on the march I found it expedient to change the order of the leading brigade, which became as follows :—

5th Goorkhas.
1 Company, 72nd Highlanders.
29th Punjab Native Infantry.

I had intended to halt the column for an hour or two during the night to rest the men; but owing to the slowness of our progress, and to the distance being greater than was anticipated, the intention had to be abandoned.

20. At a little before six o'clock on the morning of the 2nd December, the head of the column reached the foot of the Spin Gawai Kotal. Day was just breaking; and as the enemy had neglected to place a picquet down the bed of the *nullah*, our approach had so far been unobserved.

21. At this moment, two shots from the enemy's look-out sentries alarmed his picquet on the Kotal. The advance party of the 5th Goorkhas immediately formed up from column of fours into a company line, and, led by Major Fitzhugh and Captain Cook, rushed straight at a barricade which now became apparent about 50 yards in their front. The remainder of the regiment extended and swarmed round the flanks of the obstacle, which was carried in very brilliant style, the enemy firing a volley into the Goorkhas as they came up, and being nearly all killed at their posts.

22. At this time the enemy's guns from the stockades or *sungas* just above us commenced firing shells into our column, but without doing much damage.

23. The Goorkhas and 72nd Highlanders continued to advance rapidly up the steep side of the Kotal, and captured three stockades in quick succession, the enemy defending them in a very obstinate manner, and being mostly killed by the bayonet as our men jumped over the barricades.

24. No. 1 Mountain Battery was of the greatest assistance during this advance, and the guns were fought in the most determined manner, well up in the advanced line. Its gallant commander, Captain Kelso, was shot through the head whilst bringing his guns into action, just beyond the first stockade.

25. I brought up the remainder of the 72nd Highlanders as soon as the firing commenced, and I cannot praise too highly the gallant conduct of this splendid regiment, and the brilliant style in which the men were led by Lieutenant-Colonel Brownlow and the other officers of the corps.

26. Of the admirable conduct of the 5th Goorkhas, I have already spoken. They were not one whit behind their brethren of the 72nd in their eager desire to close with the enemy.

27. The 29th Punjab Native Infantry acted as a support throughout this advance, and successfully repelled an attempted attack by the enemy on our right flank.

28. By half past six o'clock the whole of the Spin Gawai barricades and stockades were in our possession, and the line of the enemy's defence was completely turned.

29. At half past seven o'clock, Captain Wynne established communication with Brigadier-General Cobbe by visual signalling, when I informed him of our progress and instructed him to co-operate vigorously from below in attacking the Kotal.

30. The 23rd Pioneers and 2nd Punjab Infantry having now come up, I continued to press the enemy and hoped to have taken the Peiwar Kotal by a direct advance upon its left flank.

31. But in this I was disappointed, for we found the enemy very numerous in our front, and our progress was slow, owing to the densely wooded hills through which the line of our advance lay, and the determined resistance which we met. During this period of the engagement the fire of the four guns of F-A., Royal Horse Artillery, which had been brought up on elephants, was found very effective. They were brought into action with great judgment by Colonel Stirling, commanding the battery.

32. About noon, under the direction of Colonel Perkins, R. E., Commanding Engineer, two guns of No. 1 Mountain Battery gained a position from which they could see the enemy's camp at Peiwar Kotal. This was shelled with such success that the tents were set on fire, and a regular flight of the enemy from its neighbourhood was witnessed.

33. Having ascertained, at one o'clock, from a reconnaissance, that the Peiwar Kotal was practically inaccessible from the northern side, on which I was operating, I resolved to withdraw the troops from this line of attack altogether, and ordered the following disposition:—

2nd Punjab Infantry to hold the hill on the north of the Kotal, which formed our present most advanced position.

29th Punjab Native Infantry to hold the hill overlooking the Spin Gawai, and protect the field hospital which had been established there.

A column, formed as follows, to march under my command in the Zabardast Kila direction, so as to threaten the enemy's line of retreat, *viz.*—

5th Goorkhas.

5th Punjab Infantry (this regiment had joined us during the day.)

No. 1 Mountain Battery 72nd Highlanders 23rd Pioneers 4 Guns F. A., R. H. A., on elephants	Under Brigadier-General Thelwall, C. B.

34. The effect of this movement was almost immediately apparent, for as soon as the march of the troops was perceived, the fire in front of the hill occupied by the 2nd Punjab Infantry slackened, and the enemy on the Peiwar Kotal became so disturbed that Colonel Barry Drew, of the 8th King's Regiment, who then commanded the troops on that side, determined to deliver his attack.

35. This was most gallantly executed, and at 2-30 P. M. the Peiwar Kotal was in our possession, and the enemy in full flight along the Ali Kheyl road, which for some distance was found strewn with abandoned guns, limber boxes, &c.

36. Brigadier-General Cobbe was, I extremely regret to say, wounded during the advance on the Peiwar Kotal, but the particulars of the attack will be found in the accompanying despatch from Colonel Drew of the 8th King's Regiment, who assumed the command of the troops when Brigadier-General Cobbe had to leave the field.

37. The Peiwar Kotal was garrisoned for the night by the 8th Foot.

38. The troops under my immediate command could not get up in time to fall on the retreating enemy, and bivouacked near the village of Zabardast Kila.

39. I annex a report from Major A. Palmer, 9th Bengal Cavalry, who commanded the Native levies during the day, in which his movements are detailed. The levies were detached to operate on the enemy's right flank, with the design of diverting his attention and of committing the Turis and other tribes to the British cause.

Major Palmer's observations on the nature of the approaches to the Kotal from the south are very valuable, as entirely confirming the intelligence which I had gained from reconnaissance and information regarding the difficulties which would attend an attack from that direction.

40. An examination of the Peiwar Kotal defences proved it to be a place of enormous natural strength, and that the enemy's dispositions for repelling any attack on it from the front were very complete and judicious. It is also evident from the enormous stores of ammunition and supplies which have been captured, that it was the intention of the Affghan Government that their troops should remain here for the winter, and that they fully expected to be able to maintain their position against the British forces. Their defeat and expulsion by a force of inferior strength from a position of their own choosing and of unusual natural advantages, may, I presume, be expected to have a very beneficial effect upon the population of the Hariab, Kurum, and Khost valleys. It is at all events quite certain that had the Affghan troops succeeded in holding their position on the Peiwar Kotal, we should never have been regarded as having full possession of the Kurum valley.

41. The enemy's strength on the Peiwar Kotal position, on the 2nd December, has been ascertained to be nearly as follows:—About 3,500 infantry, including 3 regiments which arrived from Kushi on the afternoon of the 1st December; 18 guns; and a large number of Jagis, Ghilzais, and other tribes whose exact strength cannot of course be ascertained. There was also a mule battery of six guns, which was coming up to reinforce, but did not get further than Ali Kheyl. A battery of Horse Artillery and a regiment of infantry had been left on the Shutar Gardan, having been unable to cross that pass; a regiment of cavalry was at Kushi. The total strength of the British force employed was as follows:—

Turning force, under my command	43 officers	..	2,220	men.
Co-operating column, under Brigadier-General Cobbe	30	,, ..	838	,,
Total	73	,, ..	3,058	,,

42. I may be permitted to point out that no similarity exists between the Affghan army of the former war and that which has now been put into the field. The men are now armed with excellent rifles, and provided with abundance of ammunition, bundles of cartridges having been found placed behind trees, &c., in positions intended to be held. Their shooting is good; their men are of large stature and great physical strength and courage, and are well clothed. The Affghan artillery is also well served and efficiently equipped.

43. I enclose a list of casualties, which I deeply regret should be so heavy. Of Captain Kelso I have already written; the other officer killed, Major Anderson of the 23rd Pioneers, fell at the head of his men whilst gallantly charging up the hill-side to attack the enemy. The death of these officers is mourned by the whole force, for both were well known as brave and excellent soldiers. The loss of the enemy cannot be estimated with any accuracy, but is believed to have been large. About 70 dead were counted in the Spin Gawai breastworks, and many more must have been killed in the subsequent fighting, which for the most part took place over thickly wooded hill sides. The inhabitants of the country believe the loss of the Affghans to have been heavy.

CHARASIAH 6 October 1879

From Maj-Gen Sir Frederick Roberts, KCB, VC, Commanding the Kabul Field Force, dated Bala Hissar, Kabul, 20 October 1879

My despatch No. 1122, dated Bala Hissar, Kabul, 15th October, 1879, acquainted His Excellency the Commander-in-Chief and the Government of India with the proceedings of the force under my command from the date of my arrival at Alikhel on the 12th of September, to the 2nd instant, when the column was assembled at Zargun-Shahr.

2. I purposely delayed leaving Alikhel until all necessary supplies had been conveyed to Kushi, and until everything was ready for as rapid an advance on Kabul as my limited transport would admit.

3. So long as I remained at Alikhel the people of Afghanistan were kept in doubt as to the actual intentions of the British Government. Their idea was that the season was too far advanced for troops to attempt a march on Kabul, and that, beyond occupying the Shutar Gardan and making a demonstration as far as Kushi, nothing would be done until the spring of next year.

The fact of my crossing the Shutar Gardan would, I was aware, make our plans clear to the Afghans and neighbouring tribes, and would be the signal for the assemblage of all those who had determined to oppose our advance.

4. My object was to let as short a time as possible intervene between leaving Kushi and reaching Kabul; I knew that want of carriage would prevent my moving the force as a body, and that a halt would have to be made every second day to allow of the transport animals being sent back to bring up the rear brigade. This made it more than ever necessary that I should not reach Kushi until all was ready for a start.

5. As stated in my despatch of the 15th instant, I arrived at Kushi on the 28th of September, and on the following day ordered the cavalry brigade to move to Zargun-Shahr and commence collecting supplies. On the 1st of October the last of the troops reached Kushi from Alikhel, and on the 2nd idem I marched for Zargun-Shahr with the two infantry brigades.

On the afternoon of the 5th of October the village of Charasiab, eleven miles from Kabul, was reached by the whole of the column, except two guns of No. 2 Mountain Battery, a wing of the 67th Foot, the 28th Punjab Native Infantry, and a squadron of the 5th Punjab Cavalry, which had to be left at Zahidabad to protect reserve ammunition and commissariat stores. These troops were under the command of Brigadier-General Macpherson, C.B., V.C.

6. The passage of the Logar river at Zahidabad caused some trouble; the bridge proved to be unfit for field artillery, and at first even for laden animals, while the water was deeper than I had been led to expect,—caused, I believe, by a large cut having been turned back into the river a short distance above the ford, on purpose to delay our advance.

The company of Sappers and Miners, aided by strong working parties, soon remedied matters, but the inhabitants of the near villages showed such unmistakable signs of hostility by firing on our rear-guard both on the evening of the 3rd and of the 4th of October, that I deemed it necessary to inflict summary punishment on those who had been most forward; this I did before leaving Zahidabad on the morning of the 5th idem.

7. The only casualty on our side up to this time was a slight wound received by Captain R. G. Kennedy, Deputy Assistant Quarter Master General, who was superintending the passage of the Logar river, though at one time the enemy approached so close that it became necessary for the covering companies of the 72nd Highlanders and 5th Punjab Infantry to drive them back at the point of the bayonet.

The rear-guard at this time was under the command of Major C. M. Stockwell of the 72nd Highlanders, who exercised his command with coolness and dexterity.

8. It was evident to me from the feeling and manner of the people generally, from the fact that the Shutar Gardan had been attacked immediately on the bulk of our force leaving it, and from the action of the villages near Zahidabad, that our advance on Kabul would be opposed, but I was quite unable to obtain any information as to the intentions of the enemy, although the Amir with all his principal ministers were in camp with me.

Immediately therefore on arriving at Charasiab, reconnoitring parties of cavalry were pushed forward along the three roads leading towards the city of Kabul. A few shots were fired at these parties from villages and walled enclosures, but no traces were visible of any large body of the enemy.

9. That night strong pickets were thrown out all round camp, and cavalry patrols were ordered to proceed at day-break to feel for the enemy; at the same time I determined to seize, as soon as possible after dawn, the crest of the pass known as the Sang-i-Nawishta, on the road towards Ben-i-Shahr, the one by which I had decided to continue my march towards Kabul, and which was between five and six miles in advance of our camp at Charasiab.

10. A wing of the 92nd Highlanders and the 23rd Pioneers left camp soon after day-break on the 6th, accompanied by two guns of No. 2 Mountain Battery, for the purpose of working on the road in the pass, where the cavalry patrol the previous evening had reported guns would experience difficulties; I was about to follow with a strong escort of cavalry, to examine personally the pass and the ground beyond.

Before, however, these arrangements could be carried out, and almost before any report could be received from the cavalry patrols, all doubts as to the intentions of the enemy were dissipated: troops could be seen in large numbers and regular formation crowning the crest line of the hills which extended from the narrow defile of the Sang-i-Nawishta (both sides of which were held) on their extreme left, to the heights above the Chardeh valley which formed their right.

No hurry nor confusion marked their movements; positions were taken up and guns placed with so much deliberation and coolness, that it was evident a large number of regular troops were massed against us. Soon afterwards I received reports that our cavalry patrols had been fired upon and were retiring slowly.

11. It was imperatively necessary that the enemy should be dislodged from their strong position before dark. Their occupation of the heights intervening between Charasiab and Kabul was a menace that could not be brooked, a warning that could not be disregarded.

Behind these heights lay the densely crowded city of Kabul, with the scarcely less crowded suburbs of Chardeh, Deh-i-Afghan, &c., and the numerous villages which lie thickly clustered all over the Kabul valley. Each and all of these had contributed their quota of men to assist the troops collected to fight us, and it did not require much experience of Afghans to know that the numbers already opposed to us would be very considerably increased if the enemy were allowed to remain in possession of their stronghold for a single night.

12. About this time a report was received that the road in our rear was blocked and that the march of Brigadier-General Macpherson's brigade, with its long string of baggage, would be opposed, whilst on the hills on both sides of our camp bodies of men were seen assembling, and, as I afterwards heard, were only waiting for nightfall to make a general attack upon the encampment.

Notice was sent to Brigadier-General Macpherson to keep a good look-out, and to reach Charasiab, if possible, before dark; at the same time he was reinforced by a squadron of cavalry.

Four guns of No. 2 Mountain Battery, under Captain G. Swinley, Royal Artillery.
Two Gatling guns under Captain A. Broadfoot, Royal Artillery.
7th Company of Sappers and Miners, under Lieutenant C. Nugent, Royal Engineers.
72nd Highlanders, under Lieutenant-Colonel W. H. J. Clarke.
Six companies of the 5th Goorkhas, under Major A. FitzHugh.
200 of the 5th Punjab Infantry, under Captain C. McK. Hall.

13. To Brigadier-General Baker, C.B., I entrusted the difficult task of dislodging the enemy, and placed at his disposal the troops marginally noted, making a total of about 2000 men.

Two guns of No. 2 Mountain Battery.
20 sabres, 9th Lancers, under Captain H. W. Apperly.
5th Punjab Cavalry, one squadron, under Major F. Hammond.
92nd Highlanders, one wing, under Major G. S. White.
23rd Pioneers, under Lieutenant-Colonel A. A. Currie.

Orders were now sent to the troops who had proceeded towards the Sang-i-Nawishta defile, whose strength is noted in the margin, to take up a position of defence, and to consider themselves under the command of Brigadier-General Baker.

14. Up to this period all my operations had led the enemy to expect that our attack would be directed against their left, the Sang-i-Nawishta defile, and they were seen to be concentrating their forces in that quarter. This position was so strong and could only have been carried with such loss, that I determined the real attack should be made by an outflanking movement upon the right of the enemy, while their left continued to be occupied by a feint from our right.

15. Brigadier-General Baker, who had reinforced his main attack by 450 men of the 23rd Pioneers, assembled his little column in the wooded enclosures of Charasiab, a collection of detached villages, in the most convenient of which he selected a place for his reserve ammunition, and field hospital, heliographing to me to increase the strength of the small guard he was able to leave there in charge. One hundred bayonets of the 5th Punjab Infantry were sent at once, followed by the remainder of the regiment as soon as sufficient transport could be procured for its ammunition; this only left for the protection of camp between 600 and 700 infantry and about 450 cavalry.

16. After leaving Charasiab, Brigadier-General Baker advanced over some bare undulating hills, forming a series of positions easily defensible, and flanked by steep rocky crags varying in height from 1000 to 1800 feet above the sloping plain which our troops had to cross. The main position of the enemy was at least 400 feet higher; it commanded their entire front, and was only accessible in a few places.

17. Seeing the very difficult nature of the ground in front of him, Brigadier-General Baker ordered the party on his right, which now consisted of three guns of G-3rd, Royal Artillery, under Major S. Parry, Royal Artillery, two squadrons of cavalry, made up of detachments of the 9th Lancers, 5th Punjab Cavalry and 12th Bengal Cavalry, under Major Hammond, 5th Punjab Cavalry, a wing of the 92nd Highlanders under Major J. C. Hay, and 100 rifles of the 23rd Pioneers under Captain H. Paterson, the whole commanded by Major White of the 92nd, to continue threatening the Sang-i-Nawishta, to prevent the enemy occupying any portion of the Charasiab village, to advance within artillery range of the enemy's main position, and, when, but not before, the outflanking movement was thoroughly developed and the enemy were in retreat, to push the cavalry through the pass and pursue.

These instructions were most successfully carried out by Major White, under whose orders a subsidiary movement made by Captain R. H. Oxley, of the 92nd, freed Brigadier-General Baker's right from considerable annoyance.

18. Brigadier-General Baker now moved forward his force; one company of the 72nd Highlanders, under Captain R. H. Brooke-Hunt, extended to crown the heights on the left, and speedily became engaged. The main body of the regiment attacked the enemy in front, their advance being well covered by two guns of the mountain battery. Owing, however, to the obstinate resistance of the enemy and the extremely difficult nature of the ground on the left flank, the advance was somewhat checked; the company of the 72nd was therefore re-inforced by two companies of the 5th Goorkhas under Captain J. Cook, V.C., whilst two more companies of that regiment, commanded by Major FitzHugh, and 200 men of the 5th Punjab Infantry under Captain Hall were pushed forward to strengthen the direct attack.

19. As it had now become evident to the enemy that the real attack was being directed against their right, and their troops were seen to be moving in hot haste in the latter direction, it became imperative to carry their position before it could be further reinforced. At 2 P.M., after two hours' fighting, the ridge on the left of this position was seized, and the retreating enemy exposed to a cross-fire which inflicted very heavy loss. The general advance was now sounded, and the first position gallantly carried by the 72nd Highlanders, 5th Goorkhas and 5th Punjab Infantry.

The enemy fought well to the last, and charged close up to the 5th Goorkhas, who, however, commanded by Major FitzHugh, repulsed them with heavy loss. In this affair Lieutenant and Adjutant A. R. Martin was very forward.

The 72nd Highlanders bore the brunt of the early part of the engagement on this flank, as will be seen from their casualties; they were admirably led by their company officers under the skilful direction of Lieutenant-Colonel Clarke, assisted by Lieutenant and Adjutant R. H. Murray.

20. The opposing force had now retreated to a position some 600 yards in rear of that from which they had been driven, and against this our troops advanced in rushes, covered by the fire of the mountain battery. After defending this place for half an hour, the enemy again fell back, the attack made by a company of the 23rd Pioneers under Lieutenant D. Chesney, supported by the 72nd, 5th Goorkhas and two companies of the 92nd, proving irresistible.

21. At 3-45 P.M. the high ridge was gained, and the enemy's line of defence exposed to being taken in reverse. This soon caused them to retreat from their position on the Sang-i-Nawishta, advantage of which was speedily

taken by the troops under Major White, who throughout the day conducted the operations on the right in the most satisfactory manner.

A general advance was now made, but no further resistance was offered, until a point in rear of the enemy's main position was reached.

25. Judging from the number of troops seen and from information subsequently received, I calculate that thirteen regular regiments were opposed to us, and that these, aided by contingents from the city and neighbouring villages, brought up the total force of the enemy to several thousand men. They were commanded by Sirdar Nek Mahomed Khan, son of the late Amir Dost Mahomed Khan, aided by the following Lieutenants—General Mahomed Kureem Khan (Ghilzai), General Gholam Hyder Khan (Chukri), General Mahomed Afzul Khan (Reaka), and Sirdar Mahomed Zaman Khan, Governor of Khost.

26. Their loss in killed alone is estimated at upwards of 300 men, to which must be added a large number of wounded.

27. All the guns, twenty in number, brought out from Kabul to assist in the defence of the position were captured; amongst them was an 8-inch brass howitzer presented to the Afghan State by the British Government. A large proportion of the small arms and ammunition used against us were also gifts from the same source.

28. Whilst the operations above detailed were being brought to a successful issue, large numbers of armed men were seen on the hills which lay to east and west of our camp. Patrols of cavalry were, however, sufficient to prevent their venturing down into the plain; but one party, bolder than the rest, caused so much annoyance to a picket of the 92nd Highlanders, that it became necessary to dislodge them, and this difficult service was performed in a most gallant manner by a small party of the 92nd under Lieutenant R. A. Grant. Color-Sergeant Hector Macdonald, a non-commissioned officer whose excellent and skilful management of a small detachment when opposed to immensely superior numbers in the Hazar-darakht defile was mentioned in my despatch of the 15th instant, here again distinguished himself.

29. Early on the morning of the 7th, accompanied by the cavalry brigade, F-A, Royal Horse Artillery, two guns of G-3rd, Royal Artillery, a wing of the 92nd Highlanders, the 7th Company of the Sappers and Miners, the 23rd Pioneers and the Gatling guns, I proceeded by the Sang-i-Nawishta defile to Ben-i-Shahr, where I intended to encamp my whole force prior to the final advance upon Kabul. Passing through the defile, some bands of hillmen opened fire from the opposite side of the gorge, but they were quickly silenced by our infantry.

Brigadier-General Baker with the main portion of his force arrived in camp the same afternoon.

30. On the morning of the 8th instant, having received information that those of the enemy who had not already dispersed to their homes would probably retreat towards Turkistan, I directed Brigadier-General Massy, commanding the Cavalry Brigade, to move out with his command and place himself across their line of retreat.

From Brigadier-General Massy's report attached,* it will be seen that the enemy determined upon making a final stand on the Asmai heights, which lie close to, and to the north-west of, the city, before giving up the contest as hopeless.

* Not published.

On ascertaining that such was the case, and that their intention was evidenced by the fact that a large force was in position, aided by twelve guns, on the heights referred to, I at once ordered Brigadier-General Baker to advance with the force marginally noted, attack the enemy, and compel them to fall back upon our cavalry.

Two guns, No. 2 Mountain Battery, under Lieutenant E. A. Smith, Royal Artillery.
One Gatling gun, Captain A. Broadfoot, Royal Artillery.
Two companies of the 72nd Highlanders, Captain C. W. N. Guinness.
92nd Highlanders, head-quarters wing, Lieutenant-Colonel G. H. Parker.
23rd Pioneers, Lieutenant-Colonel Currie.
Total—2 guns.
1 Gatling.
1044 rifles.

The opposing force consisted of remnants of those who had fought against us on the 6th, aided by three fresh regiments who had arrived on the 7th instant from Kohistan, and supported by numerous bad characters from the city and surrounding villages.

31. The ground over which our column had to advance was of so difficult a nature, that much delay ensued, and the day was wearing on before Brigadier-General Baker found himself near enough to engage the enemy with artillery. Reinforcements, consisting of the remainder of No. 2 Mountain Battery, a wing of the 67th Foot and two companies of the 5th Goorkhas, had been despatched to Brigadier-General Baker, but, owing to the roughness of the ground traversed, did not reach him until past 5 o'clock. That officer, although perfectly prepared to attack with the force at his disposal previous to the arrival of reinforcements, found that sufficient daylight did not remain to enable him to carry it well home, and wisely determined to postpone the delivery of the assault until day-break. In Brigadier-General Baker's decision I entirely concur.

32. About this time intelligence reached me that three regiments of infantry and twelve guns had started from Ghazni some days previously, and were endeavouring to join the troops opposed to us on the Asmai heights. I informed Brigadier-General Baker of this, and of my intention to strengthen him during the night by four guns of F-A, Royal Horse Artillery, on elephants, a wing of the 67th Foot and the 28th Native Infantry under Brigadier-General Macpherson, who would then take command. Brigadier-General Baker was at the same time informed that two guns of F-A, Royal Horse Artillery, and two squadrons of cavalry had been sent under the command of Brigadier-General Hugh Gough to watch the Kohistan road.

33. Meanwhile the cavalry brigade had crossed the low range of the Siah Sang hills, and, proceeding northwards, had entered and taken possession of the fortified cantonment of Sherpur, which had been abandoned by the enemy,—finding therein 73 guns of various calibres and 3 howitzers. Changing his line of advance towards the west, Brigadier-General Massy perceived that, in order to get in rear of the enemy's position on the Asmai heights, a considerable détour would be necessary. Making his way round to the north, he eventually debouched into the Chardeh plain and blocked the line of the enemy's retreat, which it would have been necessary for them to follow had it been attempted in military formation, and took up a position of observation to the westward of the village of Deh-i-Mozan, whence the development of the infantry attack could be seen. The line of observation occupied by the cavalry during the day was contracted at night, and the brigade bivouacked under cover of the walled enclosures, near the road running past Aliabad.

34. Brigadier-General Baker, fearing that the enemy might abandon their position during the night, despatched a strong patrol at 1-30 A.M. on the 9th to ascertain if any change had taken place, and at 4-30 A.M. it was reported to him that the camp was deserted, and twelve guns, some elephants and a large supply of camp equipage abandoned. On receipt of this information he at once com-

municated its purport to Brigadier-General Massy, and informed him that any movement of the cavalry in pursuit would be supported both by the troops under his own immediate command and by those under Brigadier-General Macpherson (who had arrived about dawn), in accordance with instructions received from me.

35. At day-break the cavalry brigade was put in motion, and throughout the entire day scoured the country in search of the fugitives, whom the villagers reported to have dispersed in small bands along the hill tracks. I further directed Brigadier-General Massy to despatch two squadrons across country up to and beyond the Kohistan road; but this party also failed to discover any trace of the enemy.

A small band was, however, overtaken at the Kotal-i-Takht, 15 miles beyond Killa Kazeh on the Ghazni road, and between 20 and 30 of them were killed by the 5th Punjab Cavalry.

Most of the men and horses having gone through very severe work on scanty food for upwards of two days, Brigadier-General Massy, after detaching two squadrons of the 12th Bengal Cavalry to push the pursuit still further, returned to the head-quarters camp, where the brigade also arrived late the same evening. There were no casualties amongst either officers or men, but several horses died from privation and fatigue. The guns and escort under Brigadier-General Gough also reached camp the same evening, as did also the troops under Brigadier-Generals Macpherson and Baker.

36. Brigadier-General Massy informs me that he has invariably received valuable aid from Captain B. A. Combe, 10th Hussars, Deputy Assistant Quarter Master General, temporarily attached to his brigade; Lieutenant J. P. Brabazon, 10th Hussars, Brigade Major; Captain S. G. Butson, 9th Lancers, Orderly Officer, and Lieutenant I. S. M. Hamilton, 92nd Highlanders, Orderly Officer; and would also testify to the excellent manner in which Major F. Hammond, 5th Punjab Cavalry, Captain F. S. Carr, of the same regiment, and Captain H. W. Apperley, 9th Lancers, led their men through the Sang-i-Nawishta defile on the 6th instant.

37. During the day of the 9th instant, the camp of the whole division was moved from Ben-i-Shahr to the heights of Siah Sang, an elevated and commanding plateau less than a mile to the east of the Bala Hissar. The 5th Goorkhas and four guns of No. 2 Mountain Battery were left on the upper Bala Hissar hill; but with these exceptions, the entire force was concentrated at Siah Sang, completely dominating the City of Kabul, which lies at our feet.

38. On the following day I visited Sherpur cantonment, and directed the 5th Punjab Cavalry to move over there for the protection of the guns and stores there. The following day I closely examined the Bala Hissar, and also the buildings occupied by the late Envoy and his suite and escort, and at noon on the 12th instant, accompanied by the heir apparent, my staff, the various heads of departments, and a large number of the most influential *sirdars* of Kabul, I proceeded to take possession of the Bala Hissar.

Both sides of the road for a distance of over a mile were lined by our troops, and, as the head of the procession entered the Fort, the British flag was run up over the gateway, and a Royal salute of 31 guns fired on the glacis. From the gateway one company of the 67th Regiment, followed by the band, led the way to the Diwan-i-Âm, the remainder of the regiment falling in immediately in rear of my personal escort.

OPERATIONS AROUND KABUL 10–23 December 1879

From Lt-Gen Sir F S Roberts, KCB, CIE, VC, Commanding in Eastern Afghanistan, dated Camp Kabul, 23 January 1880

2. It will be in your recollection that, towards the end of November, a small column under Brigadier-General Baker, C. B., visited Maidan, about 25 miles from Kabul, in the direction of Ghazni, to enforce the collection of grain and forage which is ordinarily due from that district as part of the revenues of the State, and that General Baker had met with acts of open hostility, for which he was compelled to inflict summary punishment.

3. From time to time both before and after the return of this force, information reached me that disaffection was gaining ground in the western districts, and that the people of Maidan, Logar and Wardak were in communication with the Kohistanis, in view of making a combined attack on the British position at Kabul.

4. The general political situation, as it developed itself in the early part of December, and the causes which appear to have contributed to produce it, may be briefly summarised as follows.

5. After the outbreak of last September and the massacre of our envoy, the advance of the British force from Ali Khel was too rapid to give the Afghans, as a nation, time to oppose it.

At Charasiah, the troops who had participated in the massacre, aided by large numbers of the disaffected townspeople, were conspicuously beaten in the open field; their organization as an armed body was at an end, and their leaders all sought personal safety in flight.

6. It appears probable that at this period the general expectation amongst the Afghans was that the British Government would exact a heavy retribution from the nation and city, which then lay at its mercy, and that after English vengeance had been satisfied, the army would be withdrawn.

Forty years ago, an English massacre had been followed by a temporary occupation of the city of Kabul, and as Pollock and Nott, on that occasion, had sacked and destroyed the great bazar and then retired, so now the people believed that some signal punishment would be succeeded by the withdrawal of our troops.

7. It thus happened that after the action at Charasiah there followed a period of expectation and doubt. The Afghans were waiting on events, and the time had not yet arrived when any national movement was possible.

8. But this pause was marked by certain occurrences which doubtless touched the national pride to the quick, and which were also susceptible of being used by the enemies of the British Government to excite into vivid fanaticism the religious sentiment which has ever formed a prominent trait in the Afghan character.

9. The spectacle of the prolonged occupation by foreign troops of the fortified cantonment which had been prepared by the late Amir Sher Ali for his own army; the capture of the large park of artillery, and of the vast munitions of war, which had raised the military strength of the Afghans to a standard unequalled among Asiatic nations; the measures which had been taken to dismantle the Bala Hissar, the historical fortress of the nation and the residence of its kings and principal nobles; and lastly the imprisonment and deportation to India of the ex-Amir Mahomed Yakub Khan and his leading ministers, were all circumstances which conspired to inflame to a high degree the natural antipathy felt towards a foreign invader.

10. The temper of the people being in this condition, it was clear that only mutual jealousy and distrust among the chiefs could prevent their making common cause against us, and that, if any sentiment could be found strong enough to dominate such internal dissensions, a powerful movement might be evoked, having for its object our own expulsion from the country.

11. Such an impulse was supplied by the fervent addresses to Mahomedan religious feeling made by the aged Moolla Mir Mahomed, commonly known as the Mushk-i-Alam; by the universal denunciation of the English in the mosques of every city and village; by the appeals of the ladies of Yakub Khan's family to the popular sympathies, and by the distribution of the concealed treasure which was at their command; and lastly, by the expectation of sharing in the plunder of the British camp.

12. The Moollas in short became masters of the situation, and having once succeeded in subordinating private quarrels to hatred of the common foe, the movement rapidly passed through the phase of religious enthusiasm, and culminated in nothing less than a national rising against the English invaders. The memories of the disaster of 1841-42 were appealed to; it was urged that what had happened once might happen again; and the people were assured that if they would only rise suddenly and simultaneously, the small English army in Sherpur might easily be driven from its position, and, as before, be overwhelmed in its retreat through the difficult passes which divide Afghanistan from India.

13. Such were the hopes of the chiefs and religious leaders who had now combined against the English infidels, and, according to the information which I received, their intention was to gain possession of the city and Bala Hissar, and, after occupying the numerous forts and villages in the neighbourhood of Sherpur, to surround the cantonments.

14. To attain this object, they arranged that the forces from the south, *viz.*, from Logar, Zurmat, the Mongol and Jadran districts and intervening Ghilzai country, should seize the range of hills which extend from the city towards Charasiah, and include the Bala Hissar and the high conical peak called the Takht-i-Shah; that the forces from Kohistan should occupy the Asmai heights and hills to the north of the city; while those from Maidan, Wardak, and the Ghazni direction moved upon the city from the westward.

15. As it was evident that if these several bodies once concentrated on Kabul, they would be joined by the disaffected portion of the people of the city and adjoining villages, I endeavoured to break up the combination before it came to a head, and to deal with the advancing forces in detail.

General MACPHERSON'S *Force.*
4 guns F-A, Royal Horse Artillery.
4 ,, No. 1 Mountain Battery.
6 companies 67th Regiment—(401 men.)
509 men, 3rd Sikhs.
393 ,, 5th Goorkhas.
1 squadron, 9th Lancers.
2 ,, 14th Bengal Lancers.

16. With this intent, I despatched, on the 8th December, Brigadier-General H. T. Macpherson, C. B., V. C., with a column as per margin, towards the west, *viâ* Killa Aushar and Arghandi, in order to meet the enemy and force him back on Maidan.

* *General* BAKER'S *Force.*
2½ squadrons, 5th Punjab Cavalry.
4 guns, No. 2 Mountain Battery.
25 men, Sappers and Miners.
450 men, 92nd Highlanders.
450 ,, 5th Punjab Infantry.

17. On the following day, I ordered Brigadier-General T. D. Baker, C. B., to proceed with a small force* *viâ* Charasiah and Lallidandur towards Maidan, and thus place himself across the line by which the enemy, after defeat by General Macpherson, would have to retire. To give time for the completion of this movement, and to draw the enemy forward by an appearance of hesitation, I halted General Macpherson at Killa Aushar on the 9th,

and on that day a cavalry reconnaissance by Lieutenant-Colonel W. S. A. Lockhart, Assistant Quartermaster-General, discovered that large numbers of the enemy were moving northwards from Arghandi and Paghman towards Kohistan.

18. At the same time I heard that a considerable force of Kohistanis had collected at Karez Mir, about ten miles to the north of Kabul, and feeling how desirable it was to disperse them before they could be joined by the enemy hastening from the west, I directed General Macpherson to change his line of advance and attack the Kohistanis, and as their country was unsuited to horse artillery and cavalry, I ordered him to leave this portion of his column at Killa Aushar†.

† General Macpherson took with him—
1 squadron 14th Bengal Lancers leaving at Killa Aushar.
4 guns F-A., R. H. A.
1 squadron 9th Lancers.
1 ,, 14th Bengal Lancers.

19. On reaching the Surkh Kotal, about two miles short of Karez Mir, General Macpherson found that his arrival was well timed, that the enemy from the west were still below him in the Paghman Valley, and that it was in his power to deal with the Kohistanis before a junction could be effected.

He accordingly attacked the Kohistanis vigorously and promptly, and drove them back with heavy loss.

Our casualties were one officer, Major A. FitzHugh, 5th Goorkhas, slightly wounded, and six men wounded—two severely.‡

‡ *Casualties, 10th December.*
Wounded.

Major FitzHugh, 5th Goorkhas.
1 man ,, ,,
4 men, 3rd Sikhs.
1 man, 67th Regiment.

Total.

Officer		1
Rank and File	British	1
	Native	5
		7

20. The enemy advancing from Maidan seemed inclined at first to ascend the Surkh Kotal from the Paghman Valley and assist the Kohistanis, but on seeing that our troops held all the commanding positions, and probably hearing of the defeat of their allies, they retreated towards Arghandi.

21. General Macpherson informed me of this by heliograph soon after noon on the 10th, and I at once ordered the horse artillery and cavalry from Killa Aushar to try and cut in on the enemy's line of retreat, strengthening the cavalry by two additional squadrons from Sherpur, and placing the whole under the command of Lieutenant-Colonel B. L. Gordon, Royal Horse Artillery.

This movement was unsuccessful, for as soon as the cavalry appeared, the enemy took shelter in the villages and on the skirts of the high hills which surround Paghman.

22. General Macpherson encamped on the night of the 10th at Karez Mir, and General Baker, who had steadily pursued his march by a very difficult road, halted a short distance to the west of Maidan.

23. During the day orders were sent to General Macpherson to march very early on the 11th, to follow the enemy observed retreating south and west by the Paghman Valley, and to endeavour to drive them towards General Baker; he was informed at the same time that the horse artillery and cavalry under Brigadier-General W. G. D. Massy would leave Killa Aushar at 9 A. M., and that he was to join them on the Arghandi road.

24. General Massy's orders were to advance from Killa Aushar by the road leading directly from the city of Kabul towards Arghandi and Ghazni; to proceed cautiously and quietly, feeling for the enemy; to communicate with General Macpherson, and to act in conformity with that officer's movements, but on no account to commit himself to an action until General Macpherson had engaged the enemy.

General Massy had with him four guns, F-A., R. H. A., and three squadrons of cavalry (two of the 9th Lancers and one of the 14th Bengal Lancers.)

25. Instead of gaining the Ghazni road by the ordinary route, General Massy started across country, intending to strike that road beyond the village of Killa Kazi. He sent one troop of the 9th Lancers under Captain J. J. S. Chisholme to communicate with and ascertain the movements of General Macpherson, while a second troop, under Captain Bloomfield Gough, was used as an advance guard. Captain Chisholme's troop did not again join General Massy.

26. Although, on nearing Killa Kazi, General Massy's advance guard reported to him that the enemy were in considerable force on the hills on either side of the Ghazni road, some three miles in advance, he still moved on. Shortly afterwards further reports were received by him that the enemy were coming down into the plain with the evident intention of attacking him. He then directed the horse artillery to open fire, in order to check their advance and detain them until he could hear something of General Macpherson's column.

27. Major Smyth-Windham commenced firing at a distance of 2,900 yards, but as this had not the desired effect, General Massy ordered the guns to be moved 400 yards nearer, and, finding that the enemy continued advancing, he directed the guns again to move forward. They came into action for the third time at 2,000 yards, and in this position remained until the opposing force arrived within 1,700 yards' range.

The enemy still maintaining a steady advance, General Massy dismounted 30 of the 9th Lancers, who commenced firing as soon as carbine range was reached. The enemy were in such force (General Massy reports 10,000) that the fire of the dismounted lancers "had no appreciable effect."

28. About this time I arrived on the ground, having left Sherpur with the intention of taking command of Generals Macpherson's and Massy's united forces.

Seeing the inutility of continuing a cavalry and horse artillery action against an enemy in such an overwhelming strength, and on ground so unfavorable, I ordered General Massy to retire slowly, to at once find a road by which the guns could be brought away in safety, and to watch for an opportunity for the cavalry to charge, so as to give time to extricate the guns. The order regarding the necessity of finding a line of retreat for the guns was also given to Lieutenant-Colonel Gordon, commanding the Royal Artillery, who had accompanied General Massy from Killa Aushar, where he had previously been in command.

29. The cavalry charges, gallantly led by Lieutenant-Colonel R. S. Cleland, who was dangerously wounded, and by Captain Bloomfield Gough on the flank, were well delivered and did considerable execution, but did not succeed in checking the enemy for more than a few minutes. Shortly afterwards, the artillery found their further movement in retirement stopped by a deep and narrow channel. Here, whilst searching for a passage across, I ordered a second cavalry charge, as a last hope of saving the guns; but this had still less effect than the first on the enemy, who were now coming rapidly forward, outflanking General Massy's troops on both sides, and maintaining a destructive fire. The guns could not be got over the deep channel, and it became absolutely necessary to spike and abandon them.

30. Immediately on reaching the ground, seeing that a retirement was inevitable, I had sent back orders to Sherpur to despatch 200 of the 72nd Highlanders, with the least possible delay, to hold the gap at Deh Mozang, so as to prevent the enemy gaining possession of the city, and on this point I retired with the greater portion of the cavalry, who, by manœuvring in front of the enemy and keeping them in check, gave opportunity for the 72nd Highlanders to arrive at the gorge, which they did just in time to hold it, and to bar the enemy's passage.

31. During this retirement, the squadron of the 14th Bengal Lancers, under the command of Captain J. P. C. Neville, was distinguished for its great steadiness and coolness ; every credit is due to the officers (British and Native) non-commissioned officers and men for their behaviour on this occasion. Many men had lost their horses in the charges above related, and now instances of bravery in saving wounded and dismounted men from falling into the enemy's hands were numerous.

32. The enemy, finding they were unable to enter the city, took ground to their right and occupied the Takht-i-Shah, all the slopes leading up to it and the large walled villages in Chardeh, thereby threatening the upper Bala Hissar.

The picquet on this position I had strengthened at an early hour in the day, and it was then held by 215 men of the 67th and 72nd Foot, under the command of Captain R. E. C. Jarvis, of the former regiment. During the night the enemy made repeated and determined attacks, but were on every occasion repulsed with loss; throughout, Captain Jarvis' dispositions for defence were able and soldier-like.

33. While these events were in progress, General Macpherson, who had marched from the Surkh Kotal at 8 A. M., moved in a south-westerly direction towards Arghandi, but observing large bodies of the enemy crossing his front and proceeding towards Kabul, and hearing the firing of General Massy's guns on his left, he brought his right forward, and at 12-30 P. M., or about an hour after the cavalry and artillery had commenced retiring, he found himself very nearly on the ground where General Massy's action had been fought. Here he came across the rear of the enemy, who were speedily dispersed, some making for the hills above Killa Kazi, others for the Chardeh Valley.

34. General Macpherson, not being fully informed of the result of General Massy's action, decided, about 3-30 P. M., to halt for the night at Killa Kazi. Soon afterwards he received an order from me, directing him to fall back on Deh Mozang, where he arrived at 7 P. M., thus still further securing the approach to the city.

35. When I fell back to the gap at Deh Mozang, Colonel C. M. MacGregor, C. B., Deputy Adjutant and Deputy Quartermaster-General, thinking that the infantry that had been ordered from Sherpur might take the road by the Kotal to the north by Killa Aushar, went in that direction to meet them, and observing from this point that the ground where the guns were lying had been partially cleared of the enemy by the advance of General Macpherson's troops, he with the assistance of the officers named in the margin, collected a small party of 9th Lancers, 14th Bengal Lancers, and artillery men, who had remained with him, retraced his steps, and picking up, *en route*, a few soldiers belonging to General Macpherson's baggage guard, he was enabled to recover the guns, and to bring them into cantonments before night. They had been stripped of all moveable parts, and the ammunition boxes had been emptied ; otherwise they were intact and were ready for use on the following day.

Major A. R. Badcock, Assistant Commissary-General.
H. M. Durand, Esq., C. S., Political Secretary.
Captain T. Deane, Military Department.
Captain G. W. Martin, Survey Department.
Lieutenant A. F. Liddell, R. A.

36. I returned to Sherpur by dark. In my absence Brigadier-General Hugh Gough, C. B., V. C., had been in command. His arrangements were all that could be desired, and I am much indebted to him for the quiet and order he maintained.

37. General Baker, on the morning of the 11th, started early from his encampment in the neighbourhood of Maidan, and found the enemy in considerable force, occupying the hills on either side of the Arghandi road. The main body of General Baker's force was allowed to proceed unmolested, but his rear guard and baggage were somewhat hotly attacked ; owing however to the able manner in which the

rear guard was commanded by Captain G. K. M'Callum, 92nd Highlanders, and to the energy of the officers* in charge of the Transport, the whole of the baggage was brought through in safety.

38. The advanced guard had in the meantime reached Arghandi, and found the enemy in possession of both sides of the gorge through which the road runs into the Chardeh Valley. Although late in the afternoon, it was necessary to dislodge the enemy from their position, commanding, as it did, the road to Kabul.

This was effected in a brilliant manner by a portion of the 92nd Highlanders under the command of Major G. S. White, and gallantly led by Lieutenant the Hon'ble J. Scott Napier.

General Baker encamped on the night of the 11th at Arghandi.

39. Several times during the day I tried to communicate with General Baker, in order that he might be kept acquainted with all that had been going on nearer Kabul; it was not, however, until early on the morning of the 12th, that, by means of the heliograph, he learnt that the enemy were threatening the city in very considerable strength, that I had found it necessary to withdraw General Macpherson's brigade to Deh Mozang, and that it was my wish he should return at once, as it was important that the whole force should be concentrated in the neighbourhood of the city and cantonments.

40. During the night, Colonel F. H. Jenkins, C. B., with the Guide Cavalry and Infantry arrived. Foreseeing the probability of reinforcements being required, and thinking that troops coming from the direction of India would have a good effect politically, I had ordered Colonel Jenkins on the 7th December to march on Kabul from Jagdalak.

42. Feeling that the enemy could not be permitted to retain their commanding position on the Takht-i-Shah, I directed General Macpherson, on the morning of the 12th December, to endeavour to drive them from it by an attack from the Bala Hissar and Deh Mozang directions.

Lieutenant-Colonel G. N. Money, of the 3rd Sikhs, was deputed to undertake this operation; the force placed at his disposal was—

2 guns, No. 1 Mountain Battery.
215 men, detachments 67th and 72nd Regiments.
150 ,, 3rd Sikhs.
195 ,, 5th Goorkhas.

Total 560 rifles and 2 mountain guns.

43. The crest of the Takht-i-Shah is naturally difficult; the slopes are very steep, strewn with jagged masses of rock and intersected with scarps, and the natural impediments with which the assaulting party had to contend were still further increased by breastworks which the enemy had thrown up at different points on the ascent of the peak, and behind which they were strongly posted and fought resolutely.

The position was an exceedingly formidable one, and after gallant attempts to carry it, which lasted during the greater part of the day, I ordered the assault to be deferred. I saw that to ensure success without very serious loss, and to prevent the enemy relieving and reinforcing the party holding the peak, as I had observed them to be doing during the day, it was necessary not only to attack in front, but to operate also on the enemy's line of retreat.

I therefore directed General Macpherson to hold the ground of which he had already gained possession, and informed him that on the following morning General Baker would co-operate with him from the Ben-i-Shahr side.

* Captain W. A. Wynter, 33rd Foot.
Lieutenant A. F. Cotton, 35th Native Infantry.
Lieutenant R. H. F. W. Wilson, 10th Royal Hussars.

44. On the occasion of the attack on the Bala Hissar position and the subsequent counter-attack on the Takht-i-Shah, three non-commissioned officers,—Color-Sergeant W. Macdonald, Sergeants W. Cox and R. McIlveen, all of the 72nd Highlanders,—greatly distinguished themselves, especially Color-Sergeant Macdonald, by the cool and intelligent manner in which he superintended the construction of a breastwork under a very heavy fire.

Sergeant Cox on the following day again brought himself to notice by his coolness and judgment when escorting the wounded from the Bala Hissar hill to Sherpur.

45. During this day, the 12th December, General Baker's brigade returned to Sherpur. The enemy shewed themselves in considerable force in his rear and on both flanks, and the rear guard, which was ably commanded by Major H. M. Pratt, 5th Punjab Infantry, was at first closely pressed.

On the march, the little column was skilfully protected and covered by the 5th Punjab Cavalry, who, under the command of Lieutenant-Colonel B. Williams, missed no opportunity of inflicting loss on the enemy.

47. In furtherance of my intentions of the previous day, early on the morning of the 13th December I despatched a force* under Brigadier-General Baker, with orders to proceed by the Bala Hissar road in the direction of Ben-i-Shahr, to seize the heights above that village, and to operate on the enemy's position on the Takht-i-Shah from the south-east.

* 4 guns, G-3rd, Royal Artillery.
4 ,, No. 2 Mountain Battery.
1 squadron, 9th Lancers.
5th Punjab Cavalry.
6 companies, 92nd Highlanders.
7 ,, Guides Infantry.
300 rifles, 3rd Sikhs.
Afterwards reinforced by 150 rifles, 5th Punjab Infantry.

Brigadier-General Macpherson was at the same time instructed to act in conjunction with General Baker from the north of Bala Hissar direction.

48. Soon after passing the Bala Hissar, General Baker observed the enemy streaming out of the villages immediately below the Ben-i-Shahr ridge, the centre of which he seized by a bold and rapid movement, and thus cut the enemy's forces in two.

The commencement of the attack was covered by a heavy and well-directed fire from the eight guns at General Baker's disposal, ably commanded by Majors W. R. Craster and G. Swinley.

The 92nd Highlanders led the advance under Major G. S. White, who has so frequently distinguished himself during the present campaign, and the attack on the enemy's first position was gallantly headed by Lieutenant St. John W. Forbes, who, together with the Color-Sergeant of the company, James Drummond, was killed in a hand to hand fight.

The leading men of the 92nd Highlanders were most resolutely charged by the enemy, who had a very considerable advantage both in numbers and position. After the loss of the officer and color-sergeant, there was a momentary waver, when Lieutenant W. H. Dick Cunyngham rushed forward, and, gallantly exposing himself to the full fire poured upon this point, rallied the. men by his example and cheering words.

49. A large portion of the enemy being thus prevented from uniting themselves with those occupying the Takht-i-Shah, the 92nd Highlanders and Guides, covered by the fire of Major Swinley's guns, which had by this time gained the summit of the lower ridge, and aided by that of G-3rd, Royal Artillery, from the plain below, continued the advance on the conical hill, fighting for some distance every foot of the way.

The position of the enemy was enormously strong, but by 11-30 A. M. the 92nd Highlanders and Guides had reached the summit, where they were met by some of the 72nd Highlanders, 3rd Sikhs and 5th Goorkhas under the command of Major

J. M. Sym, 5th Goorkhas, who had arrived there a few minutes before. Color-sergeant John Yule, 72nd Highlanders, was the first man up, and captured two standards. This gallant non-commissioned officer was, I regret to say, killed on the following day.

50. Large bodies of men were about this time seen issuing from the lower Bala Hissar and city, part of whom made for the heights of Siah Sang, whilst the rest, advancing towards Ben-i-Shahr, occupied two strongly fortified villages situated on either side of the road. One of these was captured by General Baker's troops on their return from the Takht-i-Shah; the other later in the day by a detachment of the 5th Punjab Infantry, under Major Pratt, which I had sent from Sherpur to keep open communication with General Baker.

51. Observing the collection of men on the Siah Sang, and thinking that General Baker might have some difficulty in dealing with so many detached parties of the enemy, I despatched Brigadier-General Massy with the cavalry brigade* to his assistance. During this operation the Guides Cavalry under Lieutenant-Colonel G. Stewart were very successful, and made a grand charge, as did the 9th Lancers under Captain S. G. Butson, who was killed, as also were Sergeant-Major Spittle and three men; Captain J. J. S. Chisholme and Lieutenant C. J. W. Trower, with eight men of the same regiment being wounded.

* General Massy took with him from Sherpur—

1	squadron ...	... 9th Lancers.
2	" ...	... 14th Bengal Lancers.

and was joined on Siah Sang by—

2	squadrons ...	... 5th Punjab Cavalry.
1	" ...	... 9th Lancers.
Total ... 6	Squadrons.	

The Guides Cavalry were an independent command.

Notwithstanding the severity of his wound, Captain Chisholme remained in the saddle, and brought his regiment out of action.

The 5th Punjab Cavalry under Lieutenant-Colonel Williams again distinguished themselves, Majors F. Hammond and J. C. Stewart both leading successful charges.

52. The result of the day's operations was very satisfactory. The enemy had been driven from the southern range, and their advance in that direction had been stopped; they had suffered greatly from our artillery and infantry fire when on the hill sides; and on the plain below they had been severely dealt with by the cavalry.

In the evening I recalled General Baker to cantonments, and directed General Macpherson to move from Deh Mozang and occupy the Bala Hissar heights, leaving the 5th Goorkhas to retain possession of the Takht-i-Shah.

54. Our success on the 13th had been so decided, and the loss inflicted upon the enemy so heavy, that I was prepared to find they would be unable or unwilling to renew their attempts; that the combination had broken up, and that the various sections had scattered and returned to their homes. But at day-light on the 14th December very large numbers of men, with numerous standards, were seen to be occupying a high hill on the Kohistan road, about a mile north of the Asmai range; and as the day advanced, they passed in great numbers from this hill, and also along the road from Kohistan, to the crest of the Asmai heights, where they were joined by many others from the direction of Chardeh and the city.

It then became apparent that foiled in their western and southern operations, the enemy had concentrated to the north-west, and were about to deliver an attack in great strength from that quarter.

55. To meet this, I determined to drive them off the Asmai heights, to cut their communications with the north, and to operate in this direction much in the same way as I had done the previous day from the south.

Accordingly, Brigadier-General Baker proceeded at 9 A. M. on the 14th, with the force named in the margin, to the eastern slope of the Asmai range, and, under cover of the fire of his field and mountain guns, which came into action close to the ruined village of Biland Khel, seized the small conical hill which forms the northern shoulder of the Aliabad Kotal.

4 guns G-3rd, R. A., under Major Craster.
4 guns No. 2 Mountain Battery, under Major Swinley.
14th Bengal Lancers.
72nd Highlanders—192 rifles.
92nd Highlanders—100 rifles.
Guides Infantry—460 rifles.
5th Punjab Infantry—470 rifles.

By this move, General Baker placed himself on the enemy's line of communication, and prevented the force on Asmai receiving support either from the large bodies on the hill to the north or on the Kohistan road.

56. General Baker commenced his attack with the force marginally noted, and in doing so, gave directions to Colonel Jenkins, who was in immediate command of the advance, that after gaining the conical hill, he was to leave there a sufficient force for its security, and was then to proceed with the remainder to attack the main body of the enemy on the Asmai heights.

194 rifles, 72nd Highlanders, under Lieut.-Col. F. Brownlow, C. B.
70 ,, 92nd ,, ,, Captain D. F. Gordon.
422 ,, Guides Infantry under Colonel Jenkins, C. B.

57. Colonel Jenkins left at the conical hill 64 men of the 72nd Highlanders and 60 of the Guides Infantry, commanded by Lieutenant-Colonel W. H. J. Clarke, 72nd Highlanders, who had led the successful attack upon this point.

With the remainder Colonel Jenkins pushed on to dislodge the enemy from the position on Asmai, the advance on this occasion being led by Lieutenant-Colonel Brownlow and the Highlanders, the Guides Infantry on the right affording assistance by continually operating on the enemy's flank.

As soon as the eastern point of the main position had been carried, General Baker directed four guns of No. 2 Mountain Battery, escorted by 100 rifles of the 5th Punjab Infantry, to reinforce the party which had been left on the conical hill, with a view of supporting the advance by engaging the enemy in the Chardeh and Kohistan directions.

The advance was also covered by the four guns of G-3rd under Major Craster, R. A., which were with General Baker, and by four guns of F-A., Royal Horse Artillery, commanded by Captain H. Pipon, which I brought into action near the south-west corner of the Sherpur cantonment. The attack was further assisted by the fire of four guns of No. 1 Mountain Battery under Captain H. R. L. Morgan, R. A., attached to Brigadier-General Macpherson's column, from the Bala Hissar hill, and by two companies of the 67th Regiment under Major G. Baker, which, crossing the Kabul river and acting on the enemy's left rear, contributed to render their position on the Asmai heights untenable.

58. The ground was most difficult and the enemy fought with the greatest obstinacy; the Highlanders and Guides were, however, not to be denied, and eventually reached, the highest peak, where a number of *ghazis* stood fast, determined to die. Here a great struggle took place, and I wish to bring to particular notice the conduct of Lance-Corporal George Sellar, 72nd Highlanders, who had rushed on well in advance of his comrades, and fell to the ground in combat with one of the *ghazis*, from whom he received a severe sword-cut on the arm.

The forward gallantry of the corporal excited the admiration of all who saw it, and I purpose addressing the Military Secretary a recommendation that he may be granted the decoration of the Victoria Cross.

Sergeant John McLaren and Corporal Edward McKay, 92nd Highlanders, also distinguished themselves by great personal gallantry on this occasion.

59. Thus, at 12-30 P. M., our troops were in possession of the whole of the Asmai heights. Shortly afterwards, I received a heliogram from Brigadier-General Macpherson, informing me that very large bodies of the enemy were moving northwards from Indiki, with the apparent intention of effecting a junction with the hostile force that still held the hills towards Kohistan, and of endeavouring to retake the original position.

Similar information was about this time communicated to General Baker by Lieutenant-Colonel T. G. Ross, commanding the cavalry, whom he had sent over the low western spurs of the conical hill to ascertain the numbers and movements of the enemy.

60. About this time I observed that the small body of our troops on the conical hill were being hotly pressed, and that a party of the 5th Punjab Infantry, under Captain C. McK. Hall, were being moved to their assistance by General Baker. Shortly afterwards, I received a heliogram from the latter officer, asking that further reinforcements might be sent to this point. I at once ordered 200 rifles of the 3rd Sikhs, that had been escorting Captain Pipon's horse artillery guns, to proceed from Sherpur with all haste and render the required aid.

Unfortunately before either of the reinforcements could reach the threatened position the enemy had gained possession of it. Their numbers were overwhelming, and though the Highlanders, Guides and 5th Punjab Infantry made a most stubborn defence, and Captain N. J. Spens, of the 72nd Highlanders, sacrificed his life in a heroic attempt to stem the advance of the enemy, it was of no avail: our troops retreated quietly and steadily down the eastern slope of the hill, unable to bring away two guns* of No. 2 Mountain Battery, that up to the very latest moment had played upon the enemy.

* These guns were eventually recovered.

No blame for the loss of these guns is in any way to be attached to the officers or men of the battery. On the other hand every credit is due to Major G. Swinley, the late Lieutenant C. A. Montanaro, and Lieutenant A. F. Liddell, the native officers, non-commissioned officers and men of the battery, for the gallant manner in which they stood to their guns to the last.

Surgeon J. Duke, in medical charge of the battery, was conspicuous for his unremitting attention to the wounded under a heavy fire; and amongst many who distintinguished themselves on this occasion, I would specially mention Major G. Swinley, R. A., Jemadar Abdul Rehman, 5th Punjab Infantry, and Lance-Naicks Dillia and Lehun, of the Guides Infantry.

61. Whilst the events above narrated were in progress, numbers of the enemy were observed (as was the case on the previous day) to be collecting on Siah Sang, and proceeding round the eastern flank of cantonments in the direction of Kohistan.

I therefore despatched a small force of cavalry and two guns of F-A., Royal Horse Artillery, under the command of Brigadier-General Hugh Gough, C. B., V. C., to disperse them. The ground however in that direction was so intersected by deep water courses that the advance of the guns was necessarily slow, and by the time the obstacles had been overcome, the enemy had got so far on the road towards Kohistan and so close to the hills, that pursuit was hopeless.

A party of the 5th Punjab Cavalry, under Captain W. J. Vousden, met with better success. This regiment was quartered in the King's garden, about a third of the way between Sherpur and the city, and I had in the morning sent orders to Lieutenant-Colonel Williams to be on the look out for any enemy that might pass in that direction. About 1 P. M., some 300 or 400 were observed moving along the left bank of the river, and Captain Vousden who, with one troop, was out on reconnaissance, most gallantly charged into the middle of them, and notwithstanding that only twelve of his men were able to follow him, six of whom were wounded (the remainder being stopped by a heavy fire which was opened on them from behind some low walls), he succeeded in dispersing the enemy, and in inflicting severe loss upon them, killing five men with his own hand. It was a most dashing little affair and reflects great credit on Captain Vousden.

62. My object throughout these operations had been either to break up the combination against us by dealing with the enemy in detail, or at least to prevent their getting command of the hills to the north and west of Kabul, and thus gain possession of the city and Bala Hissar.

Up to this time I had no reason to apprehend that the Afghans were in sufficient force to successfully cope with disciplined troops, but the resolute and determined manner in which the conical hill had been recaptured, and the information sent to me by Brigadier-General Macpherson from the signal station on the Bala Hissar that large masses of the enemy were still advancing from the north, south and west, made it evident that the numbers combined against us were too overwhelming to admit of my comparatively small force meeting them, especially on ground which still further increased the advantages they possessed from their vast numerical superiority. I therefore determined to withdraw from all isolated positions, and to concentrate the whole force at Sherpur, thus securing the safety of our large cantonments, and avoiding what had now become a useless sacrifice of life.

63. The measure was one which I was most reluctant to order, for it, of course, involved the temporary abandonment of the city and the Bala Hissar, a loss serious in itself and likely to produce a bad effect on the country at large. Under the circumstances, however, I considered that no other course was left me but to remain on the defensive, and wait until the arrival of reinforcements, or the growing confidence of the enemy, should afford me a favorable opportunity for attacking.

Orders to retire were accordingly issued to Brigadier-Generals Macpherson and Baker.

64. The withdrawal from the Bala Hissar and Asmai heights was accomplished in a manner highly creditable to the officers in command and to the discipline of the troops.

General Macpherson's brigade had to pass through a portion of the city and the suburb of Deh Afghan; his rear guard was harassed and his troops were subjected to a heavy fire as they moved along the narrow streets and through the numerous gardens and orchards, but the Brigadier-General brought off his men and baggage in perfect order, and with comparatively little loss.

68. By the evening of the 14th, all troops and baggage were within cantonments, and that night the Afghan army occupied the city and Bala Hissar.

70. In a former letter* I stated at some length the reasons which induced me to place my force at Sherpur in preference to occupying the Bala Hissar and the Siah Sang heights. Owing to recent events I will now go more fully into the grounds upon which this decision was formed.

* No. 1137, dated 30th October, to the Quartermaster-General in India.

The Bala Hissar was not sufficiently large to contain and afford shelter to the entire force, its camp followers, and many transport animals; it would have been obligatory, therefore, to have divided troops,—a measure to which I was very averse, and to have located a portion of them elsewhere, possibly upon Siah Sang, a bare and bleak plateau, nearly a mile distant from the remainder of the force, where water would have been procurable with difficulty, and where no single facility for carrying on the necessary hutting operations existed.

Again, the disastrous explosions of the 16th of October led me to regard as a grave risk the permanent settlement of the greater portion of the force close to and around a vast magazine, which there was a strong presumption was mined.

These facts, added to the existence of accommodation sufficient to at once house the commissariat stores, the entire European quota of my force and a large part of the native troops, and the rapid approach of an Afghan winter induced me, after carefully weighing the matter, to decide upon the occupation of Sherpur, and I see no reason, in the light of recent occurrences, to alter that opinion.

Sherpur, moreover, has the advantage of being on the side of the city nearest to our communications with India, and although it is situated on the left bank of the Kabul river, this river, except during very occasional spring floods, presents no difficulties to the passage of all arms.

73. On occupying Sherpur, I saw that to prevent annoyance in the event of a strong combination being directed against that place, a considerable destruction of villages and walled enclosures was advisable, so as to create an esplanade round the cantonments; but the pressure of even more important work, the collection of supplies and the provision of shelter for such of the troops as had not already been secured, combined with the scarcity of labour, compelled me in a great measure to defer this precautionary step. I was also unwilling, by what might have appeared unnecessary harshness in the destruction of villages and orchards, to give rise to any ill feeling on the part of the people of Kabul.

Indeed it has been my constant endeavour, from the first, to make our occupation of the country as little irksome to its inhabitants as the safety and welfare of my troops permitted.

Several of these villages gave considerable trouble during the events which occurred between the 15th and 23rd of December, and have since been razed to the ground. Each village is a small fortress in itself, protected by massive mud walls, impervious to all but heavy artillery, and guarded by strong loopholed flanking towers; their reduction, if resolutely held, entails certain loss.

74. As soon as it became apparent that the events of the 11th were the forerunners of a serious movement, unless the measures which I was adopting speedily broke up the combination, I took all the necessary steps for strengthening the defences of Sherpur, and made every preparation to meet the large force known to be assembling.

78. Early on the morning of the 15th December the telegraph wire was cut, but not before I had communicated our situation to His Excellency the Commander-in-Chief and the Government of India, urging the advisability of sending reinforcements as speedily as possible. At the same time I sent orders to Major-General Bright, C.B., at Jellalabad, to move Brigadier-General Charles Gough's brigade from Gandamak to Kabul without loss of time, and to send Brigadier-General Arbuthnot's brigade towards Kabul as soon as fresh troops should reach Jellalabad from India.

79. I had decided upon recalling to Sherpur the garrison of Butkak, which was in an exposed and isolated position, and not sufficiently strong to defend itself against serious attack, and I had considered the expediency of withdrawing the force at Lataband, which consisted of two mountain guns, the 28th Punjab Native Infantry and a wing of the 23rd Pioneers, the whole commanded by Colonel J. Hudson of the former regiment; but as the position was a strong one, ammunition plentiful, and sufficient supplies in hand to last over the probable date of Brigadier-General Charles Gough's arrival, and moreover, as it was in direct heliographic communica-

tion with Kabul, I decided to maintain the post. I had every confidence in Colonel Hudson, and I felt satisfied that, so long as Lataband was held, no serious opposition could be offered to General Gough's advance; it was in fact the most important link in our chain of communications, and though its occupation materially diminished my force at Sherpur, its retention was worth the sacrifice. The result justified this decision, for but slight resistance was offered to General Gough at Jagdalak, and none whatever after that point was passed.

80. On the 16th a body of about one thousand men threatened the camp at Lataband. Colonel Hudson, however, attacked and dispersed them, inflicting considerable loss in both killed and wounded. Owing to the excellent manner in which the attack was covered both by artillery and infantry fire, there were no casualties on our side. Colonel Hudson reports that the following officers did good service on this occasion —

Captain W. G. Nicholson, R. E.
Lieutenant E. A. Smith, R. A., No. 2 Mountain Battery.
Lieutenant A. A. Lane, 28th Punjab Native Infantry, and
Subadar Mehtab Singh, 23rd Pioneers.

Colonel Hudson brings to special notice the gallantry of Havildar Golab Singh, of the 23rd Pioneers, who, well in advance of his men, entered the enemy's breast-work and captured a standard there.

81. As I was very desirous of keeping open my communications with India, and as I felt it most important that Brigadier-General Charles Gough should know, from day to day, the exact position at Kabul; and further, as it was very possible that cavalry might be of great service in the advance from Lataband, I despatched the 12th Bengal Cavalry at 3 A. M. on the morning of the 22nd, to join hands with him. I instructed Major J. H. Green, who commands the regiment, that if Butkak, through which place he had to pass, was unoccupied by the enemy and proved friendly, he was to halt there, leaving a detachment to watch the Logar bridge, whilst Colonel Hudson was to push on to Butkak with the Lataband garrison as soon as the head of General Gough's column arrived at Lataband. Should it be found, however, that Butkak was hostile, Major Green was to press on to Lataband and unite with the troops there. The latter event proving to be the case, the cavalry went on as arranged, losing three men killed and three wounded in the operation, which was one of difficulty and most ably carried out by Major Green, whom I desire to bring to notice for his excellent services.

82. There were no movements of sufficient importance to need special record between the 14th and 21st December.

During that interval the enemy daily took up positions in the neighbouring forts and gardens, and firing from behind cover caused a few casualties in the camp. Each day cavalry reconnaissances were made, and some portion of the force moved out to dislodge the Afghans from any place where they could cause special annoyance; some of the forts and other cover in the immediate neighbourhood of Sherpur were also destroyed, but I confined myself to minor operations of this description, and did not undertake any sorties in force with the object of gaining possession of portions of the enemy's position. My force was not large enough to admit of my holding them, and I considered that had I replied in this way to the enemy's efforts, I should have been playing their game, and I therefore determined to wait until I could act decisively.

83. Every night information reached me that an attack was contemplated, but it was not until the 21st December that the enemy showed signs of special activity. On that day and the following large numbers of them moved from the city, and, passing round to the eastward of our position, occupied the numerous

forts in that direction in very great force. It became apparent that this movement was preparatory to an attack from that quarter. At the same time I was informed that the enemy were preparing a number of ladders, with the intention of attacking the southern and western walls by escalade.

84. The night of the 22nd passed quietly, but the songs and cries of the enemy could be heard in the surrounding villages.

I had received information that the 23rd of December, being the last day of the "Muharram," was fixed upon for their great effort, and I also knew that the flame of fanaticism would be fanned by the fact that the aged Mushk-i-Alam would, with his own hand, light the beacon fire at dawn on the Asmai heights, which was to be the signal for the commencement of the attack.

Possessing this knowledge, and knowing that the feelings of the people had been worked to the highest pitch of excitement by the preaching of their Moollas, I directed all troops to be under arms at a very early hour on the 23rd.

85. My information proved correct, and the appearance of the signal fire on the Asmai heights, shortly before day break, announced the beginning of the assault. Heavy firing almost immediately commenced against our southern and eastern faces, and by 7 o'clock A. M., an attack in force against the eastern side was fully developed, whilst a very large number of the enemy, provided with scaling ladders, were drawn up under cover of the walls to the south.

From 7 A. M. until 10 A. M. the fight was carried on vigorously; repeated attempts were made to carry the low eastern wall by escalade, but though the enemy on several occasions reached the *abattis*, they were each time repulsed, and many dead marked the spots where the assault had been most determinedly pressed home.

Soon after 10 A. M. a lull took place, as though the enemy had recoiled before the breech-loader, but at 11 A. M. the fight again grew hot, although it was not marked by the determination of the former period.

Finding that it was impossible to dislodge the enemy by any fire that could be brought to bear upon them from our defences, I determined to attack them in flank, and for this purpose directed four guns of G-3rd, Royal Artillery, and the 5th Punjab Cavalry under the command of Major W. R. Craster, Royal Artillery, and Lieutenant-Colonel B. Williams, 5th Punjab Cavalry, respectively, to move out through the gorge in the Bemaru heights.

This counter stroke at once told. The Afghans wavered and shortly afterwards broke.

86. By 1 P. M. all vigor had passed from the attack, and the time for the action of cavalry having arrived, Brigadier-General Massy was directed to proceed with every available man and horse and do his utmost against the enemy, whilst at the same time a party of infantry and sappers moved out to destroy some villages to the south, which had caused considerable annoyance and which it was necessary the enemy should be driven from to facilitate the arrival of Brigadier-General Charles Gough's brigade the following day.

This work was successfully accomplished, but I regret to say cost the lives of two gallant officers, Captain J. Dundas, V. C., R. E., and Lieutenant C. Nugent, R. E., commanding the 7th Company, Sappers and Miners, who were killed by the premature explosion of a mine.

Meanwhile a part of our cavalry had worked round to the base of Siah Sang, and succeeded in rendering a good account of the enemy in that quarter, whilst the Guides Cavalry and a squadron of the 14th Bengal Lancers, who had been manœuvring more to the eastward, had been equally fortunate.

87. By evening all fire had nearly ceased, and day-light on the 24th shewed

that the enemy, abandoning all hope of success, had dispersed, not a man being found in the adjacent villages or visible on the surrounding hills. The city was clear of them, and so precipitate was their flight that, leaving their dead unburied where they fell, by mid-day many parties of them were upwards of twenty-five miles from Kabul, the rapidity of their retreat being doubtless accelerated by the knowledge that reinforcements were near at hand.

At 5 o'clock in the morning a party of the 72nd Highlanders occupied without opposition the fort of Mahomed Sharif, and later a force under Brigadier-General Macpherson, C. B., moved out to cover, and if necessary, aid the entry of Brigadier-General Charles Gough's column, which had halted the previous evening about six miles from Sherpur.

AHMED KHEL 19 April 1880

From Lt-Gen Sir D M Stewart, KCB, Commanding the Ghazni Field Force, dated Kabul, 5 May 1880

I have the honor to report, for the information of His Excellency the Commander-in-Chief in India, that on the 19th April the troops under my command encountered and defeated an enemy holding a position at Ahmad Khel, some twenty-three miles south of Ghazni. The enemy's strength was estimated at 1000 horse and from 12,000 to 15,000 foot.

2. For several days previous a hostile gathering had been observed marching on our right flank, at a distance of about eight miles, and it was supposed that the intention of the leaders was to take part in the resistance to be expected at Ghazni itself. Meanwhile, the country from Khelat-i-Ghilzai forward was deserted by its entire population, so that not only was the supply of the troops arranged for with difficulty, but it was scarcely possible to obtain intelligence of the character of the opposition that might be offered.

3. On the morning of the 19th April the Field Force marched at daylight from the halting ground of Músháki, in the following order:—

19th Bengal Lancers, 300 sabres		Leading brigade, under the command of Brigadier-General C. H. Palliser, C.B.
A-B, Royal Horse Artillery, six 9-pr. guns		
19th Punjab Native Infantry, 470 rifles		
Field Force head-quarters	1 co. 2-60th Rifles, 63 rifles; 1 co. 25th P. N. I., 85 ,,; 1 troop 19th B. L., 50 sabres	
Nos. 4 and 10 Companies, Bengal Sappers and Miners, 80 rifles.		
59th Foot, ...	436 rifles	Under the command of Brigadier-General R. J. Hughes.
3rd Goorkha Regiment,	289 ,,	
2nd Sikh Infantry,	367 ,,	
G-4th, Royal Artillery,	Six 9-pr. guns	
6-11th, Royal Artillery,	Two 40-pr. ,,; Two 6·3-in. howitzers	
2nd Punjab Cavalry,	349 sabres	

Field Hospitals.

Ordnance and Engineer Field Parks.

Treasure.

Commissariat.

Baggage.

2-60th Rifles, ...	443 rifles	Under the command of Brigadier-General R. Barter.
15th Sikhs, ...	570 ,,	
25th Punjab Native Infantry, ...	380 ,,	
11-11th, R. A. (Mountain Battery),	Six 7-pr. guns	
1st Punjab Cavalry, ...	316 sabres	

the length of the entire column in order of march being about six miles.

4. About seven miles from camp the enemy was observed in position three miles in advance of the head of the column, when the two leading brigades were disposed as follows:—

The three batteries of artillery being in column of route upon the road, the infantry of Brigadier-General Hughes' brigade was advanced to the left, in line with the leading battery, one troop of the 19th Bengal Lancers being detached to scout on the left flank, along a range of low hills terminating in the enemy's position; the remainder of the cavalry was formed to the right of the guns in flat country stretching for some three miles as far as the Ghazni river; and the 19th Punjab Native Infantry, the two companies of Sappers and Miners, with the Lieutenant-General's escort, were placed in reserve.

5. At 7-45 A.M. orders were sent to Brigadier-General R. Barter to bring forward one-half of the infantry of his brigade, and to release two squadrons of the 1st Punjab Cavalry to join the Cavalry Brigade, then placed under the command of Brigadier-General Palliser, C.B.

6. The advance was ordered at 8 o'clock, and when the column was within a mile and a half of the enemy's line, A-B, Royal Horse Artillery, and G-4th, Royal Artillery, moved out to positions immediately to the right of the road, No. 6-11th, Royal Artillery, coming into action on a knoll 1500 yards in rear, the infantry, under the command of Brigadier-General Hughes, being formed for attack on the left of the field batteries, while the 19th Punjab Native Infantry furnished one company as escort to G-4th, Royal Artillery, and the 19th Bengal Lancers detached a squadron as escort to A-B, Royal Horse Artillery. The equipment of the sapper companies, entrenching tools of infantry regiments, &c., had, meanwhile, been placed under shelter and in rear of No. 6-11th, Royal Artillery.

59th Foot.
3rd Goorkha Regiment.
2nd Sikh Infantry.

7. At 9 o'clock, and before the intended attack of the position was developed, the crest of the range occupied by the enemy was observed to be swarming with men along a front of nearly two miles, a body of horsemen that formed the enemy's right outflanking the left of our line.

8. The guns had scarcely opened fire when, in an incredibly short space of time, an enormous mass of men with standards formed on the hill-

top, a considerable number of horsemen riding along the ridge with the intention of sweeping to the rear of our line to attack the baggage. From the central mass out rushed successive waves of swordsmen on foot, stretching out right and left, and seeming to envelop the position. The horsemen turned the left, now strengthened by a squadron of the 19th Bengal Lancers, and, pouring down two ravines which formed a V, struck the Lancers before they could charge, forcing the leading squadron to its right and rear; while the 3rd Goorkha regiment, the infantry of the left, formed rallying squares. The situation during this temporary success of the enemy was rendered critical, as the squadron could not be rallied till it had passed to the right of the line of infantry, then hotly pressed and giving way.

9. The onslaught of fanatic swordsmen was at this time so rapid, and was pushed with such desperation, that during the few minutes which followed it became necessary to place every man of the reserve in the firing line,—the two sapper companies with half a battalion of the 19th Punjab Native Infantry reinforcing the left, while a half battalion of the 19th Punjab Native Infantry, with the two companies serving on the Lieutenant-General's escort, supported the guns on their left. The enemy, however, continued to push on, and approached within a few yards of the guns, when, the whole of their case-shot being expended, both batteries were withdrawn a distance of 200 yards. The gallantry with which the batteries maintained their ground till the last moment, and the orderly manner in which the retirement was effected, reflect the greatest credit on officers and men.

At this time the infantry of the right was forced back and a fresh position was taken up, two guns of G-4th, Royal Artillery, being detached to the left centre, whither the remainder of the battery was subsequently moved.

The 2nd Punjab Cavalry relieved the escort with A-B, Royal Horse Artillery, and the remainder of the regiment moved to the left of the line, the 19th Bengal Lancers and two squadrons of the 1st Punjab Cavalry being pushed to the right towards the river, while some well-directed shell from the 40-pounder guns with No. 6-11th, Royal Artillery, checked the forward movement of the enemy's horsemen round our left flank.

10. The fighting lasted for one hour, during which the troops under Brigadier-General Barter had come up and reinforced the right centre.

11. At 10 o'clock I ordered the "cease fire" to be sounded, the enemy's attack having been effectually defeated, their entire body spreading broadcast over the country. The necessity for protecting efficiently the large parks and baggage train formed in rear of the column forced me to retain the cavalry to cover the right flank, and pursuit was checked. The regiments on the right had, however, been closely engaged.

12. The troops halted two hours, during which time the dead were buried, and the wounded received necessary attention. At 12 o'clock, however, the entire force, with its baggage in close formation, moved forward and passed over the enemy's position, completing a march of seventeen miles to Nani, where camp was pitched. My advanced cavalry entered Ghazni next day.

13. The casualties during the engagement amounted to—killed, 17; wounded, 124, of whom nine are officers. More than a thousand dead bodies of the enemy were counted on the field, and their loss is estimated at from 2,000 to 3,000.

14. Taking into consideration the character of the attack, led as it was by swarms of fanatics determined to sacrifice their own lives, the conduct of the troops engaged was beyond praise.

MAIWAND 27 July 1880

From Brig-Gen G R S Burrows, dated Kandahar 30 August 1880

I have the honor to report that, on the 26th ultimo, whilst encamped at Khushk-i-Nakhud, I received information that 2000 of the enemy's cavalry and a large number of *ghazis* had arrived at Garmao and Maiwand, and that it was Ayub Khan's intention to follow with the main body of his army immediately.

2. A sketch is attached to this report, showing the positions of Maiwand and Khushk-i-Nakhud, from which it will be seen that to carry into effect the instructions I had received,* *viz.*, to prevent Ayub Khan from passing on to Ghazni, it was incumbent on me to intercept him either at Maiwand or Khushk-i-Nakhud.

* *Vide* correspondence from the Assistant Quarter Master General, Kandahar Force, attached.

3. Hitherto I had found it impossible to obtain any reliable information regarding Ayub Khan's intended movements, for, although when the expedition set out, it was understood that we were to operate in a friendly country, and in concert with a loyal army, the actual circumstances were the reverse of this. The Wali's army had gone over to the enemy; the Wali himself was a refugee in my camp. Whatever little political influence there may previously have been in the country was at an end, and every man's hand was against us.

4. In the absence of intelligence beyond such as my cavalry patrols brought in, and from which I knew that the enemy's advanced post was at Sungboor, twelve miles in my front, on the Khushk-i-Nakhud road, I considered it advisable to await events in the position I had taken up at the latter place.

5. On learning, however, that the enemy was making for Maiwand, I determined to move on that place at once.

6. The force, strength as per margin, marched at 6-30 A. M. on the 27th July, encumbered by an enormous quantity of ordnance and commissariat stores and baggage. This was unavoidable, as the hostile state of the country rendered it impossible to leave anything behind in safety, and I could not divide my already too weak force.

E-B Royal Horse Artillery—	
Officers	5
Non-Commissioned Officers, Rank and File...	141
Horses	191
Six 9-pr. M. L. R. guns	
Smooth-bore Battery of—	
6-prs. taken from the Wali's mutinous army, and manned by 1 officer and 42 men, 66th Foot.	
66th Foot—	
Officers	19
Non-Commissioned Officers, Rank and File...	497
3rd Light Cavalry—	
Officers	6
Native Officers	13
Non-Commissioned Officers, Rank and File ..	297
Horses	306
3rd Sind Horse—	
Officers	5
Native Officers	8
Non-Commissioned Officers, Rank and File...	247
Horses	252
Sappers and Miners—	
Officer	1
European Non-Commissioned Officers ...	2
Native Officer	1
Non-Commissioned Officers, Rank and File ..	41
1st Native Infantry (Grenadiers)—	
Officers	7
Native Officers	15
Non-Commissioned Officers, Rank and File...	626
30th N. I. (Jacob's Rifles)—	
Officers	8
Native Officers	14
Non-Commissioned Officers, Rank and File...	603

Of these numbers, 34 Europeans and 50 Natives were in hospital.

7. After proceeding about eight miles, large masses of troops were discovered, about four miles distant, moving in a diagonal direction across our right front, and it was evident that a collision with Ayub Khan's army must take place before we reached our destination.

8. Advancing on a village which lay about a mile in my front, I placed my baggage there, and on the higher ground beyond I deployed my infantry into line with guns in the centre, and the cavalry on the left, covering the movement with two horse artillery guns and a troop of cavalry.

9. It was difficult, on account of the haze and dust, to estimate the number of the enemy, but judging by the extent of country covered, I believe I am within the mark when I set down his strength at 25,000 men.

10. At 11-45 A. M. the fight commenced by the advanced guns under Lieutenant H. Maclaine coming into action on our left, followed shortly by two horse artillery guns and the smooth-bore

battery in our centre. The remaining two 9-pounders were also brought up from the rear-guard.

11. In about half an hour the enemy began to reply from their right, gradually extending along their front, and concentrating the fire of thirty guns on our position.

12. The infantry were ordered to lie down, and the wing of Jacob's Rifles, which had been in reserve, was brought up on the flanks, which were threatened on the right by *ghazis*, and on the left by the enemy's regular cavalry.

13. In this position we remained for nearly three hours, our artillery making excellent practice, the cavalry holding the enemy's cavalry in check, and the infantry keeping up a steady fire on the *ghazis* on our right.

14. A large body of the enemy's regular infantry were on our left front, and about the middle of the day they advanced in line, but well-delivered volleys checked them, and they did not come on again.

15. Between 2 and 3 o'clock, the fire of the enemy's guns slackened, and swarms of *ghazis* advanced rapidly towards our centre.

16. Up to this time the casualties amongst the infantry had not been heavy, and as the men were firing steadily and the guns were sweeping the ground with case-shot, I felt confident as to the result.

17. But our fire failed to check the *ghazis*; they came on in overwhelming numbers, and making good their rush, they seized the two most advanced horse artillery guns.

18. With the exception of two companies of Jacob's Rifles, which had caused me great anxiety by their unsteadiness early in the day, the conduct of the troops had been splendid up to this point; but now at the critical moment, when a firm resistance might have achieved a victory, the infantry gave way, and commencing from the left, rolled up like a wave to the right. After vainly endeavouring to rally them, I went for the cavalry. (I was obliged to go myself, having no staff officer left.)

19. The 3rd Light Cavalry and 3rd Sind Horse were retiring slowly on our left, and I called upon them to charge across the front and so give the infantry an opportunity of reforming; but the terrible artillery fire to which they had been exposed, and from which they had suffered so severely, had so shaken them that General Nuttall was unable to give effect to my order.

20. All was now over, and I returned to the infantry to do what might be done to save them from complete annihilation.

21. After retreating across the *nullah*, and through the gardens near the village, a small walled enclosure was reached, and in this about 150 men of different corps, with several officers, made a stand and checked the enemy for a time; but seeing that we were rapidly being outflanked, and that our line of retreat would presently be cut off, I gave the order to retire.

22. A wide open plain lay before us, and with discipline utterly gone and the men all scattered, the prospect was discouraging; but we succeeded in making our way without much loss for a distance of three miles, when we joined the guns and cavalry in rear of the baggage, which was by this time stretching for miles over the country towards Kandahar.

23. Small parties of the enemy continued to hover in our rear, but no vigorous pursuit was made.

24. After daylight we were fired on from every village we passed, until we reached Kokeran, when we met a small force under General Brooke, which cleared the way for us into Kandahar.

25. Of the four horse artillery 9-pounder guns and six smooth-bore guns with which we left the field, the whole of the former and one of the latter were brought safely into Kandahar; the five other smooth-bore guns had, one by one, to be abandoned during the retreat, the horses being unable to bring them on.

26. Of the conduct of the troops, generally, I have already spoken, but I wish to bring the artillery to special notice; their behaviour was admirable; exposed to a heavy fire they served their guns coolly and steadily as on parade, and when the guns were rushed, they fought the *ghazis* with hand-spikes, sponge-rods, &c.

27. In explanation of the unfortunate loss of the two horse artillery guns, the officer commanding the battery has reported that Lieutenant Maclaine, who was in charge of them, waited to fire another round of case after the order to limber up and retire had been given, and the delay was fatal.

28. The detachment of the 66th Regiment, under Lieutenant G. De la M. Faunce, which manned the smooth-bore battery, also behaved extremely well.

29. On Major Blackwood being wounded during the action, Captain J. R. Slade, R. H. A., took command of E.-B., R. H. A.

30. I beg to bring the conduct of this officer to very special notice. Captain Slade was not only conspicuous for his gallantry during the day, but throughout the long and trying retreat of forty miles, he worked with unflagging energy, encouraging his men and tending the wounded officers and men who crowded his guns.

31. I was indebted to Major E. P. Leach, V.C., R.E., for valuable assistance during the retreat.

32. The casualty returns have already been forwarded to you.

From Brig-Gen T Nuttall, Commanding the Cavalry Brigade, dated Kandahar 3 August 1880

I have the honor to report the operations of the Cavalry Brigade under my command in the action fought in the vicinity of Maiwand on the 27th July 1880.

2. On the morning of that day, agreeably to orders, by 5-30 the camp was struck, baggage packed, and the brigade, strength as per margin, mounted at 6 o'clock and marched from Khushk-i-Nakhud on Maiwand about 6-30. My dispositions were as follows. The advanced guard was composed of a troop under the command of Lieutenant T. P. Geoghegan, 3rd Light Cavalry; in rear of the advanced guard, at about half a mile interval, followed the remainder of the 3rd Light Cavalry, with four guns of E.-B., R. H. A.; the rear guard was brought up by Colonel Malcolmson, C.B., which consisted of 96 sabres, 3rd Sind Horse, which regiment also provided parties of a troop to the left flank under Lieutenant A. M. Monteith, with another party of 50 sabres, under Lieutenant E. D. N. Smith, to the right, to protect the baggage, which marched on this flank.

E.-B., R. H. A., 6 guns.
3rd Light Cavalry, 260 sabres.
3rd Sind Horse, 200 sabres.

3. About 10 A.M., the enemy's cavalry were seen on our left front at some distance, crossing our front, and moving in the Maiwand direction, and on the nearer approach of our columns, the greater portion of them inclined in a northerly direction towards the Gúrmao Valley, their advanced parties standing fast to watch our movements.

A village stood on our left front, and Lieutenant Geoghegan, with two guns, E.-B., under Major Blackwood, were directed to clear it if occupied.

It being found unoccupied, Lieutenant Geoghegan was directed to stand fast in front of the village, and there await the arrival of the baggage, which was ordered to be collected there. In the meantime the two guns of E.-B., R. H. A., under Major Blackwood, moved on to the edge of a rather difficult broad *nullah*, that ran in front of the village. It was at this place that both Major Blackwood and myself halted to reconnoitre the enemy's position, when we noticed that Lieutenant Maclaine, who had been left with the other two guns, had crossed the *nullah* some little way to our left, and, having been joined by Lieutenant Monteith with a troop of the 3rd Sind Horse, was advancing rapidly towards the enemy.

Mounted orderlies were despatched to recall him, but before they reached he had halted and had come into action. On noting Lieutenant Maclaine's unauthorized movement, I at once, with Major Blackwood's two guns, crossed the *nullah*, and with the remainder of the 3rd Cavalry moved rapidly to the front. In the meantime, orders were sent to bring up the two guns of E.-B., R. H. A., then detached with the rear guard. After advancing some little distance, the enemy's position and forces, were distinctly seen drawn up towards Gurmao, covering some miles. Their cavalry, infantry, and the *ghazis* appeared in countless numbers, and Major Blackwood at once brought his guns into action. As I considered Lieutenant Maclaine's guns were still rather isolated, I sent orders for him to move down and take up another position nearer the main body.

The guns now advanced two or three times, when they halted and awaited the advance of the Infantry Brigade and the battery of smooth-bore guns. It was observed that large bodies of foot-men and mounted men were making towards us from the Maiwand direction, and on the guns opening on them, large numbers of foot-men streamed away along our right flank. The position now of the Cavalry Brigade was as follows:—two guns, R. H. A., on the right, supported by 130 sabres of the 3rd Light Cavalry, under Major A. P. Currie, who, with Captain M. Mayne, also watched the right flank, and two guns E.-B., R. H. A., under Lieutenant Maclaine, on the extreme left, supported by a troop, 3rd Sind Horse; and in rear, echelloned outside the guns, but with left thrown back, was a troop of the 3rd Light Cavalry under Lieutenant J. H. E. Reid, formed thus to watch a large body of the enemy's cavalry, who had formed with the evident intention of turning our left flank.

A number of cavalry, regular and irregular, were now seen moving along on our left flank towards the baggage and the rear, with which were Colonel Malcolmson, C.B., and Lieutenant Geoghegan, the former with 96 sabres, 3rd Sind Horse, and the latter with 50 sabres, 3rd Light Cavalry. Their cavalry had now completely enveloped our flank, and were threatening the rear. Fifty sabres of the Sind Horse, under Lieutenant Smith, who had originally been detached as right flanking party, joined and were now placed to watch the left flank.

Our guns opened fire about 10-50, and for half an hour no reply was made by the artillery of the enemy. However, about 11-15, the enemy replied and opened from their batteries with a well-directed fire. It will be observed that the necessities of the situation precluded my forming any reserve cavalry which could be kept out of range of the artillery, the whole available force amounting to 460 sabres, and these were fully occupied as above detailed. The configuration of the ground about was a level plain, which rendered it quite impossible to get any cover either for the guns and cavalry, which were exposed thus for three hours to a raking, well-directed and concentrated fire from five batteries.

4. Firing in the direction of the rear now told that our rear was engaged. The action had proceeded some little time, when more masses of cavalry appeared on our left flank, and to meet this movement, I placed all the cavalry that could be spared on the left flank. As the enemy, however, did not appear anxious to close with us, at my request General Burrows sent two smooth-bore guns, under Captain Slade, to this flank, who opened a well-directed fire on the masses assembled. After this the two guns under Captain Slade were moved to their former position in the front. Several demonstrations were now made from this flank by my cavalry against the enemy's cavalry, who kept firing at long ranges at us, but they only retired firing. Our men were, however, ordered every now and then to fire dismounted.

It was about this time (12-30) that the enemy succeeded in establishing a battery towards our right flank. During all this time, and till about 2 o'clock, our cavalry were losing heavily in horses and men, although I did all I could, by changing position and moving them, opening out, &c., to lessen the effect of the artillery fire.

5. Nothing could have been steadier or finer than the conduct of all ranks of the cavalry during the very severe and trying artillery cannonade to which they were exposed for about three hours, playing a passive part as escorts to the guns, and protecting the flanks from the enemy's cavalry, which literally swarmed round our left flank.

The guns of the E.-B., R. H. A., under their officers, and those of the smooth-bore battery under Captain Slade, were most admirably and steadily served, and nothing could equal, and certainly never excel, the gallant, cool and collected bearing of officers and men during the action.

6. At about 2-20 o'clock, it was evident that the immense superiority of the enemy in numbers had begun to tell with effect, for not only had the enemy swarmed round us on the left flank, and the artillery were plying us with a well-directed and destructive fire, not only from the front but from a flank, but the *ghazis*, who had led the van of the enemy's attack from the first, were advancing in overwhelming numbers in spite of our artillery and infantry fire, and were supported by a long line of infantry a short distance behind, and threatened to out-

flank the infantry. Captain Slade had withdrawn some of the guns and had moved to the rear.* About 2-30, I now perceived the infantry were in a confused state, falling back, and as their fire was slackening, I ordered the cavalry to form line, and by a charge stem the rush of *ghazis* on the infantry; but I bitterly regret to have to record that, although I was most ably seconded by the officers, only portions of the 3rd Light Cavalry and 3rd Sind Horse formed up, and we charged, but the men bearing away to the right and rear, the charge was not delivered home, and was of but little effect.

* To bring up more ammunition. G. B.

All subsequent attempts made at this time by myself and the officers to induce the men to rally and face the enemy failed.

The men seemed totally demoralized by the combined effects of the very heavy artillery fire which had, during the action, killed and wounded 149 of the horses, and about 14 per cent. of the men engaged in the front, the retreating infantry and the swarms of *ghazis* that*

There was now nothing left but to fall back on the rear-guard, which had advanced a short way towards us, but it was not till we reached the four guns, Royal Horse Artillery, brought out of action by Captain Slade, that the men, through the exertions of the officers, staff and myself, were formed up facing the enemy. Here I halted, but could see no sign of any formed body of infantry retiring; but a long stream of scattered infantry could be seen stretching away for about two miles on our right as we stood facing the enemy. I, however, sent my orderly officer, Lieutenant Monteith, to see if he could rally any stragglers, or see any officers, but after some little time, he returned with the report that the men he had met were quite disorganized and out of hand, and were making to the rear.

No cavalry came near me. I was in the rear of the retreating infantry with three or four other officers. G. B.

In the meantime, it was reported that General Burrows was amongst the slain.

I was determined, if possible, to save the guns, &c.

7. The enemy's guns had now got the range again, and commenced playing on us. Captain Slade with his guns now retired, and I covered the retreat with the cavalry, Captain Slade two or three times coming into action, and firing one or a couple of rounds. A large number of cavalry were to be seen on our left flank, about a mile off, making evidently for our rear.

I saw no cavalry between myself and the column of baggage. There may have been a few irregular horsemen. G. B.

8. After proceeding some distance the enemy's guns ceased playing on us, and I then threw out a troop of the Sind Horse to cover the retreat, which was well and ably conducted by Lieutenant Monteith.

9. After proceeding some little way, information was brought that the rear-guard was hard pressed; and leaving a troop with the guns, I returned with the 3rd Light Cavalry and 3rd Sind Horse to reinforce Lieutenant Monteith, but found all was going on well. After we had placed some tired-out and wounded men on camels and horses, we retired, agreeably to instructions, on Ata Karez, which was the nearest place where water was obtainable on the road.

10. I joined General Burrows with the rear-guard about 2 o'clock in the morning at Hauz-i-Madat. After a halt of half an hour there, General Burrows gave the order to advance. I threw out a troop of the 3rd Light Cavalry as a rear-guard, which was well commanded by Lieutenant Geoghegan. After daylight we had to fight our way to Kokeran, where a small brigade under General Brooke, which had been sent to our aid, met us.

I had been at Hauz-i-Madat upwards of an hour when Brigadier-General Nuttall joined me. G. B.

DEH KHOJAH 16 August 1880

From Lt-Gen J M Primrose, CSI, Commanding the Kandahar Force, dated Kandahar, 26 August 1880

I have the honor to report that the enemy, having clearly shewn his intention of making a complete and careful investment of Kandahar, by occupying and fortifying the adjacent villages, which are all enclosed by high mud walls, under cover of which batteries could easily have been constructed and unmasked, when required, at the shortest notice, without any one being either aware of the number of guns or their distribution to villages, and in the absence of reliable information regarding the dispositions of the enemy, whose movements were all carried out at night, it became absolutely necessary to make a sortie to cause the enemy to show his hand.

2. Before resorting to this measure, I, on two occasions, carefully searched the villages to the south and east of the city by artillery and mortar fire, but without any apparent result, a few villagers only quitting the villages after the fire had ceased.

3. I, therefore, on the 15th August, determined to bombard one village heavily, and then to put some infantry through it.

4. The village I selected was that of Deh Khojah, situated to the east of the city, exactly opposite the Bar Durani and Kabul Gates, and running almost parallel to the city wall, distant from the former gate 600 yards, and from the latter 950 yards.

5. In making the selection the following points influenced me :—

I.—The village was isolated from the main body of the enemy's regular troops, who were encamped beyond Abasabad, some four miles to the west of the city, with Kandahar between them and Deh Khojah, and therefore out of supporting distance.

II.—The only supports available for the village would have to come from the south and pass over ground on which my cavalry could act with effect.

III.—The village lies on the regular road from Mandi Hissar to Kandahar, and I was most desirous to clear and keep this road open for the advance of General Phayre, as the Kushab road was studded with villages, which, if held in succession by the enemy, could only have been forced at immense cost.

IV.—Artillery had been fired from this village completely screened, and I was very anxious to ascertain what number of guns the enemy had in position there, where they were in battery, and what was the calibre of the guns. This information was most necessary, as all reports from Maiwand agreed that Ayub Khan had with him thirty guns, including two batteries of 12-pounder Armstrongs. Up to date he had only unmasked two Armstrong guns, and it was therefore a matter of vital importance to prevent his establishing an overpowering artillery fire within one thousand yards of the walls.

V.—I wished to confine the enemy's artillery to positions perpendicular to the shorter faces of the city walls, as batteries placed opposite the east and west fronts would take these faces respectively in reverse.

VI.—The disarrangement of the enemy's dispositions to the east would practically limit his attack to the west and south fronts, as the ground to the north is open and devoid of cover.

6. On the afternoon of the 15th August, I ordered the infantry force as per margin, under the command of Brigadier-General Brooke, to attack the village early on the morning of the 16th; to force their way through it; obtain all the information they could; and, if possible, to destroy any works the enemy might have constructed under cover of the walls.

4 companies, 7th Fusiliers.
4 companies, 19th Native Infantry.
4 companies, 28th Native Infantry.
A party of Sappers, to be told off by the Commanding Royal Engineer.

The cavalry (strength as noted) under the command of Brigadier-General Nuttall, to co-operate with the infantry and to keep the ground clear to the south and east of Deh Khojah.

3rd Light Cavalry, 100 sabres.
Poona Horse, 100 „
3rd Sind Horse, 100 „

Artillery as per margin to keep up a rapid fire from the walls on the village before the attack, and to cover the advance of the infantry.

One 40-pounder.
Two 9-pounders.
Two 8"-mortars.

7. The cavalry were ordered to leave by the Eedgah Gate at 4-30 A.M., and to trot round out of musketry fire to the east of the village, and there await the result of the attack.

The artillery were ordered to open fire at 4-45 A.M., and infantry to leave by the Kabul Gate at 5 A.M.

8. Brigadier-General Brooke made his own dispositions for carrying out the attack, which were as follows:—

"I.—The Force will be divided into three columns as follows:—

1*st*.—Under Lieutenant-Colonel Daubeny, will consist of—
2 companies, 7th Fusiliers.
2 companies, 19th Native Infantry.

2*nd*.—Under Lieutenant-Colonel Nimmo—
1 company, 7th Fusiliers.
3 companies, 28th Native Infantry.

3*rd*.—Under Colonel Heathcote—
1 company, 7th Fusiliers.
2 companies, 19th Native Infantry.
1 company, 28th Native Infantry.

"II.—To each column will be attached an engineer officer, with a proportion of sappers, with tools and powder bags.

"III.—A medical officer and sick carriage will accompany each column. The reserve ammunition will remain within the Kabul Gate.

"Arrangements for carrying an ample supply of water are to be made by all commanding officers.

"IV.—The following will be the duties assigned to each column:—

The first Column will, on leaving the Kabul Gate, take the road to the right, and after proceeding 150 yards along it, advance towards the south of the village, the advance being covered by skirmishers, and the details carried out as may seem best to Colonel Daubeny, with reference to the features of the ground and the resistance offered. The object of this column is to seize a good position at the south of the village from which to advance to the north of the village, driving out all the enemy who may be met there.

"The second column will conform to, and follow the movements of, the first; but on reaching the village will seize a position on the right of that taken up by the first column. Both columns will make their advance in as open order as possible.

"The third column will remain within the Kabul Gate awaiting orders. The duty assigned to them will probably be to enter the village at the main entrance and seize the enclosure on the left of the entrance, where the gun embrasure is, and clear that part of the village. The other instructions will be issued to the commanders of the 1st and 2nd Columns by the Brigadier-General on their reaching the south of the village. The Cavalry Brigade, under Brigadier-General Nuttall, is under orders to co-operate, and will be on the east and south of the village."

9. As previously arranged, the cavalry quitted the Eedgah Gate at 4-30 A.M., and trotted round into the position assigned, a few shots being fired at them but at very long ranges and doing no damage.

10. The guns opened fire at 4-45 A.M., and at 5 A.M. the first two parties of infantry debouched from the Kabul Gate, making for the south of the village which they entered under a heavy fire of musketry at 5-30 A.M.

11. At this moment numbers of *ghazis* were seen making their way to Deh Khojah across the open ground to the south of the village.

12. They were at once charged by a troop of the 3rd Light Cavalry under Lieutenant Geoghegan, and driven back with heavy loss into broken ground, where further pursuit was hopeless.

13. The cavalry now formed up to the south of Deh Khojah waiting for another opportunity to charge, and the infantry were steadily making their way through the village, beating down all opposition.

14. Once more the *ghazis* in large numbers tried to cross from the south to the support of Deh Khojah, but Major Trench, 19th Regiment Native Infantry, met them with three well-directed volleys, which turned them, and Brigadier-General Nuttall, seizing the opportunity, charged again with the 3rd Light Cavalry and Poona Horse, dispersing and cutting up many of the enemy, who again took shelter in the *nullahs* and broken ground.

15. The enemy's fire in the village had now nearly ceased.

16. On re-forming after this charge Brigadier-General Nuttall received a note from Brigadier-General Brooke, asking him to cover the retirement of the infantry from the south of the village into the Kabul Gate.

17. In consequence of this request, the cavalry were withdrawn, and entered the city by the Kabul Gate, and it was in carrying out this movement that they suffered most of the loss sustained throughout the day, as they were exposed to infantry fire from the village (which recommenced as they were being withdrawn) in cramped ground, which prevented their being in open formation.

18. My intention had been that the cavalry should have remained out to the last in the open plain, well out of musketry fire, charging whenever opportunity should offer, and returning the same way they went out after the infantry had passed through the village.

19. The cavalry and infantry at the south end of the village being withdrawn allowed the enemy's reinforcements to move up from the south, and the fighting in the middle of the village became general and very heavy.

20. Notwithstanding the determined resistance of the enemy, who fought, under cover of their walls, with the greatest obstinacy, the infantry, under Lieutenant-Colonel Daubeny and Lieutenant-Colonel Nimmo, forced their way through the village, debouching at about 7 A.M. from the northern end, whilst the party under the command of Colonel Heathcote held their ground near the centre of the village until ordered to withdraw.

21. At 7-15 A.M. the firing had entirely ceased and the enemy were seen streaming away from Deh Khojah, carrying some of their dead with them. Their loss has been reported as very heavy, several chiefs of note having been killed, and one of the two guns in the village destroyed.

22. Whilst the fighting was going on in Deh Khojah, the enemy opened artillery fire on the city from Picket Hill, and from a gun in position about 1,200 yards from the west face of the city wall. He also attempted to form up his infantry in the old cantonments under cover of this fire; but such was the steadiness and accuracy with which our guns were served, that he was unable to do so, and within an hour his artillery fire was silenced, and one gun on Picket Hill dismounted.

23. No words of mine can express my appreciation of the cool and gallant behaviour of all ranks.

24. Brigadier-General Brooke was killed whilst attempting to save the life of Captain Cruickshank, R.E., and by his death the service and the country have suffered a heavy loss.

25. Lieutenant-Colonel W. H. Newport, 28th Native Infantry; Major R. J. Le P. Trench, 19th Native Infantry; Captain G. M. Cruickshank, R.E.; Lieutenant F. C. Stayner, 19th Native Infantry; and Second-Lieutenant F. P. F. Wood, 7th Fusiliers, all died whilst leading their men in the most forward manner; and Second-Lieutenant E. S. Marsh, 7th Fusiliers, was killed in helping to bring in Lieutenant Wood, who was then severely wounded.

26. The Reverend G. M. Gordon, Church Missionary Society, was also mortally wounded whilst attending the men under a heavy fire; and I take this opportunity of paying my small tribute of admiration to a man who, by his kindness and gentleness, had endeared himself to the whole force, and in the end died administering to their wants.

27. The sketch appended will show the movements executed. Attached is a list of our killed and wounded.

28. Whilst deeply regretting the loss of so many gallant officers and men, it would be difficult to over-estimate the effect produced on the men of the garrison and on the enemy by this affair.

29. The spirits and *morale* of the troops under my command, which had been considerably damped and shaken by the result of the action at Maiwand on the 27th July, and the continued confinement within the city walls, were raised and confidence in their superiority over the enemy restored.

30. They were convinced that even when holding a strong position and in vastly superior numbers, the enemy could not withstand their attack, and the dread of the word "*Ghazi*" was dispelled.

31. On the other hand, the overweening confidence of the enemy received a shock from which it never recovered.

32. The villagers and *ghazis*, who had been carefully instructed that there were only some eight hundred British troops in Kandahar, and that the remainder were followers dressed up as soldiers, had it conclusively proved to them that this was a fallacy.

33. The feeling of security which had hitherto marked all their movements gave place to feelings of insecurity and doubt, and they refused to remain any longer distributed about in the surrounding villages, streaming back to their camp by thousands, numbers having been reported as having gone off to their homes.

34. Hardly a shot was fired by the enemy after the 16th; and on the 24th I received intelligence that Ayub Khan had shifted his camp into the Arghandab Valley, where he was entrenching himself, and that the majority of the local contingent had dispersed.

KABUL-KANDAHAR MARCH AND BATTLE OF KANDAHAR
1 September 1880

From Lt-Gen Sir Frederick Roberts, GCB, VC, CIE, RA, Commanding the Southern Afghanistan Field Force, dated Camp Quetta 26 September 1880

Before detailing the operations on the 31st August and the 1st September, which resulted in the defeat of the Afghan army assembled at Kandahar, under the command of Sirdar Mahomed Ayúb Khan, it may be desirable to give a short account of the march from Kabul,—a distance of 318 miles,—which was accomplished in twenty-three days, including two halts.

The strength of the force, placed at my disposal at Kabul by Lieutenant-General Sir Donald Stewart, G.C B., consisted of—

3 Brigades of Infantry,
1 Brigade of Cavalry,
3 Batteries of Mountain Guns.

Major-General J. Ross, C.B., commanded the Infantry Division, the 1st, 2nd, and 3rd Brigades of which were commanded respectively by—

Brigadier-General H. T. Macpherson, C.B., V.C.
Brigadier-General T. D. Baker, C.B.
Brigadier-General C. M. MacGregor, C.B., C.S.I., C.I.E.
Brigadier-General Hugh H. Gough, C.B., V.C., commanded the Cavalry Brigade.

Colonel Alured C. Johnson commanded the artillery; Colonel Æ. Perkins, C.B., held the position of Commanding Royal Engineer, and Deputy Surgeon-General J. Hanbury, that of Principal Medical Officer.

In the detail of the forces* it will be noted that the strength in artillery was not in proportion to the strength of the other branches. But there were strong reasons which made it desirable that the artillery with the column should consist only of mountain batteries. The whole question was one of grave importance, and it was not without due consideration decided that the force should proceed to Kandahar unaccompanied by wheeled artillery.

The object was to reach Kandahar in the shortest possible time; and it was not improbable that the main road would have to be left, should the Afghan army at Kandahar endeavour to make its way towards Ghazni and Kabul by the valleys of the Argandab or the Arghastan.

*Detail of Force.

1st Infantry Brigade.

	British.	Native.
92nd Highlanders	651	...
23rd Pioneers	...	701
24th Punjab Native Infantry	...	576
2nd Goorkhas	...	501
Total ...	651	1,777

2nd Infantry Brigade.

	British.	Native.
72nd Highlanders	787	...
2nd Sikh Infantry	...	612
3rd Sikh Infantry	...	570
5th Goorkhas	...	561
Total ...	787	1,743

3rd Infantry Brigade.

	British.	Native.
2-60th Rifles	1	...
15th Sikhs	...	650
25th Punjab Native Infantry	...	629
4th Goorkhas	...	637
TOTAL ...	616	1,916

Cavalry Brigade.

	British.	Native.
9th Queen's Royal Lancers	318	...
3rd Bengal Cavalry	...	394
3rd Punjab Cavalry	...	408
Central India Horse	...	495
TOTAL ...	318	1,297

Artillery Division.

	British.	Native.	Guns.
6-8th Royal Artillery,—screw guns	95	139	6
11-9th Royal Artillery	95	139	6
No. 2 Mountain Battery ...	...	140	6
TOTAL ...	190	418	18

TOTAL OF FORCE.

British Troops	2,562
Native	7,151
British Officers	273
Guns	18
Cavalry Horses	1,779
Artillery Mules	450

The nature of the ground throughout Afghanistan is such that artillery can never be safely employed with cavalry alone, unsupported by infantry. Nor is rapidity of movement so much required of artillery in countries like Afghanistan, as the power of being able to operate over the most difficult ground without causing delay to the rest of the troops.

It was not forgotten, moreover, that on arrival at Kandahar the column would be augmented by a battery of 40-pounders, a battery of field artillery, and four guns of horse artillery.

It is unquestionable that, had either horse or field artillery accompanied the force, the march could not have been performed with the same rapidity.

Before leaving Kabul, everything that was possible was done to lighten baggage. Ten British soldiers were told off to each mountain battery tent, usually intended to hold six, and fifty to a sepoy's tent of two *páls*, 34 lbs. of kit only being allowed for each man.

To each Native soldier 20 lbs. of baggage was allowed, inclusive of camp equipage.

Each officer was allowed one mule; and one mule was allowed to every eight officers for mess.

The amount of supplies which it was determined to take with the force was as follows:—

30 days' tea, sugar, rum, and salt for Europeans.
8 days' rum for Natives drinking spirits.
5 days' flour for Europeans.
5 days' rations for Native troops.
1 day's grain, carried by cavalry horses and transport animals in addition to the ordinary load.

The force appointed for the relief of Kandahar moved into camp by brigades on the 8th August in the vicinity of Kabul, the 2nd Infantry and the Cavalry Brigade proceeding respectively to Indiki and Charasia. The 1st and 3rd Infantry Brigades encamped at Beni Hissar.

The following morning the march commenced. The route lay through the fertile Logar Valley, that line being chosen instead of the usual road by Maidan, on account of the facilities it offered for collecting supplies.

On the 15th August Ghazni was reached,—a distance of 98 miles having been marched in seven days.

I placed my own guards and sentries in and around Ghazni,—deeming it best for the preservation of order, for the prevention of collisions between the troops and people, and for the execution of our demand for supplies.

The fort was visited by numbers of officers and men, but no disturbance occurred; and before the break of the following day the force was many miles on its way towards Khelat-i-Ghilzai.

No news having reached me from either the latter place or Kandahar, I determined to push on with all possible speed.

I may here mention that I frequently despatched messengers, while on the road, with telegrams reporting our progress. I am led to think that none of these messengers ever reached their destination, except those sent from Khelat-i-Ghilzai, and from between that place and Kandahar.

On the 20th August, shortly after reaching Panjak I received a letter from Colonel Tanner, 29th Bombay Native Infantry, commanding at Khelat-i-Ghilzai, written on the 18th, to the effect that all was well with his garrison; that the neighbourhood of Khelat-i-Ghilzai was quiet, and that General Phayre, writing from Quetta on the 12th August, had stated that he hoped to be in Kandahar on the 2nd September at the latest.

The following day, at Shahjui, Captain Straton was able to open heliographic communication with Khelat-i-Ghilzai. By this means I heard of the sortie which had been made from Kandahar on the 16th August; and at the same time I received reassuring news as to the staying power of the garrison,—that they were in no straits for supplies for troops and followers, that they were all in good health and spirits, and that they had forage sufficient to hold out for a longer period than it would take the force under my command to reach Kandahar.

I decided, therefore, to push on to Khelat-i-Ghilzai, and there give the troops a well-earned rest of one day.

We arrived at Khelat-i-Ghilzai on the 23rd August, having marched from Ghazni, a distance of 134 miles, in eight days. This gives an average daily rate of $16\frac{3}{4}$ miles.

Colonel Tanner had everything in good order at Khelat-i-Ghilzai, and had been enabled to collect a fair amount of supplies.

Being of opinion that it would be inconvenient to keep open communication with Khelat-i-Ghilzai for some time to come, and seeing no immediate advantage in continuing its occupation, I determined to withdraw the garrison and take it with me to Kandahar.

All the necessary arrangements for this purpose were made during the day the force halted,—the 24th August; and the charge of the fort was handed over to Mahomed Sadik Khan, a Toki Ghilzai, who had had possession of it when the British troops under Lieutenant-General Sir Donald Stewart reached Khelat-i-Ghilzai in January, 1879.

On the 26th August, at Tirandaz, I received news from Lieutenant-General Primrose, C.S.I., commanding at Kandahar, that on the 23rd Sirdar Ayúb Khan had abandoned the villages to the east and west of Kandahar; and that on the 24th he had struck his camp and had taken up a position in the Argandab Valley between Baba Wali and Mazra, due north of the city,—thus practically giving up the investment of Kandahar.

Being anxious to open up heliographic communication with General Primrose, and if possible with General Phayre, I ordered two regiments of cavalry under Brigadier-General Hugh Gough to march the following morning (27th August) to Robat, a distance of 34 miles, the remainder of the force moving about half way.

Shortly after arrival at Robat, Brigadier-General Gough was met by Lieutenant-Colonel St. John, the Resident, and Major Adam, Assistant Quartermaster General at Kandahar. From the information brought by these officers, and from what I heard from other sources, I was led to believe that Ayúb Khan intended to make a stand, and was strengthening his position, which was said to extend from Gandizan to Kotal-i-Múrcha.

Upon receipt of this news I determined to halt for one day at Robat, and to divide the remaining distance to Kandahar, nineteen miles, into two short marches.

Soldiers, followers and transport animals were much fagged by the long and continuous marching, and somewhat exhausted by the now daily increasing heat. I was, moreover, desirous of bringing the troops into Kandahar in as fresh a state as possible, and fit for any work that might be required of them.

During the halt at Robat, on the 29th, I received a letter from Major-General Phayre, C.B., dated Kila Abdulla the 24th August, stating that he hoped his division would be assembled there on the 28th, and be able to march for Kandahar on the 30th.

I felt at once that this precluded the possibility of General Phayre's arrival at Kandahar in time to co-operate with me. I much regretted this, as I was well aware of the strenuous exertions he had made to relieve the beleaguered garrison, and the privations and hardships which he and his troops had undergone to effect this object.

On the 31st August the force reached Kandahar, having marched from Khelat-i-Ghilzai (88 miles) in seven days, including the halt at Robat.

The position I determined to take up was to the west of the city, with my right on the cantonments, and my left touching Old Kandahar.

Such a position covered the city, gave me command of a good and ample supply of water, and placed me within striking distance of Ayúb Khan's camp.

Not knowing what opposition might be expected once we advanced beyond the city, arrangements were made, in communication with Lieutenant-General Primrose, for giving the troops their breakfast outside the Shikarpore Gate, and for watering and feeding the transport animals.

At 10 A.M. the 1st and 3rd Brigades moved off from under the city walls, and took up the position as shewn in the plan attached, *viz.*, Picquet Hill, Karez Hill, and the north-eastern spur of the hill over Old Kandahar.

This movement was accomplished without opposition.

The Cavalry and the 2nd Brigade of Infantry were at this time on baggage and rear guards.

From such a cursory examination of the ground as I was able to make on arrival in the morning, I was quite satisfied that any attempt to carry the Baba Wali Kotal by a direct attack would be attended with very severe loss. I determined, therefore, if possible, to turn it.

To enable me to decide how best this operation could be carried out, it was necessary to ascertain the strength and precise extent of the position occupied by the enemy. I was anxious to obtain this information without delay, and I therefore ordered a small column* under the command of Brigadier-General Hugh Gough to start at once and make as complete a reconnaissance as possible.

* 3rd Bengal Cavalry.
15th Sikhs.
Two guns of 11-9th Royal Artillery.

Lieutenant-Colonel Chapman, Deputy Adjutant and Quarter Master General, was directed to accompany the party and to assist Brigadier-General Gough with his great local knowledge and experience.

The reconnaissance started at 1 P.M. from our left near Old Kandahar, and proceeded towards the high ground immediately above the village of Gandizan. Here the infantry and guns halted, while the cavalry advanced some two or two and a half miles, avoiding the numerous orchards and enclosures, and coming out in front of Pir Paimal village, where it was found the enemy were strongly entrenched.

As soon as the enemy's fire along this line had been drawn, the 3rd Bengal Cavalry fell back, admirably handled by their Commandant, Lieutenant-Colonel A. R. D. Mackenzie.

In the meantime the guns were brought into action, partly to test the range, and also to check the enemy, who were now observed to be passing rapidly into the gardens near Gandizan.

A retirement of the infantry and artillery of the reconnaissance to within our picquets was then ordered.

The instant our troops commenced to fall back, the enemy advanced in great strength and pressed the infantry. They eventually assembled in such large numbers, and endeavoured so persistently to follow, that the whole of the troops of the 3rd Brigade, and part of those of the 1st, were ordered under arms.

The retirement was conducted with great steadiness by the 15th Sikhs, under the command of Lieutenant-Colonel G. R. Hennessy. At the end of the day our casualties numbered only ten.

The reconnaissance of the 31st August having afforded me all the information I required, I decided on attacking the enemy the following morning.

Orders were accordingly issued for the troops to breakfast at 7 A.M., and for one day's cooked rations to be carried by all ranks.

Brigades were to be in position by 8 A.M., tents being previously struck, and, with the kits, stored in a walled enclosure.

The plan of operations was explained by me personally to the officers commanding divisions and brigades at 6 A.M.

This plan, briefly, was to threaten the enemy's left (the Baba Wali Kotal) and to attack in force by the village of Pir Paimal.

The whole of the infantry of the Kabul-Kandahar Force, upon whom devolved the duty of carrying the enemy's position, were formed up in rear of the low hills which covered the front of our camp,—the right being at Picquet Hill, and the left resting on Chilzina, while the cavalry, under the command of Brigadier-General Hugh Gough, was held in readiness, in rear of the left, to operate by Gandizan towards the bed of the Argandab river, so as to threaten the rear of Ayúb Khan's camp, and endanger his line of retreat towards Girishk and Kakrez. E-B Royal Horse Artillery (four guns), two companies of the 2-7th Fusiliers, and four companies of the 28th Bombay Native Infantry were placed at the disposal of Brigadier-General Gough to take up a position near Gandizan, and, when opportunity offered, to support his advance.

Guards for the protection of the city having been detailed, as shown in the accompanying return, marked No. 9, the remaining troops under Lieutenant-General Primrose's command were ordered to be distributed as follows:—

Brigadier-General Daubeny's brigade to hold the ground from which the Kabul Force would advance to the attack.

The remnant of Brigadier-General Burrows' brigade, with No. 5-11th Royal Artillery and the cavalry of the Bombay Force under Brigadier-General Nuttall, to take up a position north of the cantonment, from which the 40-pounders might be brought to bear directly on the Baba Wali Pass; the cavalry being instructed to watch the pass called Kotal-i-Múrcha, and to cover the city.

It was clear from a very early hour in the morning that an offensive movement was contemplated by the enemy. The villages of Gandizan and Gandi Mullah Sahibdad were held in strength; and desultory fire was brought to bear upon our front from the orchards connecting these two villages, while an ill-directed shell fire was opened from the Baba Wali Kotal, which was held in force during the greater part of the day's operations.

At 9-30 A.M. fire was opened from the 40-pounders upon the Baba Wali Pass.

Shortly afterwards the brigades of the Kabul-Kandahar Force were ordered to the attack, the 1st Brigade being on the right, the 2nd on the left, and the 3rd in reserve. Two batteries of artillery, *viz.*, C-2nd and 6-8th,—the latter being the new pattern jointed guns,—had meanwhile been placed in position to cover the advance of the infantry, and commenced shelling the village of Gandi Mullah Sahibdad.

The instructions given by Major-General Ross to Brigadier-General Macpherson were to make his first attack on that village, after which he was to clear the enemy from the enclosures which lay between the village and the low spur of the hill short of Pir Paimal. He further ordered Brigadier-General Baker to advance in a westerly direction, keeping touch with the 1st Brigade on his right, and clearing the gardens and orchards in his immediate front.

The attack upon the village of Gandi Mullah Sahibdad was made by the 2nd Goorkhas and the 92nd Highlanders, under the command of Lieutenant-Colonel A. Battye and Lieutenant-Colonel G. H. Parker respectively, the remaining two regiments of the 1st Infantry Brigade being in support. The village was carried in the most dashing style, Goorkhas and Highlanders vieing with each other in the rapidity of their advance. The enemy withdrew sullenly and leisurely, a good number remaining to the last in the village to receive a bayonet charge.

During the advance of the 1st Brigade on the village of Gandi Mullah Sahibdad, the 2nd Brigade had been threading its way through the lanes and walled enclosures, which lay in the line of its attack. The resistance it encountered was most stubborn, the enemy being well protected by high walls, which they had carefully loop-holed. The loss suffered in clearing these enclosures was necessarily severe,—Lieutenant-Colonel Brownlow, C.B., Captain Frome, and Lance-Sergeant Cameron (a grand specimen of a Highland soldier) being amongst those who fell.

Lieutenant-Colonel Brownlow met his death while gallantly leading his regiment, the 72nd Highlanders, and in him the army has experienced a great loss. He had on many occasions highly distinguished himself as a leader,—at the Peiwar Kotal, during the operations around Kabul at the latter end of 1879, and notably on the 14th December, when he won the admiration of the whole force by his brilliant conduct in the attack and capture of the Asmai Heights.

Of the regiments of this (the 2nd) brigade, the 72nd Highlanders and the 2nd Sikhs had the chief share of the fighting. They were the two leading battalions, and frequently had to fix bayonets to carry positions or to check the determined rushes of the enemy. Brigadier-General Baker speaks in high terms of the gallant behaviour of these two regiments, and notices especially the manner in which a charge of the enemy was repulsed by the 2nd Sikhs under the able and immediate command of Lieutenant-Colonel J. J. Boswell, who was well supported by Majors H. M. Pratt, J. B. Slater, and F. E. Hastings.

After severe fighting both brigades emerged at the point of the hill near Pir Paimal; and bringing their left shoulders forward, they pressed on and swept the enemy through the closely-wooded gardens and orchards which cover the western slopes of the hill.

The village of Pir Paimal was in our possession soon after noon.

When I heard from Major-General Ross of the success of the troops under his command, I determined to support his further advance by the 3rd Brigade, which had been drawn up in front of the village of Abásábad, with the double object of being a reserve to the 1st and 2nd Brigades, and of meeting a possible counter-attack by the enemy from the Baba Wali Pass.

The capture of Pir Paimal, however, brought our troops in rear of that pass; and feeling that nothing had now to be feared from the enemy's left, I pushed on with the 3rd Brigade to join Major-General Ross.

That officer, seeing the advantage gained, and knowing that he could rely upon the courage and eagerness of his troops, had very wisely determined to press forward without waiting for reinforcements.

The position to which the enemy retired, after the capture of Pir Paimal, was an entrenched camp to the south-west of the Baba Wali Kotal, commanding an open piece of ground.

This entrenchment they were evidently prepared to hold with their usual determination; reinforcements were being rapidly pushed up from their reserves, while the guns on the Baba Wali Kotal were turned round, so as to increase the heavy fire of artillery which was brought to bear upon our troops.

It became necessary to take this position at once by storm.

Recognizing this with true soldierly instinct, Major G. S. White, who was leading the advance companies of Her Majesty's 92nd Highlanders, called upon his men for just one charge more "to close the business."

The battery of screw guns, under Brevet-Major J. C. Robinson, had been shelling the enemy with a well-directed fire; under cover of which, and supported by a portion of the 2nd Goorkhas and the 23rd Pioneers, the Highlanders, responding with alacrity to their leader's call, dashed forward and drove the enemy from their entrenchments at the point of the bayonet.

The gallant and ever foremost Major White was the first to reach the enemy's guns; being closely followed by Sepoy Inderbir Lama, who, placing his rifle upon one of the guns, exclaimed that it was captured in the name of the 2nd (Prince of Wales' Own) Goorkhas.

While the 1st Brigade was advancing towards the enemy's last position, a portion of the 2nd Brigade, *viz.*, a half-battalion of the 3rd Sikhs, under Lieutenant-Colonel G. N. Money, charged a body of the enemy on the extreme left, and captured three guns.

The enemy were now completely routed; but, owing to the nature of the ground, it was impossible for Major-General Ross, who was commanding in the front line, to realise the extent of the victory he had won.

He, therefore, expecting the enemy to take up a fresh position further on, and to continue their resistance, ordered the 1st and 2nd Brigades to halt and replenish their ammunition.

When this had been done, and the troops had advanced about a mile, Major-General Ross found himself in sight of the whole of Ayúb Khan's camp, standing deserted, and apparently as it had been left in the morning, when the Afghans moved to the attack.

With his camp, Ayúb Khan lost all his artillery, numbering 32 pieces, including the two guns of E-B., Royal Horse Artillery, which had been taken by his troops at Maiwand on the 27th July.

Further pursuit with infantry being hopeless, the two brigades were halted on the far side of the village of Mazra, where they were shortly afterwards joined by the 3rd Brigade under Brigadier-General MacGregor.

I had, meanwhile, ordered the cavalry of the Bombay Force, under Brigadier-General Nuttall, to advance over the Baba Wali Kotal, and pursue the enemy up the left bank of the Argandab.

The operations of the cavalry under Brigadier-General Hugh Gough were continued throughout the day, the brigade crossing the Argandab and pushing beyond the line of the enemy's retreat towards Kakrez.

During this movement none of the regular troops were encountered, but some 350 of the fugitive *ghazis* and irregulars were killed.

With the exception of the 1st Brigade, which halted at Mazra for the night, all the troops returned to Kandahar before dark.

CASUALTY ROLL

STAFF

Brigadier-Generals

Brooke, Henry Francis, cmdg 2nd Inf Bgde k 16 Aug 1880 Deh Khojah 'whilst attempting to save the life of Captain Cruickshank RE' (D.48 & see IOM GGO 58/1881)

Cobbe, Alexander Hugh, cmdg 1st Inf Bgde sev w 2 Dec 1878 Peiwar Kotal (D.3)

Lieutenant-Colonel

Shewell, Arthur Mark, Depy Commissary-General sev w 16 Aug 1880 Deh Khojah (D.48)

Major

Cavagnari, Sir Pierre Louis Napoleon, Political Officer (Bengal Staff Corps) k 3 Sep 1879 Kabul Residency

Captains

Carthew, Charles Alfred, Deputy Asst QM General (16th Bengal Cav) sl w 11 Jun 1880 Lughman (P/1536-10533)

Harris, Thomas, Deputy Asst QM General (HM 66th Regt) w 27 Jul 1880 Maiwand (D.44)

Heath, Percy Charles, Bgde Major 1st Inf Bgde (Bombay Staff Corps) k 27 Jul 1880 Maiwand (D.44)

Kennedy, Richard George, Deputy Asst QM General sl w 5 Oct 1879 passage of Logar river (D.22)

Straton, Edward, 2nd Btn HM 22nd Regt k 1 Sep 1880 Kandahar, gs abdomen, by a ghazi springing out of a ravine close to him (D.51)

ROYAL ARTILLERY

Captains

Graves, Francis Lowry sl w 28 Feb 1880 by a young fanatic in Kandahar bazaar (P/1535-8062)

Hamilton, Constantine Henry, Staff w 14 Apr 1880 Hisarak, gs left arm (P/1537-11474)

Shafto, Edward Duncombe k 14 Oct 1879 explosion in Bala Hissar (D.29)

Waterfield, Donald Mackenzie Dunlop, attchd 3rd Sikh Inf sev w 14 Oct 1879 Sarkai Kotal, gs 'while leading a charge on the enemy' (D.30)

F / A RHA

Lieutenant

Hardy, Edward k 11 Dec 1879 Arghandi, sword cuts (D.33)

Gunners

3082 Keegan, P. sl w 11 Dec 1879 Arghandi, gs shoulder (D.33)

468 Rea, John sev w 25 Apr 1880 Charasiah, gs right forearm (D.39 & P/1537-11817)

Driver

937 Trench, J. sev w 23 Dec 1879 Kabul, gs arm (D.33)

A / B RHA

Sources D.36 & P/1537-11502

Captain

Corbett, Richard dang w 19 Apr 1880 Ahmed Khel, gs right fore-arm,compound fracture both bones

Gunner

4457 Woods, Peter sev w 19 Apr 1880 Ahmed Khel, fracture left femur,run over by wagon when carrying ammunition

E / B RHA

Source D.44

Major

Blackwood, George Frederick, cmdg k 27 Jul 1880 Maiwand, 'wounded early in the action,returned to his duty after his wound had been dressed and resumed command of the battery till he was again wounded and subsequently killed'

Lieutenants

Fowell, Newton Plomer w 27 Jul 1880 Maiwand

MacLaine, Hector captured 27 Jul 1880 Maiwand, murdered in Ayub Khan's camp 1 Sep

Osborne, Edmund George k 27 Jul 1880 Maiwand

Sergeants

4194 Burridge, Thomas w 27 Jul 1880 Maiwand, awarded DCM

4217 Wood, Michael Joseph k 27 Jul 1880 Maiwand

Collar Maker

4349 Cummings, Harry k 27 Jul 1880 Maiwand

Shoeing Smith

4186 Walker, George k 27 Jul 1880 Maiwand

Wheeler
3431 Dix, William James k 27 Jul 1880 Maiwand

actg Bombardiers
4209 Clarke, William w 27 Jul 1880 Maiwand
4430 Lowe, John k 27 Jul 1880 Maiwand

Gunners
4437 Brown, John w 27 Jul 1880 Maiwand
5062 Carver, John w 27 Jul 1880 Maiwand
4239 Dewley, John k 27 Jul 1880 Maiwand
4240 Edwards, John w 27 Jul 1880 Maiwand
4253 Jones, Richard k 27 Jul 1880 Maiwand
4257 Loughlin, James k 27 Jul 1880 Maiwand
4260 McAllister, Patrick k 27 Jul 1880 Maiwand
5082 MacDonald, Alexander k 27 Jul 1880 Maiwand
4259 Mangan, David w 27 Jul 1880 Maiwand
5071 Mathewman, Wilfred k 27 Jul 1880 Maiwand
4261 Morecroft, Samuel w 1 Sep 1880 Kandahar, gs (D.51 & P/1538-13867)
3493 Naylor, Francis J. w 27 Jul 1880 Maiwand
3422 Nicholls, William k 27 Jul 1880 Maiwand
4918 Reilly, Andrew w 27 Jul 1880 Maiwand, dow 30 Aug Kandahar
4455 Roberts, Arthur k 27 Jul 1880 Maiwand
4270 Smith, George k 27 Jul 1880 Maiwand
5070 Swinnerton, Alfred k 27 Jul 1880 Maiwand
527 Tew, James k 2 May 1880 Kandahar, by accidental discharge of a carbine (P/1537-11884)
4276 Tredgett, Joseph w 27 Jul 1880 Maiwand

Drivers
4297 Gant, Charles w 27 Jul 1880 Maiwand
722 Gove, Edward w 27 Jul 1880 Maiwand
3542 Grey, David k 27 Jul 1880 Maiwand
1634 Hornby, Thomas k 2 May 1880 Kandahar, by accidental discharge of a carbine (P/1537-11884)
4309 Istead, Picknell k 27 Jul 1880 Maiwand (see VC to Mullane)
4313 Lang, George w 27 Jul 1880 Maiwand
4686 Webster, Samuel k 27 Jul 1880 Maiwand

I/C RHA

Source D.32

Trumpeter
1997 Hill, Richard sev w 21 Nov 1878 Ali Musjid

Gunners
2007 Coonan, Timothy k 22 Nov 1878 Ali Musjid
2014 Cooper, William sl w 21 Nov 1878 Ali Musjid
1271 Fletcher, William mort w 2 Apr 1879 Fatehabad, bullet forehead, dow 25 Apr (& P/1372-6625)

C / 2 R A

Sources D.51 &
P/1538-13867

Sergeant
1450 Cox, George   sl w 1 Sep 1880 Kandahar, gs

Driver
446 Collyer, Samuel   sev w 1 Sep 1880 Kandahar, gs

G / 3 R A

Gunners
6773 Acocks, Samuel   drowned 23 Aug 1880 (MR)
7112 Holt, James   sev w Dec 1879 Kabul, gs abdomen, dow 25 Dec Kabul (D.33 & MR)

Driver
6880 Rawlins, Joseph   drowned 6 Feb 1880 Kabul (MR)

E / 4 R A

Captain
Hervey, Charles Smith   w 10 Jan 1879 Kandahar, in capturing the assassin of Lt Willis (P/1372-6054)

Lieutenant
Willis, Herbert Valiant   dang w 10 Jan 1879 Kandahar, stabbed by an assassin, dow 15 Jan (P/1372-6054 & Shadbolt)

Gunner
4928 Humphries, Charles   sev w 6 Feb 1879 camp at Kandahar (D.32)

Driver
5011 Newman, William   sev w 6 Feb 1879 camp at Kandahar (D.32)

G / 4 R A

Gunner
5270 Middleton, William   sl w 19 Apr 1880 Ahmed Khel, gs contusion right arm (D.36)

L / 5 R A

Lieutenant
Porteous, John Jones   sev w 20 May 1880 Mazina Valley, gs left thigh (D.40)

Bombardier

557 Garbett, William   sl w 20 May 1880 Mazina Valley, gs face (D.40)

6/8 RA

Source D.51

Gunner

3065 Carell, George   sev w 1 Sep 1880 Kandahar, gs chest

Drivers

Balak   sl w 1 Sep 1880 Kandahar, gs chest
Barkardar   sev w 1 Sep 1880 Kandahar, gs thigh

11/9 RA

Lieutenant

Wright, Ichabod Denman   k 29 Dec 1879 Jagdalak (D.34)

Sergeants

3764 Blackwell, Edward   sl w 21 Nov 1878 Ali Musjid; sev w 28 Jan 1879 Bazar Valley (D.32 & P/1372-5350)

1286 Pittaway, Robert   sl w 13 Apr 1880 Hisarak, sword cut (P/1537-11474)

Corporal

1292 Dalley, Richard   sl w 13 Apr 1880 Hisarak, sword cut (P/1537-11474)

Bombardier

1354 Young, William   sev w 14 Apr 1880 Hisarak, sword cut (P/1537-11474)

Gunners

1644 Akers, Henry   sev w 21 Nov 1878 Ali Musjid (D.32)
1645 Allen, Edwin   sev w 21 Nov 1878 Ali Musjid (D.32)
1648 Barker, George   sl w 13 Apr 1880 Hisarak, sword cut (P/1537-11474)
1302 Bridgeman, Benjamin   sev w 13 Apr 1880 Hisarak, sword cut (P/1537-11474)
1311 Day, William   sev w 21 Nov 1878 Ali Musjid (D.32)
1698 Sutton, George   sev w 21 Nov 1878 Ali Musjid (D.32)

13/9 RA

Sergeant

1445 Parsons, Robert   sl w 28 Nov 1878 Shagai Heights (D.32)

No 2 Mtn Bty, RA

Driver Havildar
3 Said Usman   sev w 9 Mar 1879 attack on baggage guard nr Khushdil-khan-Kakila (D.32)

ROYAL ENGINEERS

Captain
Leach, Edward Pemberton, Asst Suptd of Surveys   sl w 17 Mar 1879 Maidanak, knife cut along forearm (D.32 & P/1371-3510)

Lieutenant
Burn-Murdoch, John   sl w 23 Dec 1879 Kabul, bullet (D.33)

Sergeant
8971 Grant, T.   sev w 28 Mar 1880 nr Panizai, neck & jaw (P/1537-11401)

see also Bengal Sappers & Miners
Bombay Sappers & Miners

HM 6th DRAGOON GUARDS

The regiment lost five men drowned 5 Jan 1880 in the Kabul river nr Jellalabad (P/1534-7141)

Lance-Corporal
1851 Eves, James

Privates
1742 Friars, Frederick
1624 Slater, Thomas
1111 Stonecliffe, William R.
1680 Wood, Henry J.L.

HM 9th LANCERS

Source D.33

Lieutenant-Colonel
Cleland, Robert Stewart   sev w 11 Dec 1879 Arghandi, gs abdomen

Captains
Butson, Strange Gould   k 13 Dec 1879 Kabul, gs chest

Chisholme, John James Scott sev w 13 Dec 1879 Kabul, gs left leg,'notwithstanding the severity of his wound [he] remained in the saddle and brought his regiment out of action'

Stewart-Mackenzie, James Alexander Francis Humberston sev w 11 Dec 1879 Arghandi, gs knee

Lieutenants

Hearsey, Charles John Rumball k 11 Dec 1879 Arghandi, gs chest
Trower, Charles John William sl w 13 Dec 1879 Kabul, sword cut hand

Second Lieutenant

Ricardo, William Percy k 11 Dec 1879 Arghandi, gs chest

Sergeant-Majors

722 Spittle, Henry awarded DCM for Killa Kazi 11 Dec 1879; k 13 Dec 1879 Kabul, gs & sword cuts
705 Young, Robert sl w 11 Dec 1879 Arghandi, sword cut right thumb, awarded DCM

Trumpet-Major

1460 Potter, Harry k 11 Dec 1879 Arghandi, gs & sword cuts

Band Sergeant

728 Kent, George sev w 13 Dec 1879 Kabul, gs chest

Lance-Sergeant

1446 Shepherd, Edward k 11 Dec 1879 Arghandi, gs & sword cuts

Corporal

1575 Burn, William sev w 11 Dec 1879 Arghandi, gs fingers & chest

Lance-Corporals

1822 Bridgeman, William sev w 13 Dec 1879 Kabul, gs chest
1685 Brown, Alfred J. k 13 Dec 1879 Kabul, gs & sword cuts
1475 Doncaster, Arthur k 11 Dec 1879 Arghandi, gs & sword cuts
1593 Swann, Leonard k 11 Dec 1879 Arghandi, gs & sword cuts
1295 Tillotson, William k 11 Dec 1879 Arghandi, gs & sword cuts
1036 Wilkinson, Robert k 11 Dec 1879 Arghandi, gs & sword cuts
1924 Williamson, T. sev w 13 Dec 1879 Kabul, sword cut right arm
1531 Wright, John sev w 11 Dec 1879 Arghandi, sword cut right arm

Privates

1588 Bidwell, William sev w 11 Dec 1879 Arghandi, sword cut neck
1695 Carlisle, John k 11 Dec 1879 Arghandi, gs & sword cuts
1334 Cavanna, James sev w 11 Dec 1879 Arghandi, gs left leg
1595 Coyle, A. dang w 13 Dec 1879 Kabul, gs left thigh
1318 Gamble, John k 11 Dec 1879 Arghandi, gs & sword cuts
1800 Harris, John k 11 Dec 1879 Arghandi, gs & sword cuts
1495 Hedges, Cresswell k 11 Dec 1879 Arghandi, gs & sword cuts
1704 Holden, Thomas sev w 13 Dec 1879 Kabul, bayonet right hand
1024 Hoyle, W. sev w 13 Dec 1879 Kabul, gs left hand
489 Large, Thomas k 11 Dec 1879 Arghandi, gs & sword cuts
1628 Lloyd, Walter k 11 Dec 1879 Arghandi, gs & sword cuts

1678 Longford, James k 11 Dec 1879 Arghandi, gs & sword cuts
1010 Love, James k 13 Dec 1879 Kabul, gs & sword cuts
1819 Lowick, H. sl w 11 Dec 1879 Arghandi, contusion
1028 Mahon, Thomas k 13 Dec 1879 Kabul, gs & sword cuts
773 Newsome, William k 11 Dec 1879 Arghandi, gs & sword cuts
1230 Paice, James sev w 23 Dec 1879 Kabul, gs right foot
1899 Partington, G. sev w 13 Dec 1879 Kabul, gs left thumb
1828 Russell, Thomas k 11 Dec 1879 Arghandi, gs & sword cuts
1706 Short, James sl w 6 Oct 1879 Charasiah, bullet forehead (D.24)
1042 Simkins, George k 13 Dec 1879 Kabul, gs & sword cuts
710 Smith, Albert k 11 Dec 1879 Arghandi, gs & sword cuts
930 Smith, Thomas sev w 11 Dec 1879 Arghandi, lance in chest
1684 Tulcher, A. sev w 13 Dec 1879 Kabul, bayonet right cheek (& P/1536-10625)
1934 Wilks, C. sev w 11 Dec 1879 Arghandi, gs back
1793 Williams, R. sev w 13 Dec 1879 Kabul, gs thigh
1652 Wilson, William sev w 11 Dec 1879 Arghandi, sword cut left hand

HM 10th HUSSARS

The regiment lost one officer and forty-five men drowned 31 Mar 1879 in the Kabul river (P/1372-6646)

Sub-Lieutenant
Harford, Francis Hervey drowned

Sergeant-Major
487 Stuart, Thomas sl w 2 Apr 1879 Fatehabad (D.32)

Sergeants
977 Batten, John drowned
555 Green, P. J. drowned
1189 Hayes, H. D. drowned
1035 Keble, J. H. drowned

Lance-Sergeant (Farrier)
1050 Gilham, R. drowned

Corporals
1197 Gould, W. drowned
1042 Skinner, R. drowned

Lance-Corporal
1077 Kimble, J. drowned

Privates
1323 Allen, H. drowned
1124 Badger, E. drowned
1498 Boyes, George mort w 2 Apr 1879 Fatehabad, gs right forearm, since d (D.32 & P/1372-6625)

1641 Brisselden, Charles sl w 2 Apr 1879 Fatehabad (D.32)
823 Brown, G. H. drowned
1612 Burke, J. drowned
1380 Cant, H. drowned
816 Cappel, P. drowned
1177 Chamberlain, W. drowned
1376 Charge, W. drowned
1499 Dobin, Richard sev w 2 Apr 1879 Fatehabad, gs right leg (D.32 & P/1372-6625)
1082 Downes, T. drowned
1568 Dudley, Charles drowned
1434 Gaisford, J. drowned
1046 Gravett, T. drowned
1494 Green, G. drowned
1473 Hall, G. B. drowned
839 Hall, George sl w 2 Apr 1879 Fatehabad (D.32)
1067 Hall, John drowned
1523 Hart, James drowned
1187 Haslett, John drowned
1548 Hobbs, W. drowned
1129 Huett, F. drowned
568 Lemon, E. drowned
712 Loftus, P. drowned
1149 McKee, W. drowned
1589 Mandeville, J. drowned
1028 Massey, J. drowned
1126 May, Frederick dang w 2 Apr 1879 Fatehabad, gs abdomen (D.32 & P/1372-6625)
1302 Murrell, H. drowned
1248 Nash, W. drowned
1561 Osborne, J. drowned
870 Read, W. drowned
1519 Richards, J. drowned
1365 Roach, James Henry drowned
859 Simm, W. drowned
1271 Skevington, George drowned
452 Smith, George sl w 2 Apr 1879 Fatehabad (D.32)
1045 Tidey, G. drowned
1506 Twining, J. drowned
1199 Wilkins, W. drowned
1504 Wilson, G. drowned
1353 Wooding, C. drowned

HM 15th HUSSARS

Sources D.8, D.32 & P/1372-5813

Major

Luck, George sl w 4 Jan 1879 Saif-u-Din, sword cut contusion right arm

Sergeant-Major
475 Craddock, James sl w 4 Jan 1879 Saif-u-Din, sword cut thumb

Privates
1298 Bridgham, James sev w 4 Jan 1879 Saif-u-Din, sword cuts left wrist & elbow
1156 Collins, James sev w 4 Jan 1879 Saif-u-Din, sword cuts right wrist & left shoulder
1380 Tasker, William sl w 4 Jan 1879 Saif-u-Din, sword cut contusion right arm
1480 Taylor, Henry sl w 4 Jan 1879 Saif-u-Din, sword cut thumb
1483 Whellock, William Robert sl w 4 Jan 1879 Saif-u-Din, sword cut finger

1st Btn HM 5th REGIMENT OF FOOT (NORTHUMBERLAND FUSILIERS)

Brevet Lieutenant-Colonel
Rowland, Thomas sl w 19 May 1880 Besud, knife cut & bayonet right hand (D.41)

Colour-Sergeant
1740 Pickford, George sl w 22 Apr 1879 Kam Dakka (D.32)

Lance-Sergeant
698 Reed, William sev w 22 Apr 1879 Kam Dakka (D.32)

Privates
587 Miller, E. k 8 May 1880 nr Darounta Pass (P/1536-9901)
55 Openshaw, James sev w 19 May 1880 Besud, three knife cuts right forearm (D.41), awarded DCM
1028 Snowling, Frederick sev w 19 May 1880 Besud, deep gs left thigh (D.41)

2nd Btn HM 7th REGIMENT OF FOOT (ROYAL FUSILIERS)

Sources D.48 & P/1538-13867

Major
Vandeleur, Thomas Burton dang w 16 Aug 1880 Deh Khojah, dow 26 Aug Kandahar

Captain
Connolly, William sl w 16 Aug 1880 Deh Khojah

Second Lieutenants

De Trafford, Galfrid Aloysius Cathcart   sev w 6 Aug 1880 siege of Kandahar
Marsh, Everard Swaine   k 16 Aug 1880 Deh Khojah 'in helping to bring in Lieutenant Wood, who was then severely wounded'
Wood, Frederick Philip Forster   k 16 Aug 1880 Deh Khojah

Colour-Sergeant

750 Strong, Frederick   k 16 Aug 1880 Deh Khojah

Sergeants

1458 Quinn, John   k 16 Aug 1880 Deh Khojah
795 Shorter, William   k 16 Aug 1880 Deh Khojah
2226 Stewart, William   dang w 16 Aug 1880 Deh Khojah

Lance-Sergeants

1979 Fennell, James   k 16 Aug 1880 Deh Khojah
1394 Logan, Henry   dang w 16 Aug 1880 Deh Khojah

Corporals

825 Bennett, Henry   very sev w 16 Aug 1880 Deh Khojah
1454 Bishop, Philip   k 16 Aug 1880 Deh Khojah
2125 Cranston, William   k 16 Aug 1880 Deh Khojah

Lance-Corporal

1878 Smith, John   sev w 16 Aug 1880 Deh Khojah

Drummer

2137 Collins, Henry   sev w 9 Aug 1880 siege of Kandahar

Privates

2267 Adams, Alfred   sev w 16 Aug 1880 Deh Khojah, dow 17 Aug
812 Aldridge, Alfred   sl w 16 Aug 1880 Deh Khojah
1505 Ballard, Alfred   very sev w 16 Aug 1880 Deh Khojah
1499 Barnes, Joseph   very sev w 16 Aug 1880 Deh Khojah
1071 Cockle, Benjamin   sev w 16 Aug 1880 Deh Khojah
939 County, William   k 16 Aug 1880 Deh Khojah
2385 Cox, Thomas   sev w 16 Aug 1880 Deh Khojah
1781 Davis, George   dang w 16 Aug 1880 Deh Khojah
489 Devine, Philip   sev w 16 Aug 1880 Deh Khojah, dow same day
2134 Dixon, Charles   sev w 16 Aug 1880 Deh Khojah
891 Elliott, Charles   sl w 16 Aug 1880 Deh Khojah
2245 Farrar, Thomas   sev w 9 Aug 1880 siege of Kandahar
1077 Fitzhugh, John   k 16 Aug 1880 Deh Khojah
980 Gilmour, William   k 16 Aug 1880 Deh Khojah
1055 Goddard, William   dang w 16 Aug 1880 Deh Khojah, dow 24 Aug
1545 Gregory, William   sev w 16 Aug 1880 Deh Khojah
712 Halpin, John   k 16 Aug 1880 Deh Khojah
1631 Henniffer, James   k 16 Aug 1880 Deh Khojah
1670 Hetherington, Robert   dang w 16 Aug 1880 Deh Khojah
1002 Howe, Alfred   k 16 Aug 1880 Deh Khojah
1014 Huntley, Frederick   k 16 Aug 1880 Deh Khojah
1613 Job, John   k 16 Aug 1880 Deh Khojah
2248 Kent, George   k 16 Aug 1880 Deh Khojah

2319 Kinsella, James sl w 16 Aug 1880 Deh Khojah
1611 Kirby, Charles k 16 Aug 1880 Deh Khojah
1626 Lanning, Thomas sev w 16 Aug 1880 Deh Khojah
1196 Mabbett, Edwin very sev w 16 Aug 1880 Deh Khojah
809 McKevor, John k 16 Aug 1880 Deh Khojah
1586 Massey, William sev w 16 Aug 1880 Deh Khojah (see VCs to Ashford & Chase)
1256 Nash, George k 12 Aug 1880 siege of Kandahar
1040 New, Frederick k 16 Aug 1880 Deh Khojah
745 Newberry, Edward dang w 16 Aug 1880 Deh Khojah
774 Orton, Edward mort w 2 Aug 1880 siege of Kandahar, dow 5 Aug
440 Pringle, John k 16 Aug 1880 Deh Khojah
1207 Reilly, Terence sev w 16 Aug 1880 Deh Khojah
1917 Rushen, Thomas k 16 Aug 1880 Deh Khojah
1064 Steer, William k 16 Aug 1880 Deh Khojah
1926 Strickland, Harry dang w 16 Aug 1880 Deh Khojah, dow 17 Aug
896 Swan, Francis dang w 16 Aug 1880 Deh Khojah, dow 17 Aug
2132 Sykes, Thomas sev w 16 Aug 1880 Deh Khojah
347 Trellogan, William w 16 Aug 1880 Deh Khojah
852 Tripp, George very sev w 16 Aug 1880 Deh Khojah
1309 Trower, George k 16 Aug 1880 Deh Khojah
2100 Weaver, Henry sev w 12 Aug 1880 siege of Kandahar

2nd Btn HM 8th REGIMENT OF FOOT

Source D.32

Colour-Sergeant
1774 Innes, William sl w 2 Dec 1878 Peiwar Kotal

Sergeant
1066 Howard, James dang w 2 Dec 1878 Peiwar Kotal

Drum Major
1357 Cunningham, Owen k 2 Dec 1878 Peiwar Kotal

Lance-Corporal
1381 Savage, Thomas Storey sl w 2 Dec 1878 Peiwar Kotal

Privates
1097 Burges, Joseph sev w 2 Dec 1878 Peiwar Kotal
1324 Delany, Charles sl w 2 Dec 1878 Peiwar Kotal
685 Jones, Lewis sl w 2 Dec 1878 Peiwar Kotal
1437 Jones, Richard sl w 2 Dec 1878 Peiwar Kotal (& MR)

2nd Btn HM 9th REGIMENT OF FOOT

Source D.34

Sergeant

2353 Thompson, Joseph   w 19 Dec 1879 Jagdalak, gs head

Privates

2305 Lynch, John   sl w 25 Apr 1879 Shekabad, gs contusion muscle of left arm (D.38 & P/1537-11807)
1119 Miles, F.   w 17 Dec 1879 Jagdalak, gs right wrist
Robinson, Alfred   w 19 Dec 1879 Jagdalak Kotal, gs head, since dow
488 Sullivan, M.   w 19 Dec 1879 Jagdalak, gs hip
1312 Ward, James   w 17 Dec 1879 Jagdalak Kotal, gs right cheek

1st Btn HM 12th REGIMENT OF FOOT

Source D.32

Sergeant

1746 Stark, George   k 22 Apr 1879 Kam Dakka

Privates

32B/1098 Dunn, Richard   sl w 22 Apr 1879 Kam Dakka
32B/100 Glover, James   sev w 22 Apr 1879 Kam Dakka, d 8 Jun (MR)
32B/109 Grady, Edward   sl w 22 Apr 1879 Kam Dakka
32B/104 Longworth, Jonathan   sev w 19 May 1880 Besud, very deep knife cut back of left shoulder, deep muscles severed (D.41), awarded DCM
32B/127 Priest, James Henry   sev w 22 Apr 1879 Kam Dakka
32B/364 Taylor, Charles   sl w 22 Apr 1879 Kam Dakka
32B/473 Welsh, John   k 22 Apr 1879 Kam Dakka

2nd Btn HM 14th REGIMENT OF FOOT

Source D.40

Captain

Noyes, Arthur Walter   sl w 20 May 1880 Mazina Valley, sabre cut hand - 'there was a sanga which the guns could not reach, owing to a high bank; this position was obstinately held, but carried finally in a charge led by Captain Noyes, who was first in, killed the first man who opposed him and grappled with the second, who was bayoneted by the men, but not before he had wounded Captain Noyes in the hand'

Corporal
1867 Manning, Michael sev w 20 May 1880 Mazina Valley, gs left shoulder (& MR)

Drummer
461 Ambridge, Henry k 20 May 1880 Mazina Valley

Privates
2371 Derry, Frederick k 20 May 1880 Mazina Valley
1352 Hollingdrake, Thomas sev w 20 May 1880 Mazina Valley, gs left thigh
2206 Humphries, Reuben sl w 20 May 1880 Mazina Valley, gs

2nd Btn HM 15th REGIMENT OF FOOT

Lieutenant
Wood, Hastings, Transport Dept dang w 16 Aug 1880 Deh Khojah, gs (P/1538-13867)

1st Btn HM 17th REGIMENT OF FOOT

Sources D.32, P/1372-5297 & P/1372-6625

Lieutenant
Wiseman, Nicholas Cuthbert k 2 Apr 1879 Fatehabad, 'a gallant charge captured the standard but at the cost of the life of this gallant young officer' (& D.18)

Sergeant
638 Halpin, John sl w 2 Apr 1879 Fatehabad, neck

Lance-Corporal
1811 Moore, Frederick dang w 2 Apr 1879 Fatehabad, gs left thigh,ring & little fingers left hand

Privates
1661 Bashford, Thomas mort w 21 Dec 1878 Bazar Valley, gs thigh,bone fractured, dow 22 Dec
1627 Benwell, William k 19 Mar 1879 nr Dakka
1760 Bradbury, Edward k 19 Mar 1879 nr Dakka
1807 Clarke, John sev w 2 Apr 1879 Fatehabad, contusion left shoulder
522 Gavin, Michael sl w 2 Apr 1879 Fatehabad, hand
1879 Good, Henry k 2 Apr 1879 Fatehabad
27B/287 Powell, John sev w 21 Dec 1878 Bazar Valley, gs fractured thigh; k 22 Dec while in a doolie on the march

1st Btn HM 25th REGIMENT OF FOOT

Source D.32

Drummer

6B/606 Colbeck, Samuel sl w 26 Jan 1879 Bazar Valley

Privates

6B/455 Birmingham, John sl w 29 Jan 1879 Bazar Valley
6B/27 Flute, Thomas dang w 26 Jan 1879 Bazar Valley
6B/858 Gregson, Thomas sl w 18 May 1879 attack on picquet at Landi Kotal
6B/1317 McMullen, Robert k 26 Jan 1879 Bazar Valley
757 Murray, Martin k 6 Jul 1880 nr Surwak village, gs through body (P/1538-14089)

HM 51st KING'S OWN LIGHT INFANTRY REGIMENT

Sources D.32, P/1536 -10533 & P/1537-11474

Major

Burnaby, Eustace B. sl w 11 Jun 1880 Lughman

Captains

Kennett, Brackley Herbert Burington sl w 16 Apr 1880 Hisarak, contusion from spent ball
Nugent, John Vesey w 12/16 Apr 1880 Hisarak, contusion from spent ball

Lieutenant

Thackwell, Colquhoun Grant Roche sev w 30 Jun 1880 on convoy duty between Pezwan & Jagdalak Kotal, gs left chest,clavicle exposed (P/1537-12272)

Second Lieutenants

Reid, Herbert A. S. sl w 15 Apr 1880 Hisarak, head
Thurlow, Benjamin Smith k 22 Mar 1880 (MR)

Sergeants

881 Binge, William sev w 28 Nov 1878 attack on picquet at Ali Musjid
1790 McCarthy, James k 13 Apr 1880 Hisarak
2747 Rawkins, Matthew sl w 16 Apr 1880 Hisarak, gs leg

Lance-Corporals

8B/847 Darter, John H. sl w 28 Nov 1878 attack on picquet at Ali Musjid
8B/938 Holland, Joseph sl w 21 Nov 1878 Ali Musjid
1337 Shard, William sl w 11 Jun 1880 Lughman

Privates

1493 Atkinson, Charles A. sl w 16 Apr 1880 Hisarak, gs thigh

1352 Chapman, Charles sl w 16 Apr 1880 Hisarak, gs wrist
951 Cleary, Michael w 13 Apr 1880 Hisarak, contusion from spent ball
720 Dowling, John w 13 Apr 1880 Hisarak, contusion from spent ball
8B/882 Downey, Robert sev w 19 Jan 1879 attack on picquet at Ali Musjid
2727 Drury, Samuel sl w 28 Nov 1878 attack on picquet at Ali Musjid
8B/956 Gall, James sev w 19 Jan 1879 attack on picquet at Ali Musjid
978 Moore, Patrick sev w 16 Apr 1880 Hisarak, gs left elbow
8B/169 Nelson, John k 21 Nov 1878 Ali Musjid
2026 Talbot, Robert sev w 21 Nov 1878 Ali Musjid
2165 White, Thomas sl w 28 Nov 1878 attack on picquet at Ali Musjid
8B/146 White, William sl w 28 Nov 1878 attack on picquet at Ali Musjid

HM 59th REGIMENT OF FOOT

Sources D.36, D.48 & P/1537-11502

Brevet Lieutenant-Colonel

Lawson, James sev w 19 Apr 1880 Ahmed Khel, gs left breast

Captain

Sartorius, Euston Henry w 24 Oct 1879 Shahjui, sword cuts both hands (P/1537-6652), awarded VC

Lieutenant

Watson, Stephen, Adjutant sl w 19 Apr 1880 Ahmed Khel, gs back of left hand

Sergeants

1590 Donovan, John sev w 6 Feb 1879 attack on camp Kandahar (D.32)
373 Thompson, Frederick sev w 19 Apr 1880 Ahmed Khel, gs

Corporal

1186 McGarry, Felix, attchd HM 66th Regt k 27 Jul 1880 Maiwand (MR)

Drummer

838 Butler, James sev w 19 Apr 1880 Ahmed Khel, gs

Privates

893 Atterwill, James dang w 16 Aug 1880 Deh Khojah, dow 3 Sep
167 Callaghan, John sl w 19 Apr 1880 Ahmed Khel, gs
1222 Carruthers, James k 24 Oct 1879 Shahjui (P/1537-6652)
207 Carten, James k 16 Aug 1880 Deh Khojah
657 Collier, William sl w 6 Feb 1879 attack on camp Kandahar (D.32)

1205 Connolly, Thomas sev w 19 Apr 1880 Ahmed Khel, gs
278 Daley, Lawrence sev w 19 Apr 1880 Ahmed Khel, gs
814 Friend, John k 6 Feb 1879 attack on camp Kandahar (D.32)
384 Kidney, Patrick k 16 Aug 1880 Deh Khojah
890 Lunn, Allen sev w 19 Apr 1880 Ahmed Khel, sword cuts
670 Oliver, Patrick sl w 19 Apr 1880 Ahmed Khel, gs
1299 Rutherford, George k 19 Apr 1880 Ahmed Khel, sword cuts
1241 Saunders, John sev w 19 Apr 1880 Ahmed Khel, gs (MR '1314')
231 Ward, Thomas w 15 Aug 1880 Deh Khojah, dow same day
1313 Wardall, Thomas mort w 6 Feb 1879 attack on camp Kandahar, dow 7 Feb (D.32)
216 Wood, John mort w 19 Apr 1880 Ahmed Khel, gs, dow 20 Apr
1338 Worthington, William sev w 19 Apr 1880 Ahmed Khel, gs

2nd Btn HM 60th (KING'S ROYAL RIFLE CORPS) REGIMENT OF FOOT

Sources D.36 & P/1537-11502

Colour-Sergeant

1482 Chessum, John H. k 19 Apr 1880 Ahmed Khel, sword

Bugler

837 Fitzpatrick, John dang w 19 Apr 1880 Ahmed Khel, gs neck & shoulder,bullet passed through trachea

Privates

785 Blake, William k 19 Apr 1880 Ahmed Khel, gs & sword
1183 Bungey, John sev w 19 Apr 1880 Ahmed Khel, gs left hip
2009 Crook, Worthy k 23 Apr 1880 Arzu, bullet (D.37)
192 Dean, James sev w 1 Sep 1880 Kandahar, gs foot (D.51)
1806 Tripp, George sl w 1 Sep 1880 Kandahar, gs foot
2091 Ward, George k 19 Apr 1880 Ahmed Khel, gs & sword

HM 66th REGIMENT OF FOOT

Privates

545 Ball, Tom sev w 14 Jul 1880 Girishk, gs through left thigh (D.43)
493 Cunningham, Joseph sev w 10 Aug 1880 siege of Kandahar, gs, d 21 Aug pneumonia (D.48 & P/1538-13867)
B.665 Holmes, John D.44 = k at Maiwand, but D.48 & MR = d 11 Aug 1880 Kandahar, diarrhoea
1628 Pike, James sl w 14 Jul 1880 Girishk, bayonet left hand (D.43), awarded DCM

603 Robbins, William — dang w 14 Jul 1880 Girishk, gs through upper left thigh & right buttock (P/1538-12852)

1658 White, George — sev w 14 Jul 1880 Girishk, gs through left thigh, since dow (D.43)

The regiment suffered the following casualties at Maiwand 27 Jul 1880 (D.44 & D.45)

Lieutenant-Colonel

Galbraith, James k 'last seen on the nullah bank, kneeling on one knee, with a color in his hand, officers and men rallying round him; and on this spot his body was found'

Captains

Cullen, Francis James k
Garratt, Ernest Stephen k 'both killed on the field in front of the nullah, up to the last moment commanding their companies and giving their orders with as much coolness as if on an ordinary regimental parade'

Harris, Thomas, Deputy Asst QM General w

McMath, William Hamilton k

Roberts, Walter k 'mortally wounded in the garden where the last stand was made'

Lieutenants

Chute, Richard Trevor k 'fell in the garden where the last stand was made'

Lynch, Hyacinth w

Rayner, Maurice Edward k 'fell in the garden where the last stand was made'

Second Lieutenants

Barr, Henry James Outram k 'shot dead over one of the colors'

Honywood, Arthur k 'shot down in the garden where the last stand was made, whilst holding a color high above his head, shouting - Men, what shall we do to save this!'

Olivey, Walter Rice k 'in the garden where the last stand was made, holding up the colors as rallying points'

Surgeon-Major

Preston, Alexander Preston w

Sergeant-Major

1171 Cuppage, Alexander k 'shot dead outside the garden where the last stand was made, whilst carrying a color'

Colour-Sergeants

1410 Apthorpe, John k
B.640 Bayne, James k
1397 Connor, James sl w
1011 Gover, Frederick k
1340 Scadding, Samuel k

Sergeants

245 Colley, Robert, Armourer Sgt k
890 Connolly, Michael, Band Sgt sl w
1436 Cosgrove, John k
770 Cruise, John W. k
726 Davis, Thomas H., Master Tailor k
1615 Fitzgerald, Richard k
1485 Guntrip, William k
1336 Kelly, William sev w
1296 Lockwood, Charles sev w
1466 Rice, George k
1416 Rollings, Jesse k
B.672 Spencer, Isaac J., Pioneer Sgt k
1635 Symonds, William k
1598 Tyrell, Thomas sl w
1072 Walker, James k

Lance-Sergeants

1276 Burnes, Patrick sl w
1185 Ireland, Robert, actg Drum Major k
1386 Kelly, Peter sl w
B.227 Stewart, William sl w

Corporals

1011 Ayling, James k
1495 Bolton, George k
B.200 Brennan, Michael k
1276 Byrnes, Patrick w (MR)
4146 Connolly, Richard k
725 Davis, Eli k
1493 Hanks, Charles, actg Pay Master Sgt k
1386 Kelly, Peter w (MR)
1621 Mahoney, Eugene k
1643 Millsome, William k
B.677 Morecroft, Enoch, Band Corp k
1476 Smith, William k
1423 Travers, Hugh k

Lance-Corporals

897 Gosslin, Tressilian very sev w
1786 Ireland, Henry sl w
B.1396 Williams, Frederick sl w, awarded DCM
849 Willis, James sl w

Drummers

975 Cain, James sl w
B.1644 Cohen, Henry k
1497 Darby, Michael k
941 Goddard, George k
1639 Groves, John k
B.175 Johnston, James k

Privates

B.1440 Ackins, John k
B.1253 Acott, Henry k
B.678 Adams, John k
B.147 Adams, Patrick k
B.591 Allen, Edward k
B.1437 Allen, Edwin k
3381 Almond, Robert k
B.520 Ambrose, Thomas k
1519 Anderson, George k
B.688 Ashton, Samuel k
997 Atkins, Edward sev w
114 Barrett, Crispin k
B.1310 Basden, Alfred k
850 Beard, James k
1175 Beard, John k
1096 Beeck, David k
966 Beggs, Edward k
B.392 Belcher, Abraham k
B.312 Bennett, James k
833 Bentley, George k
1632 Biffin, George k
1129 Blake, Francis k
B.577 Bolton, Edwin k
1387 Boon, Samuel k
B.29 Boucher, Henry k
1408 Bracken, Michael k
1380 Brown, Henry k
1646 Brown, James k
B.1474 Brown, Thomas k
B.488 Brown, William k
1071 Bryant, Benjamin k
B.644 Bullock, David k
B.77 Burgess, John k
B.419 Burke, Edmund k
B.1438 Burling, William k
B.147 Burton, James k
B.1395 Butler, Joseph k
B.1327 Campbell, John k
B.187 Cannings, John k
B.651 Capel, Charles k
B.473 Carter, George k
639 Casey, Patrick k
B.1277 Castle, Alfred k
B.81 Chamberlain, Charles k
B.315 Charman, John k
1213 Cheeseman, William k
1672 Churcher, George k
1361 Clarke, James k
B.616 Cobern, William k
B.1544 Coleman, John k
828 Collins, William k
1155 Connolly, Richard k
B.349 Cooke, Charles k
1304 Cooke, William k
B.1460 Cooney, John k
B.1486 Cooper, Joshua k
B.405 Cope, Joseph k
1075 Corke, James k
B.274 Croft, Charles k
1241 Daniels, William k
B.710 Davis, Charles sl w
B.1421 Davis, George k
B.159 Davis, John k
B.1531 Dawson, Frederick k
1229 Dawson, John k
B.615 Dewe, Albert k
1347 Diamond, Martin k
1433 Didcock, Job k
B.1499 Donigan, Peter k
845 Donnon, Robert k
1471 Donoghue, Charles k
1279 Doran, Edward k
B.1434 Downes, Patrick k
1273 Downey, Owen k

1567 Doyle, James k
B.301 Drew, Albert k
1262 Drewitt, Philip k
1645 Dudman, James k
B.1487 Duffy, Edward k
1203 Dunn, Andrew k
B.420 Dunne, Andrew k
B.1714 Durrant, Daniel k
B.216 Eaton, John k
B.1401 Edwards, John k
886 Elvidge, Mark k
B.566 Evans, John k
1364 Evans, John k
B.1495 Evars, David k
3452 Fahey, Edward k
B.1494 Faulkner, Joseph k
B.109 Feeney, John k
1159 Fields, John k
B.288 Fisher, Frederick k
1660 Fitzgerald, John k
1320 Fitzpatrick, James k
B.1630 Fleming, William k
B.1491 Foley, Patrick k
1512 Ford, John k
B.429 Fraher, Michael k
B.260 Froude, Henry k
B.1561 Gibson, William k
1243 Gilbert, Frederick k
1493 Gray, Jacob k
B.1403 Green, Henry k
1339 Green, Thomas sev w
B.687 Green, William k
B.430 Greenstock, Joseph k
B.318 Grimshaw, Joseph k
B.163 Grist, Levi k
B.1508 Gunney, George k
1461 Hanson, Joseph k
B.352 Harding, Henry k
B.1330 Harmsworth, Thomas k
1527 Harvey, George sl w
B.192 Harwood, Oliver sev w
B.1407 Hazzell, William k
1097 Healey, James k
B.1381 Hill, Charles k
B.1422 Hill, Frank sev w
B.291 Hines, Robert k
816 Hinton, George k
B.1413 Hoare, John k
1479 Holloway, Thomas k
925 Hoskins, William k
1223 Houlihan, Edward k
1206 Hughes, Thomas k
B.1273 Hume, Benjamin k
B.691 Huzzey, Andrew k
B.686 Ingerfield, George k
1449 Jackson, Joseph k
B.607 Jackson, William k
B.407 Jacobs, Edward k
B.275 James, Isaac k
B.498 James, William k
B.1550 Jeffries, Alfred k
1268 Jenkins, John k
1667 Jones, George k
831 Jones, Joseph k
166 Jones, William k
1407 Kelly, James k
B.1510 Kelly, Thomas k
905 Kent, John k
1066 King, John k
B.1374 King, John very sev w, dow 28 Jul Kandahar
B.1506 King, Thomas k
B.468 Knight, Daniel k
B.1329 Laing, Henry k
1281 Lambert, Reuben k
1480 Lawrence, George k
1031 Leach, Robert Daniel k
B.706 Lee, Richard k
B.1583 Lennon, William k
B.1319 Leonard, Henry k
B.1378 Lewis, Henry k
B.1391 Lock, John k
1596 McCaffery, Owen k
1257 McDermott, John k
B.433 McGinley, John k
B.231 McGlashan, James sl w
1404 McLaren, James k
B.1637 McManus, James k
B.1640 McQuade, Michael sl w
1576 McQuade, Peter sev w
1380 Maloney, Cornelius k
B.654 Mannons, John k
B.707 Martin, Henry k
B.141 Martin, John k
B.580 Masterson, John A. k
B.1294 Matthews, David k
B.261 Mead, William k
B.219 Meadhurst, Frederick k
B.306 Merritt, James k
1298 Morgan, Joseph k
B.373 Munday, Walter k
1555 Murrell, Henry k
1616 Neal, Martin k

B.492 Newton, Thomas k
B.1580 Noon, Martin sl w
973 Northcott, Alfred k
1411 Olley, Joseph k
1464 O'Neil, Thomas k
B.1339 O'Reilly, Michael k
1529 Orris, Arthur k
970 Palmer, John k
B.123 Partington, Matthew k
B.341 Perkins, William k
B.326 Perris, Frederick k
1673 Pettit, Oscar k
B.575 Pike, William sev w
1546 Pooley, Philip k
B.181 Pound, John k
B.680 Proctor, Joseph k
974 Ravenscroft, Joseph k
B.1638 Reichell, John k
B.206 Richardson, James k
1231 Ritchie, John k
B.470 Roach, Joseph k
B.603 Robbins, William w (but also = dang w 14 Jul 1880 Girishk, gs through upper left thigh & right buttock)
1420 Robinson, David sev w
B.1419 Rolf, Charles k
B.1787 Ryan, Alfred k
B.416 Seery, Patrick k
B.1488 Sharp, Richard k
B.1341 Shead, Joseph sl w
B.1426 Shelly, Shadrack k
B.590 Sherville, Henry k
B.640 Shiner, Henry k
968 Shute, Edwin k
B.461 Sibson, George k
B.448 Sims, Thomas k
1604 Slevin, John k
B.434 Smith, Daniel k
B.444 Smith, Edwin k
B.436 Smith, James k
B.400 Smith, John k
1254 Smith, John k
B.1670 Stacey, Thomas k
B.447 Stallard, William k
B.367 Staymaker, William k
1513 Stephens, Joseph k
1295 Stevens, George k
B.411 Stroud, Henry k
1248 Sutton, James k
1224 Thompson, Charles k
1655 Thorne, Enos k
1322 Tippin, Emanuel k

B.1409 Townshend, John k
B.205 Trewinhard, William J. k
1642 Tuttle, George k
B.439 Veeney, William k
B.531 Vernum, Arthur k
1660 Vigors, Harry k
B.410 Waight, Harry k
B.555 Wakefield, James k
B.1496 Walsh, John k
1509 Ward, Patrick k
B.207 Wardle, Henry sl w
B.533 Warren, Henry sl w
B.568 Watts, Joshua k
B.1262 Wayne, John k
1123 Webb, Harry k
B.1315 Webb, William k
B.391 Welsh, Samuel k
B.179 Werrell, Frederick k
824 West, George k
B.1523 Weston, Lester k
1536 White, Henry k
1550 Whiting, Charles k
B.1280 Wiggins, Thomas k
B.128 Willett, James kld
1362 Williams, Edward k
1593 Wilson, Henry k
B.1641 Wilson, James k
B.210 Wilson, William k
B.332 Winter, Isaac k
25 Wolstenholme, Richard k
1451 Wood, William k
1370 Yandell, George k

HM 67th REGIMENT OF FOOT

Sources D.33 & P/1535-8191

Captain
Poole, Arthur James sev w 10 Nov 1879 Doaba, bullet,calf of right leg

Colour-Sergent
1255 Hennessy, James sev w 11 Dec 1879 Arghandi, gs scalp

Sergeants
1908 Brown, Richard, Army Signalling Dept sl w 2 Oct 1879 Shutar Gardan (D.21)
1859 Edwards, George sev w 10 Nov 1879 Doaba, bullet right calf

Corporals
2439 Bray, Frederick k 14 Oct 1879 explosion in Bala Hissar (D.29)
1475 Heath, William dang w 10 Nov 1879 Doaba, bullet right leg,since amputated, awarded DCM
40B/89 Woolley, Michael sl w 10 Nov 1879 Doaba, left thigh, awarded DCM

Lance-Corporal
429 Gannon, T. sev w 14 Dec 1879 Kabul, gs right leg

Privates
40B/403 Burton, Ananias k 10 Nov 1879 Doaba, bullet left hip
1994 Cannon, Henry sl w 14 Dec 1879 Kabul, gs contusion
487 Clery, W. sl w 23 Dec 1879 Kabul, gs
1969 Cook, Frank sev w 19 Dec 1879 Kabul, gs eyebrow
1762 Goodyear, James sev w 19 Dec 1879 Kabul, gs leg, since d (& MR)
2445 Heaney, Terence sev w 12 Nov 1879 Doaba, bullet right thigh
40B/183 Kearle, John k 10 Nov 1879 Doaba
40B/1057 Kimber, Henry sl w 14 Dec 1879 Kabul, gs left ankle
40B/802 Knaggs, Alfred J. sev w 19 Dec 1879 Kabul, gs knee
2393 Lever, William sev w 19 Dec 1879 Kabul, gs face, since d (& MR)
476 Lower, J. sev w 14 Dec 1879 Kabul, gs right leg
1634 May, George sl w 10 Dec 1879 Paghman Valley, sword cut head, since d (& MR)
1751 Palmer, Samuel k 10 Nov 1879 Doaba, bullet left side of neck
1472 Smith, Henry sev w 21 Dec 1879 Kabul, gs thigh
40B/193 Thornhill, Stephen sev w 19 Dec 1879 Kabul, gs elbow
40B/478 Ward, Tom Cooper sl w 18 Dec 1879 Kabul, gs thumb, since d (& MR)
2341 Webb, Charles sl w 14 Dec 1879 Kabul, gs ankle

HM 70th (SURREY) REGIMENT

Private
2029 Turner, James   sev w 6 Feb 1879 attack on camp at Kandahar (D.32)

HM 72nd (DUKE OF ALBANY'S OWN HIGHLANDERS) REGIMENT OF FOOT

Sources D.24, D.32 D.33 & D.51

Colonel
Brownlow, Francis   k 1 Sep 1880 Kandahar, gs chest

Captains
Frome, St John Thomas   k 1 Sep 1880 Kandahar, gs chest
Murray, Robert Hunter   sev w 1 Sep 1880 Kandahar
Spens, Nathaniel James   k 14 Dec 1879 Kabul, sword cuts, 'in an heroic attempt to stem the advance of the enemy'

Lieutenants
Egerton, Granville George Algernon   sev w 14 Dec 1879 Kabul, gs chest
Fergusson, Charles Hamilton   sl w 6 Oct 1879 Charasiah, bullet contusion left leg; sev w 12 Dec 1879 Sherpur, gs face
Gaisford, Cecil Henry   k 14 Dec 1879 Kabul, gs chest
Monro, Seymour Charles Hale   sl w 2 Dec 1878 Peiwar Kotal; sev w 1 Sep 1880 Kandahar

Second Lieutenant
Sunderland, Lister   sl w 18 Dec 1879 Kabul, gs right heel

Colour-Sergeants
514 Jacobs, George   awarded DCM for Kabul; sev w 1 Sep 1880 Kandahar, gs groin, awarded bar to DCM
1400 Yule, John   k 14 Dec 1879 Kabul, gs pelvis

Sergeants
1029 Leisk, John   sev w 6 Oct 1879 Charasiah, bullet right leg
429 Patterson, Abraham   sl w 2 Dec 1878 Peiwar Kotal
891 Smart, John   sev w 6 Oct 1879 Charasiah, bullet left forearm
651 Watt, George   k 6 Oct 1879 Charasiah, bullet through head

Lance-Sergent
1583 Cameron, William   k 1 Sep 1880 Kandahar, gs abdomen - 'a grand specimen of a Highland soldier'

Corporals
968 Adams, William   sl w 14 Dec 1879 Kabul, gs contusion
1298 Darling, David   sev w 2 Dec 1878 Peiwar Kotal

1633 Doughty, William sl w 14 Dec 1879 Kabul, gs left foot
218 Newton, Robert sl w 11 Dec 1879 Arghandi, gs right shoulder (MR = '1371')
1302 Thomson, Arthur sl w 1 Sep 1880 Kandahar, gs abrasion ear
58B/23 Wilson, Alfred k 14 Dec 1879 Kabul, gs left thigh

Lance-Corporals

1746 Brown, William mort w 2 Dec 1878 Peiwar Kotal, dow 16 Dec
967 Eyre, John sev w 1 Sep 1880, gs abrasion breast
1547 Fraser, John sl w 6 Oct 1879 Charasiah, bullet
1263 Gannon, William k 1 Sep 1880 Kandahar, gs abdomen
58B/2065 McIlvenna, Josiah k 1 Sep 1880 Kandahar, gs shoulder
179 McKenzie, George sl w 6 Oct 1879 Charasiah, bullet left foot
574 McManus, James sl w 6 Oct 1879 Charasiah, face contusion from bullet
594 McManus, Peter sev w 14 Dec 1879 Kabul, gs right leg
2018 Philip, Robert sev w 1 Sep 1880 Kandahar, gs forearm
1111 Pottie, George sev w 6 Oct 1879 Charasiah, bullet in jaw
1499 Sellar, George sev w 14 Dec 1879 Asmai Heights,Kabul, gs,sword cut on arm in combat with a ghazi, awarded VC

Piper

1614 Macpherson, James k 6 Oct 1879 Charasiah, bullet in thigh

Drummers

1502 Adams, Edward sev w 6 Oct 1879 Charasiah, bullet right leg
2022 Adams, Frederick k 14 Dec 1879 Kabul, gs chest
1917 Girvan, Peter k 14 Dec 1879 Kabul, gs head

Privates

183 Allan, Andrew sev w 6 Oct 1879 Charasiah, bullet right thumb
1436 Allison, Samuel sev w 1 Sep 1880 Kandahar, gs knee
922 Anderson, James sev w 6 Oct 1879 Charasiah, bullet left breast & right forearm
1149 Auld, William sl w 6 Oct 1879 Charasiah, bullet leg
1576 Barnett, George sl w 2 Dec 1878 Peiwar Kotal
58B/468 Beagan, James dang w 1 Sep 1880 Kandahar, gs chest, dow 2 Sep (MR = Baggan)
58B/2686 Bell, John suicide 21 Aug 1880 Kabul (MR)
1679 Black, George sev w 1 Sep 1880 Kandahar, gs neck & chest
1489 Bonar, Daniel awarded DCM for Peiwar Kotal; sl w 6 Oct 1879 Charasiah, bullet left arm
1988 Bridges, James sl w 14 Dec 1879 Kabul, gs left breast
63 Cairns, John sev w 6 Oct 1879 Charasiah, bullet right shoulder

56B/191 Cole, John sev w 14 Dec 1879 Kabul, gs through neck
2026 Colville, David sev w 1 Sep 1880 Kandahar, gs left shoulder
975 Conn, John sev w 6 Oct 1879 Charasiah, bullet left breast, dow 31 Oct Kabul (& P/1372-6650)
1232 Cooper, Robert sl w 2 Dec 1878 Peiwar Kotal
205 Cracknell, Henry k 6 Oct 1879 Charasiah, bullet in neck
1350 Douglas, John dang w 1 Sep 1880 Kandahar, gs breast & arm, dow 8 Sep (& MR)
764 Duffy, Daniel sev w 14 Dec 1879 Kabul, gs right thigh
58B/2653 Erskine, William k 1 Sep 1880 Kandahar, gs abdomen
1604 Fitzgerald, William sev w 14 Dec 1879 Kabul, gs neck
1255 Forbes, William sev w 6 Oct 1879 Charasiah, bullet through thigh
1760 Foster, William sev w 14 Dec 1879 Kabul, gs right knee
58B/568 Fraser, John k 14 Dec 1879 Kabul, gs chest
58B/368 Fulton, William sl w 1 Sep 1880 Kandahar, gs head
1290 Glen, Peter k 12 Dec 1879 Sherpur, gs chin (MR = dow 21 Dec)
1699 Gordon, John sev w 1 Sep 1880 Kandahar, gs hip
1165 Gray, Jesse k 14 Dec 1879 Kabul, gs abdomen
58B/115 Guthrie, William dang w 6 Oct 1879 Charasiah, bullet right temple
1483 Halkett, Charles sev w 11 Dec 1879 Arghandi, gs contusion
58B/32 Hariarty, Richard sev w 14 Dec 1879 Kabul, gs right thigh
199 Harris, Charles sl w 6 Oct 1879 Charasiah, bullet head
58B/2040 Heffernan, Patrick sev w 1 Sep 1880 Kandahar, gs contusion shoulder
58B/472 Henry, William k 14 Dec 1879 Kabul, gs abdomen
1980 Heseltine, George dang w 1 Sep 1880 Kandahar, gs arm, since d
58B/381 Hodge, Alexander k 1 Sep 1880 Kandahar, gs abdomen
2054 Hogg, James dang w 6 Oct 1879 Charasiah, bullet left shoulder, dow 8 Oct
58B/237 Hone, James sev w 2 Dec 1878 Peiwar Kotal
Johnstone, Hugh sl w 19 Dec 1879 Jagdalak, gs (D.34) (MR = 58B/105 <u>or</u> 883)
974 Kelly, John sev w 6 Oct 1879 Charasiah, bullet both thighs
695 Kennard, Robert sev w 14 Dec 1879 Kabul, gs left knee
1836 Kettle, George sev w 2 Dec 1878 Peiwar Kotal
1590 Knox, James sl w 14 Dec 1879 Kabul, gs left arm
900 Lees, Joseph k 14 Dec 1879 Kabul, gs abdomen
1673 Light, Josiah k 14 Dec 1879 Kabul, gs chest
1117 Lowe, John sl w 6 Oct 1879 Charasiah, bullet neck
562 McCallum, John sev w 6 Oct 1879 Charasiah, bullet in knee cap
1530 McCready, Edward mort w 14 Oct 1879 Shutar Gardan, dow 31 Oct Kabul (MR & P/1372-6650)
1571 MacDonald, Alexander sev w 6 Oct 1879 Charasiah, bullet left forearm

465 McGomlick, John sev w 11 Dec 1879 Arghandi, gs right arm
58B/153 McGowan, James k 1 Sep 1880 Kandahar, gs head
1950 McKenzie, Robert sev w 6 Oct 1879 Charasiah, contusion chest
58B/1039 McKinlay, James sev w 14 Dec 1879 Kabul, gs
1470 McLaren, Alexander sev w 1 Sep 1880 Kandahar, gs instep
58B/690 McLeish, Neil sev w 1 Sep 1880 Kandahar, gs forearm
58B/415 McQueen, James k 1 Sep 1880 Kandahar, gs head
1335 McQuellan, Francis sl w 18 Dec 1879 Kabul, gs face
58B/40 Maguire, James sev w 1 Sep 1880 Kandahar, gs breast, dow 16 Sep (& MR)
1903 Malley, Martin k 14 Dec 1879 Kabul, gs chest
1618 May, Isaac sev w 6 Oct 1879 Charasiah, bullet right instep
58B/177 Mellis, John sev w 14 Dec 1879 Kabul, gs left thigh
1426 Miller, George k 14 Dec 1879 Kabul, gs & sword cuts
58B/394 Mitchell, Alexander dang w 6 Oct 1879 Charasiah, bullet forehead, dow 17 (MR = 18) Oct (& P/1372-5894)
259 Oliver, William sl w 6 Oct 1879 Charasiah, bullet ear & cheek
1966 Osborn, Charles sev w 12 Dec 1879 Sherpur, gs left calf
746 Pattison, James sev w 14 Dec 1879 Kabul, gs left hand
1674 Power, David k 2 Dec 1878 Peiwar Kotal
58B/1924 Raper, William sev w 1 Sep 1880 Kandahar, gs hand
58B/145 Rattray, William sev w 2 Dec 1878 Peiwar Kotal
987 Reid, Peter sl w 6 Oct 1879 Charasiah, bullet foot
1161 Ritchie, William k 14 Dec 1879 Kabul, gs body
271 Robertson, George sl w 6 Oct 1879 Charasiah, contusion chest
1573 Robertson, John sl w 6 Oct 1879 Charasiah, bullet leg
1954 Smith, David sl w 1 Sep 1880 Kandahar, gs contusion thigh
906 Smith, Francis sev w 11 Dec 1879 Arghandi, gs face
2649 Sorley, James sev w 1 Sep 1880 Kandahar, gs scalp
1960 Steel, James sl w 1 Sep 1880 Kandahar, gs abrasion back
58B/323 Stewart, James k 2 Dec 1878 Peiwar Kotal
58B/31 Stewart, William sl w 2 Dec 1878 Peiwar Kotal; sev w 14 Dec 1879 Kabul, gs face & hand
1132 Taylor, John k 14 Dec 1879 Kabul, gs head
1294 Thompson, Edward k 14 Dec 1879 Kabul, gs head
94 Vine, John sl w 6 Oct 1879 Charasiah, bullet cheek
2056 Walker, George dang w 6 Oct 1879 Charasiah, bullet through chin, dow 8 Oct
559 Wallace, Davidson sl w 6 Oct 1879 Charasiah, bullet left index finger
58B/236 West, Charles sev w 6 Oct 1879 Charasiah, bullet in leg
58B/149 Wilson, John sev w 6 Oct 1879 Charasiah, bullet forehead
58B/612 Woods, Thomas sev w 13 Dec 1878 Sapari Pass (& D.6)

HM 81st REGIMENT OF FOOT

Privates

1616	McCann, Michael	k 28 Nov 1878 Sarkai Pass (D.32)
12B/547	McMahon, John	sev w 29 Nov 1878 Khyber Pass (D.32)

HM 85th KING'S LIGHT INFANTRY

Privates

42B/327	Allsworth, F.	k Jul 1880 (MR)
1640	Smith, Patrick	k 13 Sep 1880 nr Shalozan, gs left side & sword cuts left palm (P/1538-14317)

HM 86th REGIMENT OF FOOT

Lieutenant

Tobin, Frederick John — badly w 9 Aug 1880 by Marri marauders nr Kuchali, left elbow (P/1538-13016)

HM 92nd (GORDON HIGHLANDERS) REGIMENT OF FOOT

Sources D.24, D.33, D.39
D.51 & P/1537-11817

Captain

Gordon, Duncan Forbes — sev w 14 Dec 1879 Kabul, gs chest

Lieutenants

Forbes, St John William — k 13 Dec 1879 Kabul, gs head in a hand-to-hand fight

Menzies, Stuart Alexander — sev w 1 Sep 1880 Kandahar

Second Lieutenant

Stewart, Donald William — sev w 1 Sep 1880 Kandahar

Colour-Sergeants

488	Drummond, James	k 13 Dec 1879 Kabul, gs abdomen in a hand-to-hand fight
304	Fraser, Richard	k 1 Sep 1880 Kandahar, gs head
1402	Hart, Robert	sev w 13 Dec 1879 Kabul, gs right wrist
1566	Smith, Thomas	dang w 25 Apr 1880 Charasiah, gs abdomen, since dow
1192	Stewart, William	sl w 13 Dec 1879 Kabul, gs right knee

Sergeants

1971 Adams, Henry sev w 1 Sep 1880 Kandahar, gs left knee joint, dow 22 Sep (& MR)
2053 Coutts, James sl w 1 Sep 1880 Kandahar, gs lung
730 Innes, James sl w 1 Sep 1880 Kandahar, gs contusion
2030 McGill, William sl w 1 Sep 1880 Kandahar, gs shoulder
1983 MacNally, John sl w 1 Sep 1880 Kandahar, gs hand
1938 Thomson, Matthew sl w 13 Dec 1879 Kabul, gs right leg; sl w 1 Sep 1880 Kandahar, gs left thumb
2058 Wilson, James sl w 1 Sep 1880 Kandahar, gs thumb

Lance-Sergeants

2347 Anderson, Alexander sl w 1 Sep 1880 Kandahar, gs left shoulder
1244 Lawson, James sev w 25 Apr 1880 Charasiah, gs left side of neck

Corporals

2340 Calder, James sl w 14 Dec 1879 Kabul, sword cut left hand
56B/335 Friendship, Lewis k 1 Sep 1880 Kandahar, gs lung (325?)
2069 Gamble, Matthew sl w 1 Sep 1880 Kandahar, gs forearm
900 Kilkenny, Edward sev w 13 Dec 1879 Kabul, gs left thigh
1539 McGillivray, William dang w 1 Sep 1880 Kandahar, gs left arm, awarded DCM
56B/362 McPhail, Donald sev w 1 Sep 1880 Kandahar, gs left lung, dow 30 Sep (& MR)

Lance-Corporals

89 Hunter, John sl w 1 Sep 1880 Kandahar, gs shoulder
2011 Innes, Robert sl w 1 Sep 1880 Kandahar, gs abdomen
56B/174 Mackinnon, James sev w 1 Sep 1880 Kandahar, gs both thighs
56B/706 Macpherson, Paul sl w 1 Sep 1880 Kandahar, gs temple
1748 Saunders, Henry dang w 1 Sep 1880 Kandahar, gs lower jaw
1921 Vassie, John sev w 1 Sep 1880 Kandahar, gs thigh

Drummer

1473 Jardine, Thomas sev w 25 Apr 1880 Charasiah, gs right forearm

Privates

1597 Aitken, Thomas sev w 25 Apr 1880 Charasiah, gs left side of chest
56B/484 Alexander, Joseph sl w 1 Sep 1880 Kandahar, gs graze abdomen
56B/388 Allan, James sev w 1 Sep 1880 Kandahar, gs knee
1388 Balcarres, John W. sev w 1 Sep 1880 Kandahar, gs arm
56B/194 Barrie, Alexander sl w 1 Sep 1880 Kandahar, gs right hand
56B/956 Baxter, James sl w 1 Sep 1880 Kandahar, gs thigh & chest
56B/206 Brady, Thomas sl w 1 Sep 1880 Kandahar, gs forearm

1644 Bridgman, Joseph sl w 13 Dec 1879 Kabul, gs abrasure (MR = Brightman)
1359 Brimber, Duncan dang w 1 Sep 1880 Kandahar, gs thigh, dow 22 Sep (& MR)
1277 Brown, James sl w 14 Dec 1879 Kabul, gs right forearm; sl w 25 Apr 1880 Charasiah, gs contusion right leg
59 Burness, Henry k 6 Oct 1879 Charasiah, bullet in chest
56B/1078 Calton, Charles sev w 1 Sep 1880 Kandahar, gs right leg
614 Carston, Adam sev w 23 Dec 1879 Kabul, gs arm
56B/193 Cockburn, John dang w 6 Oct 1879 Charasiah, bullet left thigh, dow 1 Nov (& MR)
56B/1070 Coverdale, Charles sl w 1 Sep 1880 Kandahar, gs wrist
2136 Davis, William sev w 13 Dec 1879 Kabul, gs chest, dow 28 Dec (& MR)
56B/1305 Dean, Joseph dang w 1 Sep 1880 Kandahar, gs head
1163 Dennis, John sl w 1 Sep 1880 Kandahar, sword cuts head,wrist & knee, awarded DCM
1659 Devlin, William dang w 1 Sep 1880 Kandahar, gs left arm, dow 8 Sep (& MR)
1691 Dexter, Joseph sev w 1 Sep 1880 Kandahar, gs left hand
2342 Dick, James sl w 6 Oct 1879 Charasiah, bullet left shoulder
56B/83 Dirick, William k 13 Dec 1879 Kabul, gs body
1638 Dixon, William dang w 1 Sep 1880 Kandahar, gs abdomen, dow 3 Sep (& MR)
2065 Easton, Alexander k 1 Sep 1880 Kandahar, gs head
56B/27 Falconer, David sl w 1 Sep 1880 Kandahar, gs shoulder
56B/172 Forrester, George sev w 1 Sep 1880 Kandahar, gs leg
56B/124 Forster, Robert sev w 1 Sep 1880 Kandahar, gs forehead
56B/404 Galletley, Malcolm k 6 Oct 1879 Charasiah, shell wound front of neck
665 Gemmell, Alexander sev w 25 Dec 1879 Kabul, gs leg
2181 Gillanders, Charles sev w 1 Sep 1880 Kandahar, gs foot
1951 Glacken, Peter sl w 1 Sep 1880 Kandahar, gs left arm
56B/174 Gordon, James R. dang w 1 Sep 1880 Kandahar, gs knee, thigh & thumb
82 Gould, John sev w 14 Dec 1879 Kabul, gs back
1838 Graham, William sev w 1 Sep 1880 Kandahar, gs right leg
56B/449 Grant, William sl w 12 Dec 1879 Sherpur, gs right leg
1058 Hawkes, Henry sl w 13 Dec 1879 Kabul, gs abrasure
1704 Henderson, William sl w 23 Dec 1879 Kabul, gs left shoulder
56B/18 Henderson, William dang w 1 Sep 1880 Kandahar, gs head, dow 2 Sep (& MR)
1321 Hensley, Charles sev w 13 Dec 1879 Kabul, gs arm
56B/553 Hoey, Peter dang w 1 Sep 1880 Kandahar, gs right side, since d (MR = k)
2348 Hull, George F. sev w 1 Sep 1880 Kandahar, gs thigh
56B/289 Irvine, Samuel sev w 1 Sep 1880 Kandahar, gs shoulder
627 Jeffries, Charles sl w 13 Dec 1879 Kabul, gs left wrist
1712 Jerwood, John sl w 13 Dec 1879 Kabul, gs right knee

1846 Johnston, James sl w 13 Dec 1879 Kabul, gs abrasure
1664 Keane, John k 25 Apr 1880 Charasiah, gs head
56B/242 Kerr, Thomas k 1 Sep 1880 Kandahar, gs lung
56B/791 Laing, John sev w 1 Sep 1880 Kandahar, gs foot
56B/432 Lamb, Adam sl w 1 Sep 1880 Kandahar, gs nose
1260 McDonald, Allan sev w 1 Sep 1880 Kandahar, gs head, dow 8 Sep (& MR)
1489 McFarlane, Thomas sl w 1 Sep 1880 Kandahar, gs left arm
56B/99 McGinley, John sev w 1 Sep 1880 Kandahar, gs head
56B/249 McIntosh, John sl w 1 Sep 1880 Kandahar, gs right leg, awarded DCM
56B/298 McKay, John sl w 1 Sep 1880 Kandahar, gs leg
698 Mackenzie, Hugh sl w 13 Dec 1879 Kabul, gs right wrist
1370 Mackenzie, John k 1 Sep 1880 Kandahar, gs abdomen
2027 Mackenzie, John sl w 1 Sep 1880 Kandahar, gs thigh
56B/505 Mackenzie, Robert k 1 Sep 1880 Kandahar, gs head & breast
1883 Mackenzie, William sev w 12 Dec 1879 Sherpur, gs right knee
1561 McLaren, John sl w 1 Sep 1880 Kandahar, gs head
56B/1111 McLaughlan, Martin sev w 1 Sep 1880 Kandahar, sword cuts head & arm
514 McLennan, Duncan sl w 13 Dec 1879 Kabul, gs abdomen
589 McNab, John sev w 6 Oct 1879 Charasiah, bullet right hip
56B/31 Macpherson, Alexander sev w 1 Sep 1880 Kandahar, gs lung
2251 MacRae, Gregor dang w 1 Sep 1880 Kandahar, gs right temple
88 Masterton, John sev w 23 Dec 1879 Kabul, gs arm
908 Meek, James k 6 Oct 1879 Charasiah, gs chest (MR = 918)
1178 Middlemas, William sl w 25 Apr 1880 Charasiah, gs contusion right breast
56B/279 Muir, William sl w 1 Sep 1880 Kandahar, gs left foot
56B/113 Muirhead, Alexander sl w 1 Sep 1880 Kandahar, gs right hand
1269 Munro, John sev w 13 Dec 1879 Kabul, gs abdomen
1800 Murray, James sl w 1 Sep 1880 Kandahar, gs thigh
2314 Neilson, Hugh sl w 1 Sep 1880 Kandahar, gs right leg
190 Norman, William sev w 13 Dec 1879 Kabul, gs abdomen
1530 Park, Alexander P. sl w 1 Sep 1880 Kandahar, gs pelvis
1777 Reid, David sl w 1 Sep 1880 Kandahar, gs lip
2332 Reid, Josiah sl w 1 Sep 1880 Kandahar, gs thigh
56B/111 Reid, William k 1 Sep 1880 Kandahar, gs abdomen
159 Robertson, Thomas sl w 13 Dec 1879 Kabul, gs right thumb
56B/534 Ronald, Alexander sl w 1 Sep 1880 Kandahar, gs shoulder
1907 Ross, Neil k 1 Sep 1880 Kandahar, gs head
1748 Saunders, Henry sl w 25 Apr 1880 Charasiah, gs right hand
56B/248 Scott, James sev w 13 Dec 1879 Kabul, gs abdomen
2022 Scott, James k 1 Sep 1880 Kandahar, gs abdomen
56B/105 Sharp, James sev w 13 Dec 1879 Kabul, gs left leg

1853	Sherran, William	sev w 6 Oct 1879 Charasiah, bullet left leg
56B/323	Simpson, Daniel	sl w 6 Oct 1879 Charasiah, bullet right ankle
1250	Simpson, Robert	sev w 1 Sep 1880 Kandahar, gs left thigh
1165	Sinclair, John	sl w 13 Dec 1879 Kabul, gs right ankle
1672	Smith, Francis	sev w 1 Sep 1880 Kandahar, gs foot
2023	Smith, William	sev w 1 Sep 1880 Kandahar, gs right hand
2140	Steel, Henry	sl w 1 Sep 1880 Kandahar, gs shoulder
2034	Stewart, Alexander	sl w 6 Oct 1879 Charasiah, bullet in neck
978	Stewart, James	dang w 1 Sep 1880 Kandahar, gs arm
905	Strachan, John	k 1 Sep 1880 Kandahar, gs abdomen (MR = 995)
2066	White, Thomas	k 23 Dec 1879 Kabul, gs heart
1593	Wilson, James	dang w 1 Sep 1880 Kandahar, gs right side, dow 2 Sep (& MR)
1928	Wilson, William	k 1 Sep 1880 Kandahar, gs heart
56B/614	Wood, John S.	k 20 Dec 1879 Kabul, gs arm (MR = dow 27 Dec)
56B/152	Woods, Daniel	sl w 1 Sep 1880 Kandahar, gs left foot
2026	Wright, James	sl w 14 Dec 1879 Kabul, gs spine & chest

1st BENGAL CAVALRY

Sowar

Yakub Khan   w 1 May 1880 Chapri, since d (P/1536-9901)

3rd BENGAL CAVALRY

Major

Willock, George Woodward   sl w 31 Aug 1880 Kandahar (D.51 & P/1538-12960)

Sowar

Sewa Sing   w 1 Sep 1880 Kandahar, since dow (D.51)

5th BENGAL CAVALRY

Lieutenant

Kinloch, Francis Garden   k 29 Sep 1879 on road between Chapri & Manduri, gs (P/1534-7547)

10th BENGAL LANCERS

Captain

Barrow, Seymour Duncan   sev w 1 Jul 1880 Patkao Shana, incisions right forearm & left hand 'in a personal encounter with a nephew of Sultan Mahomed' (D.42)

Lance-Daffadar

740 Ahmed Khan   sl w 22 Apr 1879 Kam Dakka (D.32)

Sowars

Bhagwan Sing   sev w 16 Dec 1879 Jagdalak, gs leg (D.34), awarded IOM 3rd Class

Kirpal Sing   k 16 Dec 1879 Jagdalak, gs (D.34)

11th BENGAL LANCERS

Source D.32

Ressaidar

20 Sardul Sing   sl w 24 Mar 1879 Deh Sarak (& D.15)

Daffadar

53 Fazel Khan   sl w 24 Mar 1879 Deh Sarak

Sowars

1176 Atar Sing   k 24 Mar 1879 Deh Sarak

1335 Atra   sl w 24 Mar 1879 Deh Sarak

1376 Attah Mahomed sl w 24 Mar 1879 Deh Sarak
1460 Bishen Sing sl w 24 Mar 1879 Deh Sarak
1505 Ganga Ram sl w 24 Mar 1879 Deh Sarak
1531 Gurdit Sing sl w 24 Mar 1879 Deh Sarak
1195 Jiwand Sing sl w 24 Mar 1879 Deh Sarak
1325 Kala Sing sl w 24 Mar 1879 Deh Sarak
1551 Kala Sing sev w 29 Nov 1878 Shagai
917 Kanh Sing sl w 24 Mar 1879 Deh Sarak
1407 Mohta Sing sev w 24 Mar 1879 Deh Sarak
1150 Punjab Sing sev w 24 Mar 1879 Deh Sarak

12th BENGAL CAVALRY

Source D.33

Trumpeter
Zareem Khan sl w 14 Oct 1879 Ali Khel, sword cut (P/1372-6654 & P/1534-7969)

Sowars
Alladad Khan sev w 23 Dec 1879 Kabul, gs leg
Goormuk Sing sev w 22 Dec 1879 Lataband, Kabul, gs shoulder
Jewant Sing k 22 Dec 1879 Lataband, Kabul, gs, body not recovered
Kirpal Sing k 22 Dec 1879 Lataband, Kabul, gs, body not recovered
Kishen Chand k 22 Dec 1879 Lataband, Kabul, body not recovered
Kishen Sing sev w 22 Dec 1879 Lataband, Kabul, gs face
Mussar Sing sev w 19 Dec 1879 Kabul, gs arm

13th BENGAL LANCERS

Lieutenant
Lumsden, Gordon Hugh murdered 19 Feb 1880 Kuram Valley, stabbed by a thief (Shadbolt)

Daffadar
80 Kala Sing k 24 Mar 1879 Deh Sarak (D.32)

Sowars
Goman Sing k 1 May 1880 Chapri (P/1536-9901)
Khoosial Sing sl w 14 Oct 1879 Ali Khel, sword cut (P/1372-6654 & P/1534-7969)
490 Kishen Sing k 31 Jan 1879 Bazar Valley (D.32)

14th BENGAL LANCERS

Source D.33

Lieutenant
Forbes, Oswald Eric S. k 11 Dec 1879 Arghandi, Kabul, sword cuts

Jemadar
Gopal Sing dang w 14 Dec 1879 Kabul, gs temple, dow, awarded IOM 3rd Class

Daffadars
Kulloo sev w 11 Dec 1879 Arghandi,Kabul, gs thigh
Umra Sing k 11 Dec 1879 Arghandi,Kabul, sword cuts,gs thigh

Sowars
Bhopal Sing sev w 14 Dec 1879 Kabul, gs shoulder
Burt Sing sev w 11 Dec 1879 Arghandi,Kabul, gs arm
Duttoo Ram sev w 11 Dec 1879 Arghandi,Kabul, gs leg
Jusram dang w 14 Dec 1879 Kabul, gs right hand
Kishen Ram k 11 Dec 1879 Arghandi,Kabul, gs thigh
Kubbi Ram k 11 Dec 1879 Arghandi,Kabul, sword cuts,gs thigh
Mottee Ram sev w 13 Dec 1879 Kabul, gs chest
Munjoo Ram k 11 Dec 1879 Arghandi,Kabul, sword cuts,gs thigh
Ram Jellal sev w 14 Dec 1879 Kabul, gs leg
1020 Ram Lall k 14 Dec 1879 Kabul, gs
1183 Ram Lall dang w 14 Dec 1879 Kabul, gs chest, since d
Sowal Sing k 11 Dec 1879 Arghandi,Kabul, sword cuts,gs thigh
Sulwunt Sing k 11 Dec 1879 Arghandi,Kabul, sword cuts,gs thigh

19th BENGAL LANCERS

Sources D.36 & 42
P/1537-11502 & 11382

Colonel
Yorke, Philip Sidney sl w 19 Apr 1880 Ahmed Khel, abrasion from lance point,sword cut right arm (see IOM GGO 563/1880)

Lieutenants
Gordon, Stewart Douglas sl w 19 Apr 1880 Ahmed Khel, sword cut left hand
Massy, Harry Stanley sl w 19 Apr 1880 Ahmed Khel, contusion right side
Young, Edward Archibald dang w 19 Apr 1880 Ahmed Khel, eight serious sword cuts & one bullet wound

Ressaidars
15 Jowahir Sing sl w 19 Apr 1880 Ahmed Khel, incision right forearm, awarded IOM 3rd Class
16 Mahomed Shahriar sl w 19 Apr 1880 Ahmed Khel, cut over left shoulder

Jemadar
253 Gulab Sing sl w 19 Apr 1880 Ahmed Khel, incision right forearm (see IOM GGO 563/1880)

Kot-Daffadars
238 Habub Sing sl w 19 Apr 1880 Ahmed Khel, incision finger awarded IOM 3rd Class
24 Karam Sing sev w 19 Apr 1880 Ahmed Khel, incision over right shoulder (see IOM GGO 563/1880)

Daffadars
1074 Budha Sing sev w 19 Apr 1880 Ahmed Khel, incision scalp

70 Dewa Sing k 19 Apr 1880 Ahmed Khel, bullet in abdomen, skull split by tulwar
197 Hardat Sing sev w 19 Apr 1880 Ahmed Khel, incision forearm,dividing ulna, awarded IOM 3rd Class
474 Hassan Ali sev w 19 Apr 1880 Ahmed Khel, sword cut in palm & almost severing little finger
496 Hukam Sing sev w 19 Apr 1880 Ahmed Khel, incision scalp
1130 Mahomed Ishak sl w 19 Apr 1880 Ahmed Khel, sword cut forehead, awarded IOM 3rd Class
Nowshad Khan sl w 19 Apr 1880 Ahmed Khel, contusion left arm
244 Shaik Kallu sl w 1 Jul 1880 Patkao Shana, incision right forearm
677 Wazir Khan k 19 Apr 1880 Ahmed Khel, two bullets through heart

Lance-Daffadars
1126 Atar Singh (2) sev w 19 Apr 1880 Ahmed Khel, incision left shoulder & wrist; sl w 1 Jul 1880 Patkao Shana, abrasion over left tibia
753 Buta Singh sev w 1 Jul 1880 Patkao Shana, two stabs in chest
83 Sant Sing sl w 19 Apr 1880 Ahmed Khel, cut over left scapula
503 Santokh Sing sev w 19 Apr 1880 Ahmed Khel, bullet right thigh
1185 Sirdar Sing sl w 19 Apr 1880 Ahmed Khel, sword cut palm, awarded IOM 3rd Class

Sowars
945 Abdulla sev w 19 Apr 1880 Ahmed Khel, incision right side of face
1196 Amar Sing sev w 19 Apr 1880 Ahmed Khel, incision right wrist
916 Atar Sing (1) sev w 19 Apr 1880 Ahmed Khel, two sword cuts left hand
1349 Barkat Rai k 19 Apr 1880 Ahmed Khel, skull split by tulwar
1195 Buta Sing k 19 Apr 1880 Ahmed Khel, bullet left chest,skull split by tulwar
1087 Chowkis sl w 19 Apr 1880 Ahmed Khel, abrasion neck
1193 Dabi Dial sl w 19 Apr 1880 Ahmed Khel, lance wound right eyebrow
1055 Dabi Dita sl w 19 Apr 1880 Ahmed Khel, incision forehead
990 Dalpat sl w 19 Apr 1880 Ahmed Khel, incision finger
1252 Dewan Singh sev w 1 Jul 1880 Patkao Shana, incision scalp, two stabs over chest
1398 Enaiat Khan sev w 1 Jul 1880 Patkao Shana, incision right hand,gs scalp & gs biceps
995 Fateh Mahomed sev w 19 Apr 1880 Ahmed Khel, sword cut forearm,fractured
1411 Fazl Ahmed k 1 Jul 1880 Patkao Shana, gs penetrating chest
1341 Ganda Sing sev w 19 Apr 1880 Ahmed Khel, incision root of neck
1203 Gopal Sing sl w 19 Apr 1880 Ahmed Khel, contusion right eye
1168 Haiatulla sl w 19 Apr 1880 Ahmed Khel, incision scalp

1187 Hasham Khan sev w 19 Apr 1880 Ahmed Khel, incision right forearm

1098 Jehan Khan (1) sl w 19 Apr 1880 Ahmed Khel, incision right forearm

1114 Jewand Singh dang w 1 Jul 1880 Patkao Shana, gs penetrating abdomen, dow same night

1376 Jhanda Khan sl w 19 Apr 1880 Ahmed Khel, incision left hand

1135 Jit Ram sl w 19 Apr 1880 Ahmed Khel, contusion right temple

1073 Kaisar Singh sl w 1 Jul 1880 Patkao Shana, incision forearm

1223 Kait Ram sl w 19 Apr 1880 Ahmed Khel, incision face, awarded IOM 3rd Class

1173 Kalian Sing sev w 19 Apr 1880 Ahmed Khel, incision scalp

1293 Kashi Ram sev w 19 Apr 1880 Ahmed Khel, incision scalp

1396 Khan Jan Khan sl w 19 Apr 1880 Ahmed Khel, incision left hand, awarded IOM 3rd Class

915 Khushal Sing sl w 19 Apr 1880 Ahmed Khel, abrasion right hand, awarded IOM 3rd Class

595 Lachman sl w 19 Apr 1880 Ahmed Khel, cut right thumb

1053 Lal Sing sev w 19 Apr 1880 Ahmed Khel, incision right arm

1281 Mehrdin sev w 19 Apr 1880 Ahmed Khel, incision forearm,both bones divided

1063 Nand Lal Sing sl w 19 Apr 1880 Ahmed Khel, abrasion right leg

1381 Narain Sing k 19 Apr 1880 Ahmed Khel, bullet in abdomen

994 Nehal Chand k 20 Jan 1879 Jaldak

136 Nehal Sing sl w 19 Apr 1880 Ahmed Khel, sword cut right hand

968 Parsa Ram sl w 19 Apr 1880 Ahmed Khel, sword cut face

708 Sher Singh (1) k 1 Jul 1880 Patkao Shana, gs penetrating chest

1447 Sher Singh (2) sev w 1 Jul 1880 Patkao Shana, gs finger

1331 Shib Dial sev w 19 Apr 1880 Ahmed Khel, incision right temple

1086 Subah Sing sl w 19 Apr 1880 Ahmed Khel, sword cut left shoulder

849 Suchet Ram sev w 19 Apr 1880 Ahmed Khel, incision neck & back

BENGAL SAPPERS & MINERS

Major

Thackeray, Edward Talbot VC RE sev w 23 Dec 1879 Jagdalak Kotal (D.34)

Captain

Dundas, James VC RE 7th Co k 23 Dec 1879 Kabul, premature explosion of a mine (D.33)

Lieutenant

Nugent, Charles RE 7th Co k 23 Dec 1879 Kabul, premature explosion of a mine (D.33)

Sergeant
9807 Jones, John RE sl w 19 Apr 1880 Ahmed Khel, bullet through left hand (D.36 & P/1537-11502)

Sepoys
1940 Abdulla Khan 8th Co sev w 22 Dec 1878 Bazar Valley, gs forearm,fractured (D.7, D.32 & P/1372-5297)

Karbeer 7th Co dang w 6 Oct 1879 Charasiah, gs chest, dow 7 Oct (D.24 & P/1372-5894)

1773 Nek Mahomed Khan 4th Co sl w 28 Mar 1879 attack on telegraph train nr Kandahar (D.32)

Ramdin Sing 7th Co sev w 6 Oct 1879 Charasiah, gs left shoulder (D.24)

Roora sev w Dec 1879 Kabul, gs chest (D.33)

5th BENGAL NATIVE INFANTRY

Source P/1536-9901

Naik
Katwaru Sing w 1 May 1880 Chapri

Sepoys
Ganpat Sing k 1 May 1880 Chapri
Khubi Sing w 1 May 1880 Chapri
Madho Sing w 1 May 1880 Chapri

6th BENGAL NATIVE INFANTRY

Source D.32

Sepoys
1573 Baktawar Ram k 29 Nov 1878 Khyber Pass
1470 Jowala Sing sev w 11 Jun 1879 nr Fort Ali Musjid
Malay Khan k 1 Jan 1879 attack on camp at Ali Musjid
1582 Tiloki mort w 5 Apr 1879 attack on grazing ground nr Ali Musjid, dow same day

8th BENGAL NATIVE INFANTRY

Jemadar
Bahadar Khan k 15 Jan 1880 Kam Dakka, shot through head (P/1537-11397)

Sepoys
Dabi Singh w 13 Apr 1880 Hisarak, gs thigh, since dow (P/1536-11474)

Saiad Ashgar sev w 12 Apr 1880 Hisarak, gs thigh (P/1537-11474)

11th BENGAL NATIVE INFANTRY

Sources P/1372-6654 & P/1534-7969

Sepoys

2412 Kinzia Sookul sl w 14 Oct 1879 Ali Khel, gs
Seonarain Pandy sl w 14 Oct 1879 Ali Khel, gs

14th BENGAL NATIVE INFANTRY

Source D.32

Captain

MacLean, John George sev w 21 Nov 1878 Ali Musjid (& D.1, see also IOM GGO 164/1879)

Subadar

Suhel Sing sl w 21 Nov 1878 Ali Musjid

Havildars

231 Dharam Sing k 21 Nov 1878 Ali Musjid
305 Maun Sing sev w 21 Nov 1878 Ali Musjid, awarded IOM 3rd Class
62 Prem Sing sev w 21 Nov 1878 Ali Musjid
88 Rur Sing k 21 Nov 1878 Ali Musjid
167 Supah Sing sev w 21 Nov 1878 Ali Musjid

Naik

204 Chart Sing k 21 Nov 1878 Ali Musjid

Drummer

Bhagwan Sing sev w 21 Nov 1878 Ali Musjid

Sepoys

431 Atar Sing sev w 21 Nov 1878 Ali Musjid
479 Atar Sing sev w 21 Nov 1878 Ali Musjid
423 Bhagwan Sing k 21 Nov 1878 Ali Musjid
343 Buta Sing sev w 21 Nov 1878 Ali Musjid
621 Ganesha Sing sev w 21 Nov 1878 Ali Musjid
364 Gour Khan sev w 21 Nov 1878 Ali Musjid, awarded IOM 3rd Class
810 Gurmukh Sing k 21 Nov 1878 Ali Musjid
956 Jagat Sing k 21 Nov 1878 Ali Musjid
674 Kala Sing k 21 Nov 1878 Ali Musjid
737 Karam Sing sev w 21 Nov 1878 Ali Musjid
959 Mal Sing sev w 21 Nov 1878 Ali Musjid
510 Panjab Sing sev w 21 Nov 1878 Ali Musjid
693 Santoke Sing sev w 21 Nov 1878 Ali Musjid
895 Subha Sing sev w 21 Nov 1878 Ali Musjid
667 Sujan Sing sev w 21 Nov 1878 Ali Musjid
858 Tilok Sing sl w 21 Nov 1878 Ali Musjid
872 Wazir Sing k 21 Nov 1878 Ali Musjid

15th BENGAL NATIVE INFANTRY

Source D.51

Havildar

619 Anok Sing dang w 31 Aug 1880 Kandahar, gs chest, since d

Lance-Naik

819 Ram Sing k 31 Aug 1880 Kandahar, gs chest

Sepoys

1822 Bishambar Sing sev w 31 Aug 1880 Kandahar, gs head
1957 Harnam Sing sl w 31 Aug 1880 Kandahar, gs leg
1495 Syeemal Sing k 31 Aug 1880 Kandahar, gs abdomen
1724 Wazir Sing sev w 31 Aug 1880 Kandahar, gs hand

19th (PUNJAB) BENGAL NATIVE INFANTRY

Sources D.36 & P/1537-11502

Havildar

1310 Kharak Sing sl w 19 Apr 1880 Ahmed Khel, gs contusion nose

Sepoys

1795 Gulab Khan mort w 19 Apr 1880 Ahmed Khel, gs right lung, dow 21 Apr
2086 Jowahir Sing k 19 Apr 1880 Ahmed Khel, gs heart
Mehrban Shah sl w 19 Apr 1880 Ahmed Khel, gs leg
Nehal Shah sev w 12 Aug 1880 siege of Kandahar attchd 19th Bombay NI, gs right hand (D.48 & P/1538-13867)
Prem Sing sev w 16 Aug 1880 Deh Khojah attchd 19th Bombay NI, gs right wrist (D.48 & P/1538-13867)

20th (PUNJAB) BENGAL NATIVE INFANTRY

Sepoy

2174 Baktawar Sing sev w 21 Nov 1878 Ali Musjid (D.32)

21st (PUNJAB) BENGAL NATIVE INFANTRY

Subadar

Bhagel Sing k 28 Jun 1879 Badesh-Khel (D.32)

Sepoys

1551 Atra k 28 Jun 1879 Badesh-Khel (D.32)
Fateh Khan sev w 14 Oct 1879 Shutar Gardan, gs (D.30)
1911 Habib Khan k 14 Oct 1879 Shutar Gardan, gs (D.30)

1858 Hashmat Ali k 7 Jan 1879 Matun, bullet in head (D9 & 32)
1563 Kesar Sing sl w 18/19 Oct 1879 Shutar Gardan, gs (D.30)
Khair Din k 14 Oct 1879 Shutar Gardan, gs (D.30)
1956 Rakhmat Shah sl w 14 Oct 1879 Shutar Gardan, gs (D.30)
1786 Rehmatullah Khan sev w 7 Jan 1879 Matun, bullet in ankle (D.9 & 32)
1846 Thakur Sing sev w 14 Oct 1879 Shutar Gardan, gs (D.30)

23rd (PUNJAB) BENGAL NATIVE INFANTRY (PIONEERS)

Major
Anderson, Alexander Dunlop offic 2-i-c k 2 Dec 1878 Peiwar Kotal, 'at the head of his men whilst gallantly charging up the hillside to attack the enemy' (D.3)

Lieutenant
Chesney, Duncan sl w 1 Sep 1880 Kandahar (D.51)

Surgeon
Duncan, Andrew sev w 6 Oct 1879 Charasiah, bullet in chest (D.24)

Havildars
Bussawa Sing sev w Dec 1879 Kabul, gs face (D.33)
1354 Kharak Sing k 2 Dec 1878 Peiwar Kotal (D.32)
1405 Sawan Sing sl w 1 Sep 1880 Kandahar, gs contusion (D.51)

Naik
776 Bur Sing sl w 2 Dec 1878 Peiwar Kotal (D.32)

Lance-Naik
1566 Jita k 2 Dec 1878 Peiwar Kotal (D.32)

Bugler
1397 Sham Sing sev w 1 Sep 1880 Kandahar, gs contusion (D.51)

Sepoys
1319 Atar Sing sl w 1 Sep 1880 Kandahar, shell burst,arm & loin (D.51)
1917 Bhag Sing k 1 Sep 1880 Kandahar, gs chest (D.51)
2002 Bur Sing sev w 2 Dec 1878 Peiwar Kotal (D.32)
1894 Dewa Sing sev w 1 Sep 1880 Kandahar, right leg & foot shattered by shell (D.51)
1379 Dula Sing sl w 1 Sep 1880 Kandahar, gs abdomen (D.51)
2038 Fateh Sing sev w 2 Dec 1878 Peiwar Kotal (D.32)
1851 Gopal Sing sl w 1 Sep 1880 Kandahar, gs shoulder (D.51)
Gunda Sing k 6 Oct 1879 Charasiah, bullet
1226 Hira Sing sl w 1 Sep 1880 Kandahar, shell contusion (D.51)
2145 Jagat Sing k 1 Sep 1880 Kandahar, gs head (D.51)
2166 Jowahir Sing sev w 2 Dec 1878 Peiwar Kotal (D.32)
1287 Jowala Sing mort w 12 Apr 1879 attack on camp Ali Khel, dow 12 May (D.32)

1978 Jowala Sing sev w 2 Dec 1878 Peiwar Kotal (D.32)
2386 Kesar Sing sev w 1 Sep 1880 Kandahar, gs scalp (D.51)
1420 Lehna Sing sl w 1 Sep 1880 Kandahar, shell burst, shoulder (D.51)
2349 Lehna Sing sl w 1 Sep 1880 Kandahar, shell contusion, foot (D.51)
2273 Magghar Sing sev w 1 Sep 1880 Kandahar, gs arm & side (D.51)
Nehal Sing sev w 6 Oct 1879 Charasiah, bullet (D.24)
1406 Prem Sing sev w 2 Dec 1878 Peiwar Kotal (D.32)
1034 Ram Sing k 2 Dec 1878 Peiwar Kotal (D.32)
2023 Teja Sing sev w 1 Sep 1880 Kandahar, gs scalp (D.51)

24th (PUNJAB) BENGAL NATIVE INFANTRY

Subadar
Sultan Sing sl w 1 Sep 1880 Kandahar, gs right leg (D.51)

Lance-Havildar
Chet Sing sl w 1 Sep 1880 Kandahar (D.51)

Naik
1139 Dewa Sing k 28 Feb 1879 nr Michni (D.32)

Sepoys
1785 Ahmed Khan sl w 27 Jan 1879 Bazar Valley (D.32)
1635 Daiah Sing k 28 Feb 1879 nr Michni (D.32)
2176 Dewa Sing sev w 1 Sep 1880 Kandahar, gs (D.51)
1929 Fateh Khan sl w 1 Sep 1880 Kandahar, gs contusion (D.51)
Fazl Ahmed sl w 19 Dec 1879 Jagdalak, gs (D.34)
Fazl Ahmed sl w 1 Sep 1880 Kandahar, contusion (D.51)
2101 Gholam Mahomed sl w 1 Sep 1880 Kandahar, gs contusion (D.51)
1827 Gurmukh Sing sev w 29 Jan 1879 Bazar Valley (D.32)
1641 Haji k 2 Feb 1879 Bazar Valley (D.32 & P/1372-5350)
Issar Sing sev w 1 Sep 1880 Kandahar, gs (D.51)
2011 Khan Mahomed sl w 28 Feb 1879 nr Michni (D.32)
1732 Mahomed Baksh k 1 Sep 1880 Kandahar (D.51)
1765 Maruf Shah sl w 1 Sep 1880 Kandahar, gs contusion (D.51), awarded IOM 3rd Class
2002 Miah Sing sev w 28 Feb 1879 nr Michni (D.32)
2121 Nathu sev w 31 Aug 1880 Kandahar, gs left elbow (D.51)
2122 Rajab Ali sev w 1 Sep 1880 Kandahar, gs (D.51)
1177 Sejawal k 29 Mar 1879 nr Jamrud (D.32)
Sher Gul sl w 1 Sep 1880 Kandahar, gs (D.51)
1051 Suruf Sing sl w 28 Feb 1879 nr Michni (D.32)

25th (PUNJAB) BENGAL NATIVE INFANTRY

Subadar

Bhikam Sing sl w 1 Sep 1880 Kandahar, gs contusion thigh (D.51)

Sepoys

Kapur Sing k 19 Apr 1880 Ahmed Khel, sword (D.36 & P/1537-11502)

Nand Singh k 19 Apr 1880 Ahmed Khel, gs & sword (D.36 & P/1537-11502)

639 Natha Sing sl w 31 Aug 1880 Kandahar, contusion face (D.51)

Shahabudin dang w 12 Aug 1880 siege of Kandahar attchd 19th Bombay NI, gs right thigh (D.48 & P/1538-13867)

247 Sudh Sing k 1879 attack on baggage guard at camp Selim (D.32)

26th (PUNJAB) BENGAL NATIVE INFANTRY

Sepoy

1071 Jowahir Sing sev w 17 Mar 1879 attack on convoy in Bolan Pass (D.32)

27th (PUNJAB) BENGAL NATIVE INFANTRY

Source D.32

Major

Birch, Henry Holwell offic Cmdt k 21 Nov 1878 Ali Musjid (D.1 & see IOM GGO 164/1879)

Lieutenant

Fitzgerald, Thomas Otho QM k 21 Nov 1878 Ali Musjid (D.1 & see IOM GGO 230/1879)

Subadar

Deo sl w 21 Nov 1878 Ali Musjid, awarded IOM 3rd Class

Havildars

744 Gulab Sing sl w 21 Nov 1878 Ali Musjid

764 Mahomed Roshan sev w 21 Nov 1878 Ali Musjid

Naik

761 Himmat Sing mort w 22 Dec 1878 Bazar Valley, gs right thigh & left knee, dow 8 Jan 1879 (& P/1372-5297)

Sepoys

1749 Ammer Nath sl w 22 Dec 1878 Bazar Valley, contusion (& P/1372-5297)

1471 Badawa Sing k 21 Nov 1878 Ali Musjid

1114 Gulab Sing dang w 21 Nov 1878 Ali Musjid

1380 Haiat sl w 22 Dec 1878 Bazar Valley, contusion (& P/1372-5297)

1229 Jowahir Sing k 21 Nov 1878 Ali Musjid (& see IOM GGO 230/1879)

1293 Khushial Sing sev w 21 Nov 1878 Ali Musjid
1590 Kishen Sing k 29 Nov 1878 Khyber Pass
1311 Lalu sl w 22 Dec 1878 Bazar Valley, contusion (& P/1372-5297)
1816 Lalu sl w 21 Nov 1878 Ali Musjid
1394 Mohbin sev w 29 Nov 1878 Khyber Pass
1306 Narain Sing k 18 Jun 1879 Haft Chah
774 Nathu mort w 21 Nov 1878 Ali Musjid, dow 22 Nov (& see IOM GGO 230/1879)
248 Sunder Sing dang w 18 Jun 1879 Haft Chah
1653 Surat sl w 21 Nov 1878 Ali Musjid

28th (PUNJAB) BENGAL NATIVE INFANTRY

Jemadar
Fazl Ahmed w 13 Dec 1879 Zaimukht, sword cut head & back (P/1535-8361)

Havildar
Ram Sing sev w Dec 1879 Kabul, gs face (D.33)

Sepoys
1578 Nutha Sing w 10 Nov 1879 nr Daba, gs through cheek (P/1535-8191)
Sobhan w 12 Dec 1879 Zaimukht, since d (P/1535-8361)

29th (PUNJAB) BENGAL NATIVE INFANTRY

Source D.32

Lieutenant
Reid, Alexander John Forsyth dang w 28 Nov 1878 Peiwar (& see IOM GGO 89/1879)

Naik
1000 Prem Sing sev w 28 Nov 1878 Peiwar

Sepoys
1487 Atar Sing sev w 2 Dec 1878 Peiwar Kotal
1552 Badawa Sing k 2 Dec 1878 Peiwar Kotal
1438 Budh Sing k 2 Dec 1878 Peiwar Kotal
1493 Dewa Sing dang w 28 Nov 1878 Peiwar
1574 Dewa Sing sl w 2 Dec 1878 Peiwar Kotal
1560 Fateh Sing sl w 2 Dec 1878 Peiwar Kotal
Hurnam Sing sl w 14 Oct 1879 Ali Khel, gs (P/1372-6654 & P/1534-7969)
1621 Jagat Sing sl w 2 Dec 1878 Peiwar Kotal
1331 Jita Sing mort w 2 Dec 1878 Peiwar Kotal, dow 12 Dec
1612 Jiwan Sing dang w 2 Dec 1878 Peiwar Kotal
1858 Jiwan Sing k 2 Dec 1878 Peiwar Kotal
416 Kadir Baksh k 2 Dec 1878 Peiwar Kotal

1505 Mana Sing sl w 28 Nov 1878 Peiwar
1824 Nauranga sl w 2 Dec 1878 Peiwar Kotal
1315 Nehal Sing k 2 Dec 1878 Peiwar Kotal
1477 Rada sl w 28 Nov 1878 Peiwar
1747 Ranj Khan sl w 2 Dec 1878 Peiwar Kotal
1595 Saiad Gulam sl w 28 Nov 1878 Peiwar
1156 Sharif Khan mort w 2 Dec 1878 Peiwar Kotal, dow 13 Dec
1475 Sher Mahomed sl w 2 Dec 1878 Peiwar Kotal

30th (PUNJAB) BENGAL NATIVE INFANTRY

Source P/1537-11397

Havildar

814 Hamira sl w 15 Jan 1880 Kam Dakka, side of neck,rock fragts

Lance-Naik

1492 Fakir Mahomed sev w 15 Jan 1880 Kam Dakka, gs side of arm & back

Sepoy

1898 Dewa Singh sl w 15 Jan 1880 Kam Dakka, gs left hand

31st (PUNJAB) BENGAL NATIVE INFANTRY

Source P/1537-11180

Lieutenant

Angelo, Frederick Canning Cortlandt k 26 Mar 1880 Fort Battye, gs head

Havildar

Jewand Sing sl w 26 Mar 1880 Fort Battye, sword

Naik

Baddhan Singh k 26 Mar 1880 Fort Battye, gs head

Lance-Naik

Bhadawa Sing sl w 26 Mar 1880 Fort Battye, sword

Sepoys

Bhag Sing sl w 26 Mar 1880 Fort Battye, sword
Gopi k 26 Mar 1880 Fort Battye, bullet & sword
Hazaru k 26 Mar 1880 Fort Battye, gs head
Hira Sing sl w 26 Mar 1880 Fort Battye, gs
Jhanda Singh sl w 26 Mar 1880 Fort Battye, sword
Soba Sing sl w 26 Mar 1880 Fort Battye, sword
Taraija sl w 26 Mar 1880 Fort Battye, gs
Tika sl w 26 Mar 1880 Fort Battye, sword

32nd BENGAL NATIVE INFANTRY

Sepoy

1509 Kharak Singh sev w 20 May 1880 Mazina Valley, gs right forearm (D.40)

39th BENGAL NATIVE INFANTRY

Source D.32

Sepoys

1896 Harnam Sing sl w 29 Apr 1879 attack on grazing ground nr Ali Musjid

1818 Nanicka sev w 10 May 1879 nr Ali Musjid

45th (RATTRAY'S SIKHS) BENGAL NATIVE INFANTRY

Lieutenants

Barclay, Francis Miles mort w 17 Mar 1879 Maidanak, musket shot right shoulder & lung, dow 1 Apr Landi Kotal (D.32, P/1371-3510 & see VC to Leach)

Holmes, Henry Richard Longcroft sev w 28 Jan 1879 Bazar Valley (D.12)

Havildars

1059 Dewa Sing k 17 Mar 1879 Maidanak (D.32)

665 Kharak Sing k 16 Jun 1879 attack on post at Dakka (D.32)

Sepoys

458 Atar Sing sl w 25 Apr 1880 Charasiah, gs contusion,head (D.39 & P/1537-11817)

1214 Dassaunda Sing sev w 22 Dec 1878 Bazar Valley, contusion (D.32 & P/1372-5297)

1368 Jhanda Sing sl w 25 Apr 1880 Charasiah, gs third finger right hand (D.39 & P/1537-11817)

1595 Kishen Sing sev w 17 Mar 1879 Maidanak (D.32)

1474 Mewa Sing sl w 28 Nov 1878 Shagai; sl w 17 Mar 1879 Maidanak (D.32)

415 Rur Sing sl w 25 Apr 1880 Charasiah, gs right elbow (D.39 & P/1537-11817)

1057 Rura sev w 29 Nov 1878 Khyber Pass; sev w 28 Jan 1879 Bazar Valley (D.32)

1417 Wasawa Sing sl w 17 Mar 1879 Maidanak (D.32)

1st GURKHA REGIMENT

Naik
Diaram Nagarkoti sl w 11 Jun 1880 Lughman (P/1536-10533)

Sepoys
Dhanbir Rana sl w 11 Jun 1880 Lughman (P/1536-10533)
Harkison Thapa sl w 16 Apr 1880 Hisarak, gs thigh (P/1537-11474)

2nd GURKHA (SIRMOOR RIFLE) REGIMENT

Lieutenant-Colonel
Battye, Arthur sl w 1 Sep 1880 Kandahar (D.51)

Jemadar
Mohan Sing Maharah sev w 1 Sep 1880 Kandahar, gs right leg (D.51)

Naiks
Gungaram Alleh sev w 1 Sep 1880 Kandahar, since d (D.51)
Kharakdhoj Sahi k 1 Sep 1880 Kandahar (D.51)
Kheema Newar sl w 17 Dec 1879 Jagdalak, gs (D.34)
Nurbir Karki sev w 1 Sep 1880 Kandahar (D.51)

Bugler
Kasi Lohar sev w 1 Sep 1880 Kandahar (D.51)

Sepoys
1319 Bisram Thapa sev w 1 Sep 1880 Kandahar, since d (D.51), awarded IOM 3rd Class
Dillu Kawas sl w 1 Sep 1880 Kandahar (D.51)
Fateh Kwas k 1 Sep 1880 Kandahar (D.51)
975 Gajbir Gurung sl w 29 Jan 1879 Bazar Valley (D.32)
948 Gangabir Gharti sev w 26 Jan 1879 Bazar Valley (D.32 & P/1372-5350)
Gobardham Bandari sl w 1 Sep 1880 Kandahar (D.51)
Gungabir Rana sl w 1 Sep 1880 Kandahar (D.51)
Jagarnath Sahi k 1 Sep 1880 Kandahar (D.51)
Jagatram Thapa sl w 1 Sep 1880 Kandahar (D.51)
Jangbir Thapa sev w 1 Sep 1880 Kandahar (D.51)
1195 Jangbir Thapa k 29 Jan 1879 Bazar Valley (D.32)
1017 Kalu Gurung sl w 26 Jan 1879 Bazar Valley (D.32)
Kasiram Gharti k 1 Sep 1880 Kandahar (D.51)
Kasiram Gurung sl w 1 Sep 1880 Kandahar (D.51)
Kethar Sing Gurung sl w 1 Sep 1880 Kandahar (D.51)
Maiteah Chand sl w 1 Sep 1880 Kandahar (D.51)
Man Sing Alleh sev w 1 Sep 1880 Kandahar (D.51)
Mohandar Sing Khatri k 1 Sep 1880 Kandahar (D.51)
1360 Mukhareah Rana sl w 1 Sep 1880 Kandahar (D.51), awarded IOM 3rd Class
584 Mungal Joyser sev w 1 Sep 1880 Kandahar (D.51), awarded IOM 3rd Class

Narsing Gurung k 1 Sep 1880 Kandahar (D.51)
Nowbeer Sahie sl w 18 Dec 1879 Jagdalak, gs (D.34)
Parbal Thapa sev w 1 Sep 1880 Kandahar (D.51)
1059 Punbhadar Thapa sev w 18 Dec 1878 attack on grazing ground in the Khyber (D.32)
Puranbir Thapa sl w 1 Sep 1880 Kandahar (D.51)
Ransur Thapa sev w 1 Sep 1880 Kandahar (D.51)
Sadhu Rana sev w 1 Sep 1880 Kandahar (D.51)
Santbir Thapa k 1 Sep 1880 Kandahar (D.51)
858 Sarjin Pun mort w 22 Dec 1878 Bazar Valley, dow same day (D.32)
Sher Sing Thappa w 19 Dec 1879 Jagdalak, gs head, dow (D.34)
1041 Thakur Sain sl w 26 Apr 1879 attack on picquet at Basawal, d 9 May (D.32)
Tularam Gurung k 1 Sep 1880 Kandahar (D.51)
Ussun Rana sl w 1 Sep 1880 Kandahar (D.51)
901 Wazir Sing Nagarkoti sl w 1 Sep 1880 Kandahar (D.51), awarded IOM 3rd Class

3rd (THE KUMAON) GURKHA REGIMENT

Sources D.48 & P/1538-13867

Sepoys attchd 19th Bombay NI
Har Sing sev w 16 Aug 1880 Deh Khojah, gs contusion right side
Sham Lall sev w 16 Aug 1880 Deh Khojah, gs right thigh

4th GURKHA REGIMENT

Lieutenant-Colonel
Rowcroft, Frederick Francis sl w 31 Aug 1880 Kandahar (D.51)

Subadar
Ran Sing Rana dang w 31 Aug 1880 Kandahar, gs left upper arm (D.51)

Naik
Johar Sing Thapa sl w 25 Apr 1880 Shekabad (P/1536-9899)

Sepoys
Bajbir Thapa w 25 Apr 1879 Shekabad, gs right shoulder (D.38)
1640 Danbir Gharti k 31 Aug 1880 Kandahar, gs chest (D.51)
Danbir Khanka sl w 31 Aug 1880 Kandahar (D.51)
Dhanbir Thapa w 25 Apr 1879 Shekabad, gs contusion left loin (D.38)
2112 Dulbir Rana sev w 31 Aug 1880 Kandahar, gs hip (D.51)
Gujia Rana w 25 Apr 1879 Shekabad, gs forehead (D.38)
1525 Hari Gurung k 27 Jan 1879 Bazar Valley (D.32)
1788 Kallu Nagarkoti sl w 31 Aug 1880 Kandahar, gs left hand (D.51)

Musthan Thapa dang w 31 Aug 1880 Kandahar, gs right eye (D.51)
Sobhitman Gurung k 25 Apr 1879 Shekabad, tulwar across vortex, cutting into brain (D.38)
Surrubjeet Thapa sl w 17 Dec 1879 Jagdalak, gs forearm (D.34)

5th GURKHA REGIMENT

Sources D.32 & 33
P/1372-5896

Brevet Lieutenant-Colonel
Fitzhugh, Alfred sl w 10 Dec 1879 Paghman Valley, gs

Major
Cook, John awarded VC for Peiwar Kotal 2 Dec 1878; dang w 12 Dec 1879 Kabul, gs left leg, 'while leading the attack on a high conical hill, the Takht-i-Shah peak', dow 19 Dec Sherpur

Captain
Powell, Charles Folliott very sev w 13 Dec 1878 Sapari Pass, gs, 'most forward and gallant in the fight', dow 18 Dec (& D.6)

Subadar-Major
Bhageeram Gurung k 14 Oct 1879 explosion in Bala Hissar

Subadars
Balbhudder Negi sev w 2 Dec 1878 Peiwar Kotal (D.3)
Ragubir Nagarkoti sl w 2 Dec 1878 Peiwar Kotal, awarded IOM 3rd Class

Havildars
Badhibul Rama k 14 Oct 1879 explosion in Bala Hissar
541 Balbahadur Jaisi sev w 2 Dec 1878 Peiwar Kotal
892 Birband Sahai sev w 14 Dec 1879 Kabul, gs arm
Garaibir Rai w 14 Oct 1879 explosion in Bala Hissar
Hansaram Jaisi k 14 Oct 1879 explosion in Bala Hissar
Inderbir Jaisi k 14 Oct 1879 explosion in Bala Hissar
Jasbir Gurung k 14 Oct 1879 explosion in Bala Hissar
Kassi Chund sev w 6 Oct 1879 Charasiah, gs (D.24)
623 Nar Sing Mohat sl w 13 Dec 1878 Sapari Pass
Nund Ram Jaisi sev w 14 Dec 1879 Kabul, gs face
Pershad Sing k 6 Oct 1879 Charasiah, gs
Wazir Sing Adhikari k 14 Oct 1879 explosion in Bala Hissar

Naiks
670 Birbal Sing Thakur sev w 2 Dec 1878 Peiwar Kotal
Dasi Chund k 14 Oct 1879 explosion in Bala Hissar
1005 Ibran Gurung sl w 2 Dec 1878 Peiwar Kotal

Buglers
Chooni Damai sl w 6 Oct 1879 Charasiah, gs (D.24), awarded IOM 3rd Class
61 Kalu Lohar sl w 2 Dec 1878 Peiwar Kotal

Sepoys

Ameeroodeen Thappa w 14 Oct 1879 explosion in Bala Hissar
1582 Atibal Khawas sl w 2 Dec 1878 Peiwar Kotal
1605 Bagbir Nagarkoti k 2 Dec 1878 Peiwar Kotal
1732 Bhabeshwar Gharti sl w 10 Dec 1879 Paghman Valley, gs thigh
Bhairab Sing Thakoor w 14 Oct 1879 explosion in Bala Hissar
Biraj Ghirta sev w 6 Oct 1879 Charasiah, gs (D.24)
1601 Bishnu Thapa sev w 2 Dec 1878 Peiwar Kotal
984 Dalbir Thapa k 13 Dec 1878 Sapari Pass
1754 Dalbir Thapa sl w 2 Dec 1878 Peiwar Kotal
1543 Daljit Rai sl w 13 Dec 1878 Sapari Pass
Dela Thapa sl w 13 Dec 1878 Sapari Pass (D.6)
1468 Deo Narain sev w 28 Nov 1878 Peiwar
1200 Dhanbir Rana k 13 Dec 1878 Sapari Pass
Dhaniram Gurung w 14 Oct 1879 explosion in Bala Hissar
1394 Dhaniram Gurung k 12 Dec 1879 Kabul
1862 Dharam Dhoj Achai sev w 13 Dec 1878 Sapari Pass
Dhurm Baz sev w 13 Dec 1878 Sapari Pass
1722 Dilaram Thapa sev w 2 Dec 1878 Peiwar Kotal
Dillia Allia sl w 6 Oct 1879 Charasiah, gs (D.24)
Dulbeer Thapa sl w 13 Dec 1878 Sapari Pass (D.6)
984 Dulbir Thapa k 13 Dec 1879 Sapari Pass
1192 Dulbir Thapa k 14 Dec 1879 Kabul, gs thighs
Duljeet Rai sl w 13 Dec 1878 Sapari Pass (D.6)
1280 Dunber Lohar sl w 10 Dec 1879 Paghman Valley, gs right ear
Dungit Gurung k 6 Oct 1879 Charasiah, gs (D.24 & P/1372-5894)
Gunnia Bora Thappa k 14 Oct 1879 explosion in Bala Hissar
1630 Hawaria Gharti sev w 13 Dec 1878 Sapari Pass
1677 Hirabir Gurung sev w 1 Sep 1880 Kandahar, gs left forearm (D.51)
1537 Indarbir Gharti sev w 13 Dec 1878 Sapari Pass
1044 Indarbir Thapa sev w 2 Dec 1878 Peiwar Kotal
Inderbir Ghalea sev w 6 Oct 1879 Charasiah, gs (D.24)
Jasbir Sing Katri sev w 6 Oct 1879 Charasiah, gs (D.24)
Jasbir Thappa k 6 Oct 1879 Charasiah, gs (D.24)
1352 Jitman Aliah k 2 Dec 1878 Peiwar Kotal
Kabiraj Adkari sl w 6 Oct 1879 Charasiah, gs (D.24)
Kabiraj Thappa w 14 Oct 1879 explosion in Bala Hissar
1326 Kalar Thapa k 1 Sep 1880 Kandahar, gs chest (D.51)
1271 Kalu Kawas sev w 1 Sep 1880 Kandahar, gs throat (D.51)
1595 Kalu Thapa sev w 2 Dec 1878 Peiwar Kotal
Kaman Sing Ghurtee k 14 Oct 1879 explosion in Bala Hissar
Kasar Thappa k 14 Oct 1879 explosion in Bala Hissar
1290 Kashiram Burathoki sl w 2 Dec 1878 Peiwar Kotal
Kishenbir Akoti sl w 6 Oct 1879 Charasiah, gs (D.24)
Kulbir sev w 14 Dec 1879 Kabul, gs cheek
1557 Kulbir Thapa sev w 14 Dec 1879, gs cheek (same man ?)
1075 Kunbir Bhist sl w 10 Dec 1879 Paghman Valley, gs arm
1614 Lachman Thapa sl w 13 Dec 1878 Sapari Pass
1471 Lalbir Gurung sl w 2 Dec 1878 Peiwar Kotal

1857 Lanto Burathoki w 11 Dec 1879 Kabul; k 17 Dec 1879 Kabul (P/1536-10625)
Lutchman Thapa sl w 13 Dec 1878 Sapari Pass (D.6)
1474 Manaraj sev w 10 Dec 1879 Paghman Valley, gs leg
1546 Man Bahadur Gurung sl w 2 Dec 1878 Peiwar Kotal
1888 Mohepatte Sahai sl w 10 Dec 1879 Paghman Valley, gs ear
Mohun Sing Rana sev w 6 Oct 1879 Charasiah, gs (D.24)
1501 Nandia Thapa mort w 2 Dec 1878 Peiwar Kotal, dow 15 Dec
Narain Thappa k 6 Oct 1879 Charasiah, gs (D.24)
1818 Nar Sing Rana mort w 13 Dec 1878 Sapari Pass, dow 15 Dec
1772 Nathu Gurung sev w 2 Dec 1878 Peiwar Kotal
1885 Nunbir Thappa sl w 10 Dec 1879 Paghman Valley, gs eyelid
1202 Pahalwan Kasai sl w 2 Dec 1878 Peiwar Kotal
Panorea Thappa k 14 Oct 1879 explosion in Bala Hissar
Pooran Sing sev w 10 Dec 1879 Paghman Valley, gs head
Poorun Thappa w 14 Oct 1879 explosion in Bala Hissar
1728 Puran Sing Thapa k 14 Dec 1879 Kabul, gs chest
1746 Rabilal Thapa sev w 13 Dec 1878 Sapari Pass
Rada Kishen sl w 10 Dec 1879 Paghman Valley, gs shoulder
44 Raghubir Nagarkoti k 14 Dec 1879 Kabul, gs chest
Rajman Nagarkoti w 14 Oct 1879 explosion in Bala Hissar
1633 Ramia Thapa sev w 13 Dec 1878 Sapari Pass
1403 Rania Khawas sev w 2 Dec 1878 Peiwar Kotal
Rannia Thappa k 14 Oct 1879 explosion in Bala Hissar
1354 Sahajbir Gurung k 13 Dec 1878 Sapari Pass
1581 Shewdul sev w 10 Dec 1879 Paghman Valley, gs head
1175 Shibram Gurung sl w 13 Dec 1878 Sapari Pass
Sing Bir sl w 6 Oct 1879 Charasiah, gs (D.24)
1295 Sitia Lohar sl w 2 Dec 1878 Peiwar Kotal
1042 Surabjit Thapa sl w 13 Dec 1878 Sapari Pass

BENGAL COMMISSARIAT DEPARTMENT

Lieutenant

Edmund, Palmer w 14 Apr 1880 Hisarak, dow 15 Apr (P/1537-11474)

BENGAL MEDICAL SERVICE

Deputy Surgeon-General

Townsend, Stephen Chapman sev w 28 Sep 1878 pass between Jagi Thanna & Karatiga, bullet right cheek (D.20)

Surgeons

Duncan, Andrew 23rd Bengal NI sev w 6 Oct 1879 Charasiah, bullet in chest (D.24)

Kelly, Ambrose Hamilton   k 3 Sep 1879 Kabul Residency (P/1372-5281)

McCartie, Charles Joseph   2nd Punjab Cav   w 2 Mar 1880 while out riding nr Kandahar, gs shoulder (P/1535-8062)

Smyth, William Beatty   murdered 25 Jun 1879 Chapri, sword cuts inflicted by thieves (P/1371-4799)

PUNJAB FRONTIER FORCE

1st PUNJAB CAVALRY, P F F

Jemadar

Haknewaz Khan   sl w 4 Jan 1879 Saif-u-Din, sword cut right hand 'in a personal encounter with one of the enemy, whom he killed' (D.8, D.32 & P/1372-5813)

Daffadars

1066 Abdul Baki Khan   k 1 Jul 1880 Patkao Shana, gs neck (D.42)

1456 Gulam Haidar Khan   sl w 27 Mar 1879 Saiad-Bud (D.32)

688 Gulam Jelani   sl w 1 Jul 1880 Patkao Shana, incisions,hand (D.42), awarded IOM 3rd Class

1660 Mazar Ali Khan   sl w 27 Mar 1879 Saiad-Bud (D.32)

1503 Mir Alam Khan   sl w 19 Apr 1880 Ahmed Khel,sword cut right thumb (D.36 & P/1537-11502)

1264 Sabdil Khan   sev w 27 Mar 1879 Saiad-Bud (D.32 & P/1372-5837)

Lance-Daffadars

1255 Buta Singh   dang w 1 Jul 1880 Patkao Shana, gs wrist (D.42)

1576 Mobariz Khan   sev w 23 Apr 1880 Arzu, sword cut head & hand (D.37 & P/1537-11502)

1422 Mowaz Khan   sl w 19 Apr 1880 Ahmed Khel, sword cuts both hands (D.36 & P/1537-11502), awarded IOM 3rd Class

1034 Sohan Sing   sl w 19 Apr 1880 Ahmed Khel, abrasion right temple (D.36 & P/1537-11502)

Sowars

Abdul Rehman   sl w 19 Apr 1880 Ahmed Khel, sword cuts middle & little fingers (D.36 & P/1537-11502)

1474 Ahmed Khan   sev w 19 Apr 1880 Ahmed Khel, sword cut back of right hand & right side of head (D.36 & P/1537-11502)

1637 Ajab Khan   sl w 19 Apr 1880 Ahmed Khel, abrsaion left hand (D.36 & P/1537-11502)

1688 Amanulla Khan   sev w 19 Apr 1880 Ahmed Khel, sword cut left hand,little finger amputated (D.36 & P/1537-11502)

1392 Bhagwan Singh sev w 1 Jul 1880 Patkao Shana, incision shoulder (D.42)
1255 Buta Sing sl w 23 Apr 1880 Arzu, sword cut hand (D.37 & P/1537-11502), awarded IOM 3rd Class
1710 Dalla Khan dang w 1 Jul 1880 Patkao Shana, incision head (D.42)
1145 Dhain Sing sev w 19 Apr 1880 Ahmed Khel, contusion head (D.36 & P/1537-11502)
1767 Emam Buksh sl w 19 Apr 1880 Ahmed Khel, sword cuts middle & little fingers; sl w 1 Jul 1880 Patkao Shana, puncture in hand (D.36, D.42 & P/1537-11502)
Fateh Khan sev w 21 Jan 1879 Nur Khan (D.32)
1807 Fazl Khan sl w 1 Jul 1880 Patkao Shana, incision hand (D.42), awarded IOM 3rd Class
1679 Gopal Sing sl w 19 Apr 1880 Ahmed Khel, sword cut inner side of forearm (D.36 & P/1537-11502)
1805 Gulab Khan sl w 1 Jul 1880 Patkao Shana, incision hand (D.42)
1332 Gulam Ali Khan sev w 19 Apr 1880 Ahmed Khel, sword cut,right ulna fractured (D.36 & P/1537-11502)
1813 Gulzar Khan sl w 19 Apr 1880 Ahmed Khel, abrasion left knee (D.36 & P/1537-11502)
1740 Isfand Yar Khan sev w 1 Jul 1880 Patkao Shana, incision arm (D.42)
1571 Jagat Sing sl w 19 Apr 1880 Ahmed Khel, right temple; sl w 1 Jul 1880 Patkao Shana, incision temple (D.36, D.42 & P/1537-11502)
1221 Jhanda Khan k 23 Apr 1880 Arzu, gs chest (D.37 & P/1537-11502)
1487 Jiwand Sing sl w 4 Jan 1879 Saif-u-Din, sword cut hand (D.32 & P/1372-5813)
1698 Karam Khan sl w 1 Jul 1880 Patkao Shana, incision forearm (D.42)
1228 Kashi Ram sev w 1 Jul 1880 Patkao Shana, incision hand (D.42)
1809 Khair Mahomed sl w 1 Jul 1880 Patkao Shana, contusion hand (D.42)
1498 Khan Zaman Khan sl w 19 Apr 1880 Ahmed Khel, sword cuts left hand & cheek (D.36 & P/1537-11502)
1275 Lakhmir Khan mort w 27 Mar 1879 Saiad-Bud, dow 11 May (D.32)
1629 Mahomed Faiaz sl w 23 Apr 1880 Arzu, sword cut forehead (D.37 & P/1537-11502)
1666 Mahomed Taki sl w 23 Apr 1880 Arzu, sword cut left forearm (D.37 & P/1537-11502)
1720 Maula Baksh sl w 23 Apr 1880 Arzu, contusion of chest by spent bullet (D.37 & P/1537-11502)
1382 Mehtab Roy sl w 27 Mar 1879 Saiad-Bud (D.32)
1648 Mir Alam Khan dang w 1 Jul 1880 Patkao Shana, gs chest (D.42)
1849 Mirdad sl w 19 Apr 1880 Ahmed Khel, sword cut left forearm (D.36 & P/1537-11502)
1345 Multan Sing sev w 19 Apr 1880 Ahmed Khel, laceration cheek (D.36 & P/1537-11502)
1773 Mushki Khan dang w 19 Apr 1880 Ahmed Khel, bayonet in groin (D.36 & P/1537-11502)

1811 Nadir Khan sl w 23 Apr 1880 Arzu, sword cut hand (D.37 & P/1537-11502)

1800 Nawab Khan sl w 1 Jul 1880 Patkao Shana, incision forearm (D.42)

1549 Ram Rakha sev w 4 Jan 1879 Saif-u-Din, sword cut left elbow 'gallantly rescuing a dismounted trooper of the 15th Hussars' (D.8, D.32 & P/1372-5813)

1616 Rehmatulla Khan sl w 23 Apr 1880 Arzu, gs graze forearm (D.37 & P/1537-11502)

1458 Samand Khan sl w 19 Apr 1880 Ahmed Khel, nose (D.36 & P/1537-11502)

1721 Sarfaraz Khan sev w 19 Apr 1880 Ahmed Khel, sword cuts fracturing right ulna,detaching large flap on left arm (D.36 & P/1537-11502)

1745 Sekander Khan sl w 1 Jul 1880 Patkao Shana, incision arm (D.42)

1318 Shah Pasand sl w 4 Jan 1879 Saif-u-Din, sword cut hand (D.32 & P/1372-5813)

1504 Sirbuland Khan dang w 1 Jul 1880 Patkao Shana, gs arm (D.42), awarded IOM 3rd Class

1851 Wazir Singh sev w 1 Jul 1880 Patkao Shana, incision arm (D.42)

2nd PUNJAB CAVALRY, P F F

Sources D.36, P/1372-6652 & P/1537-11502

Captain

Broome, John Howard w 24 Oct 1879 Shahjui; sl w 19 Apr 1880 Ahmed Khel, bullet graze

Lieutenant

Stuart, Charles John Lewis sev w 19 Apr 1880 Ahmed Khel, sword cut right forearm

Surgeon

McCartie, Charles Joseph w 2 Mar 1880 while out riding nr Kandahar, gs shoulder (P/1535-8062)

Rissaldar

Lahrasad Khan w 24 Oct 1879 Shahjui (see IOM GGO 336/1880)

Ressaidar

Shere Sing w 24 Oct 1879 Shahjui

Kot-Daffadars

Emanatoollah Khan w 24 Oct 1879 Shahjui

Sobha Sing w 24 Oct 1879 Shahjui

Daffadars

Abdul Rehman w 24 Oct 1879 Shahjui, since d

Dharam Sing sl w 1 Jul 1880 Patkao Shana, sabre,right arm (D.42)

Faizulla Khan dang w 19 Apr 1880 Ahmed Khel, sword cuts head, arms & face
Gholam Haider w 24 Oct 1879 Shahjui
Partab Sing k 19 Apr 1880 Ahmed Khel, sword cut head
Soba Sing sl w 19 Apr 1880 Ahmed Khel, bullet head

Lance-Daffadars

1821 Abbas Khan sev w 19 Apr 1880 Ahmed Khel, sword cut left hand
1759 Amir Shah sl w 19 Apr 1880 Ahmed Khel, sword cut back of neck
1530 Amir Sing sev w 19 Apr 1880 Ahmed Khel, sword cut right thigh
1663 Azizulla Khan dang w 19 Apr 1880 Ahmed Khel, sword cut back of head
Chet Sing w 24 Oct 1879 Shahjui
Karamdad w 24 Oct 1879 Shahjui
Makallan w 24 Oct 1879 Shahjui
Oomdeh Sing w 24 Oct 1879 Shahjui
Salim-u-din k 24 Oct 1879 Shahjui
Sawan Sing dang w 19 Apr 1880 Ahmed Khel, sword cut back of head

Trumpeter

Jowala Sing k 19 Apr 1880 Ahmed Khel, sword cut head & face

Sowars

1385 Agdeh Sing sl w 1 Jul 1880 Patkao Shana, gs back (D.42)
2076 Aludin sev w 19 Apr 1880 Ahmed Khel, sword cut back of head
Amir Shah w 24 Oct 1879 Shahjui
1994 Baidulla Khan dang w 19 Apr 1880 Ahmed Khel, sword cut face
1626 Bakshish Sing sev w 1 Jul 1880 Patkao Shana, sabre right hand, & sl w chest (D.42)
Bishn Sing w 24 Oct 1879 Shahjui
2027 Buali Buksh sev w 19 Apr 1880 Ahmed Khel, sword cuts both hands
1536 Dewa Sing sl w 19 Apr 1880 Ahmed Khel, sword cuts both hands
2096 Dewa Sing sev w 19 Apr 1880 Ahmed Khel, sword cut left hand
Fateh Ali w 24 Oct 1879 Shahjui
Jafar Khan w 24 Oct 1879 Shahjui
Jagat Sing w 24 Oct 1879 Shahjui
1726 Jewan Sing sev w 19 Apr 1880 Ahmed Khel, sword cut right hand
2066 Jewan Sing sev w 19 Apr 1880 Ahmed Khel, sword cut left hand
2147 Jilal Khan sl w 19 Apr 1880 Ahmed Khel, sword cut right hand
Jowalla Sing w 24 Oct 1879 Shahjui
Kishn Sing w 24 Oct 1879 Shahjui
Mahomed Ali w 24 Oct 1879 Shahjui
Mahomed Husain w 24 Oct 1879 Shahjui
Mahomed Khan dang w 23 Apr 1880 Arzu, gs left temple (D.37)
Makhan Sing w 24 Oct 1879 Shahjui
Mula Sing w 24 Oct 1879 Shahjui
1848 Nizamudin sev w 19 Apr 1880 Ahmed Khel, sword cut left hand

2039 Nur Ahmad sl w 19 Apr 1880 Ahmed Khel, sword cut right hand
Oomer Buksh w 24 Oct 1879 Shahjui
1727 Ram Sing k 19 Apr 1880 Ahmed Khel, sword cut head & face
Sawan Sing (1) w 24 Oct 1879 Shahjui
1882 Sawan Sing (2) w 24 Oct 1879 Shahjui; dang w 19 Apr 1880 Ahmed Khel, bullet right shoulder
Shaftur Khan w 24 Oct 1879 Shahjui
2008 Torabaz Khan sl w 19 Apr 1880 Ahmed Khel, sword cut left hand
1784 Zain Khan sl w 19 Apr 1880 Ahmed Khel, sword cut right leg
Zarif Khan w 24 Oct 1879 Shahjui

3rd PUNJAB CAVALRY, P F F

Source D.51

Lieutenant

Baker, Louis Samuel Hyde sl w 1 Sep 1880 Kandahar

Daffadars

Arjun Sing sl w 1 Sep 1880 Kandahar, punctured eyebrow
Mansur Khan dang w 1 Sep 1880 Kandahar, lance left breast

Sowars

Barkar Khan dang w 1 Sep 1880 Kandahar, sword cut amputating four fingers left hand, sword cut skull
Fateh Khan dang w 1 Sep 1880 Kandahar, sword cut dividing nose & part of skull & exposing left eye-ball
Haidar Khan sl w 1 Sep 1880 Kandahar, puncture right forearm
Yusaf Khan sl w 1 Sep 1880 Kandahar, sword cut scalp

4th PUNJAB CAVALRY, P F F

Source P/1534-6873

Captain

Shephard, Thomas sl w 5 Jan 1879 nr Tank, sword cut neck

Jemadar

Shere Beg sl w 5 Jan 1879 nr Tank, sword cut arm

Trumpeter

Neha_ Singh k 5 Jan 1879 nr Tank

Sowars

Bur Singh sev w 5 Jan 1879 nr Tank, gs leg
837 Bussaun Singh sev w 5 Jan 1879 nr Tank, spear in hand
580 Ismail sev w 5 Jan 1879 nr Tank, sword cut arm, compound fracture
663 Kishen Sing sev w 5 Jan 1879 nr Tank, sword cut head

5th PUNJAB CAVALRY, P F F

Sources D.32 & D.33

Lieutenant

Gambier, Claude Frederic sev w 23 Dec 1879 Kabul, gs thigh

Rissaldars

Ameer Ali Shah sev w 14 Dec 1879 Kabul, gs chest, awarded IOM 3rd Class

Jemajat Sing sl w 20 Dec 1879 Kabul, puncture face

Jemadar

Jhunda Sing sev w 14 Dec 1879 Kabul, gs arm

Kot-Daffadars

Jewant Sing k 14 Dec 1879 Kabul

Sahail Khan sev w 14 Dec 1879 Kabul, gs head

Daffadars

Goormuk Sing k 12 Dec 1879 Sherpur, gs body

167 Hashmat Sing dang w 7 Jan 1879 Matun, bullet in leg (& D.9)

187 Hassan Khan k 7 Jan 1879 Matun, shot through heart (& D.9)

Trumpeter

Jungar sl w 14 Oct 1879 Ali Khel, sword cut (P/1372-6654 & P/1534-7969)

Sowars

Akmut Khan sev w 20 Dec 1879 Kabul, gs thigh

1604 Bhup Sing sev w 7 Jan 1879 Matun, bullet arm & chest (& D.9)

Budri sev w 20 Dec 1879 Kabul, sword cut face

1371 Bussawar Sing sev w 14 Dec 1879 Kabul, gs wrist, awarded IOM 3rd Class

Chet Sing sev w 20 Dec 1879 Kabul, gs foot

Chettoo Misser sev w 6 Oct 1879 Charasiah, bullet left cheek (D.24)

Gholam Shah k 13 Dec 1879 Kabul, gs chest

Golab Sing sl w 14 Oct 1879 Ali Khel, sword cut (P/1372-6654 & P/1534-7969)

Goojor Sing sev w 14 Dec 1879 Kabul, gs thigh

1756 Harsa Sing sl w 6 Oct 1879 Charasiah, abrasion right heel (D.24), awarded IOM 3rd Class

Jai Sing k 6 Oct 1879 Charasiah, bullet (D.24)

Jewun Sing k 13 Dec 1879 Kabul, gs, carried off by the enemy

1445 Jhanda Sing sl w 7 Jan 1879 Matun, sword cut right wrist (& D.9)

Kadir Bux sl w 20 Dec 1879 Kabul, sword cut chest

Luckoo Sing sl w 20 Dec 1879 Kabul, sword cut face

1678 Miah Sing sev w 14 Dec 1879 Kabul, gs groin, awarded IOM 3rd Class

Ram Sing k 13 Dec 1879 Kabul, gs, carried off by the enemy

Sunt Sing sev w 12 Dec 1879 Kabul, gs foot

Urjun Khan sl w 20 Dec 1879 Kabul, sword cut scalp

Ursa Sing sev w 14 Dec 1879 Kabul, gs thigh

1804 Yetbar Shah sl w 7 Jan 1879 Matun, sword cut left knee (& D.9)

CORPS OF GUIDES, P F F

Sources D.18, D.32, D.33, D.39, P/1372-6625 & P/1537-11817. Kabul Residency casualties appear in Historical records of the services of the Queen's Own Corps of Guides (Lahore, 1886).

CAVALRY

Major
Battye, Wigram, offic Cmdt   k 2 Apr 1879 Fatehabad, 'charging at the head of his men, first receiving two bullets in his left hip and shortly after another in the chest'

Lieutenant
Hamilton, Walter Richard Pollock   awarded VC for Fatehabad 2 Apr 1879; k 3 Sep 1879 Kabul Residency

Ressaidars
Dhuni Chand   sl w 2 Apr 1879 Fatehabad, spear
Kala Sing   sl w 2 Apr 1879 Fatehabad, sword cut
10 Mahomed Khan   k 2 Apr 1879 Fatehabad

Jemadars
Bishen Das   sl w 2 Apr 1879 Fatehabad, contusion left elbow
Jewand Sing   sl w 2 Apr 1879 Fatehabad, sword cut; k 3 Sep 1879 Kabul Residency

Kot-Daffadars
66 Atar Sing   mort w 2 Apr 1879 Fatehabad, sword cut, dow 6 Apr
242 Boop Sing   sl w 13 Dec 1879 Kabul, gs arm
137 Tangi   dang w 25 Apr 1880 Charasiah, gs abdomen

Daffadars
325 Buta   mort w 2 Apr 1879 Fatehabad, sword cut, dow 19 Apr
244 Hira Singh   k 3 Sep 1879 Kabul Residency
180 Nur Mahomed   k 2 Apr 1879 Fatehabad
482 Sada Sing   sl w 2 Apr 1879 Fatehabad, sword cut
184½ Suchet Sing   sl w 2 Apr 1879 Fatehabad, sword cut
233 Teja Sing   sl w 2 Apr 1879 Fatehabad, sword cut; sev w 25 Apr 1880 Charasiah, gs shoulder

Lance-Daffadars
505 Amir Chand   k 25 Apr 1880 Charasiah, gs neck
585 Chatar Sing   sl w 2 Apr 1879 Fatehabad, sword cut
748 Dhalip Chand   dang w 25 Apr 1880 Charasiah, gs neck
625 Faiz Talab   sev w 25 Apr 1880 Charasiah, gs left arm

Farrier
783 Amirulla   k 3 Sep 1879 Kabul Residency

Trumpeter
525 Kirpa Ram   sev w 13 Dec 1879 Kabul, gs leg

Sowars

529 Abdulla sl w 13 Dec 1879 Kabul, bayonet thigh
766 Ahmed Ali dang w 25 Apr 1880 Charasiah, gs abdomen
793 Akbar k 3 Sep 1879 Kabul Residency
725 Akbar Khan k 3 Sep 1879 Kabul Residency
551 Amar Singh k 3 Sep 1879 Kabul Residency
774 Amir Hyder k 3 Sep 1879 Kabul Residency
709 Bhola Sing sl w 2 Apr 1879 Fatehabad
659 Bishen Das sl w 2 Apr 1879 Fatehabad
Budh Sing k 13 Dec 1879 Kabul, sword cuts
Chet Sing k 23 Dec 1879 Kabul, gs spine
502 Chogat Sing sl w 2 Apr 1879 Fatehabad (502½?); k 13 Dec 1879 Kabul
Darmanda Sing sl w 13 Dec 1879 Kabul, sword cut head & shoulders
544 Deo Raj k 25 Apr 1880 Charasiah, gs skull
787 Dewa Singh k 3 Sep 1879 Kabul Residency
708 Dial Sing dang w 2 Apr 1879 Fatehabad
788 Duswana Singh sl w 13 Dec 1879 Kabul
903 Ganesh Das k 13 Dec 1879 Kabul, sword cuts
845 Ghulam Habib k 3 Sep 1879 Kabul Residency
781 Gokal Chand sl w 2 Apr 1879 Fatehabad, thigh; sev w 25 Apr 1880 Charasiah, gs thumb
672 Gul Ahmed k 3 Sep 1879 Kabul Residency
492 Gulab Sing dang w 2 Apr 1879 Fatehabad
611 Harnam Sing sl w 2 Apr 1879 Fatehabad, sword cuts; k 3 Sep 1879 Kabul Residency
565 Himaiat Khan sl w 2 Apr 1879 Fatehabad
641 Hira Nund Sing sl w 2 Apr 1879 Fatehabad, sword cut hand
771 Hukam Sing sev w 25 Apr 1880 Charasiah, gs face
470 Jiwan Singh k 3 Sep 1879 Kabul Residency
Juggut Sing k 13 Dec 1879 Kabul, sword cuts
808 Kandu Sing sev w 2 Apr 1879 Fatehabad
220 Kesar Sing sl w 2 Apr 1879 Fatehabad, hand
700 Khairulla k 3 Sep 1879 Kabul Residency
476 Kirpal Sing sl w 2 Apr 1879 Fatehabad, contusion back
562 Maddat sev w 25 Apr 1880 Charasiah, gs finger
694 Mahomed Amin k 3 Sep 1879 Kabul Residency
704 Mahomed Hussun k 3 Sep 1879 Kabul Residency
639 Makan Sing sl w 25 Apr 1880 Charasiah, gs chest
753 Mal Sing sl w 2 Apr 1879 Fatehabad, sword cut hand
802 Miroh k 3 Sep 1879 Kabul Residency
753 Mul Singh k 3 Sep 1879 Kabul Residency
558 Nadir Singh sev w 2 Apr 1879 Fatehabad, sword cut
891 Natha Sing sev w 13 Dec 1879 Kabul, gs arm
475 Nihal Sing dang w 2 Apr 1879 Fatehabad, spear in abdomen
546 Pars Ram k 3 Sep 1879 Kabul Residency
608 Ratan Singh k 3 Sep 1879 Kabul Residency
719 Sant Ram sl w 2 Apr 1879 Fatehabad, sword cut
744 Sarmukh Sing sev w 2 Apr 1879 Fatehabad
730 Shahdad Khan mort w 2 Apr 1879 Fatehabad, dow 5 Apr
624 Shamur Sing k 2 Apr 1879 Fatehabad

525 Suleiman sl w 13 Dec 1879 Kabul, gs hand
419 Thakur Sing sev w 25 Apr 1880 Charasiah, gs right arm
684 Thakur Singh k 3 Sep 1879 Kabul Residency
710 Wadawa Sing sl w 2 Apr 1879 Fatehabad, sword cut
750 Wadhama Sing sev w 13 Dec 1879 Kabul, gs arm
572 Wazir Singh k 3 Sep 1879 Kabul Residency
855 Yakut sev w 2 Apr 1879 Fatehabad
702 Zaidulla sev w 13 Dec 1879 Kabul, gs arm, awarded IOM 3rd Class
822 Zamin Shah sev w 25 Apr 1880 Charasiah, gs leg
859 Zarghun Shah sev w 25 Apr 1880 Charasiah, gs leg, since d

INFANTRY

Captain
Battye, Frederick Drummond dang w 14 Dec 1879 Kabul, gs

Subadars
Jowala Sing dang w 14 Dec 1879 Kabul, gs thigh, dow 18 Dec
Rup Sing k 14 Dec 1879 Kabul, gs chest

Jemadars
Jung Bahadur dang w 23 Dec 1879 Kabul, gs neck, dow 24 Dec
Mehtab Sing k 3 Sep 1879 Kabul Residency

Hospital Assistants
Gulam Haidar Khan sev w 25 Apr 1880 Charasiah, gs ankle
Rahman Baksh k 3 Sep 1879 Kabul Residency

Havildars
1319 Bahadur Sing sl w 14 Dec 1879 Kabul, gs thigh
1244 Hazara Singh k 3 Sep 1879 Kabul Residency
560 Husen k 3 Sep 1879 Kabul Residency
447 Jowala Sing sl w 14 Dec 1879 Kabul, gs abdomen, awarded IOM 3rd Class
874 Kharak Singh k 3 Sep 1879 Kabul Residency
814 Mohan Bir sev w 25 Apr 1880 Charasiah, gs arm
1217 Narain Sing k 14 Dec 1879 Kabul, gs chest
760 Narain Sing sl w 14 Dec 1879 Kabul, gs eyelid
302 Tail Sing k 14 Dec 1879 Kabul, gs heart

Naiks
953 Kallu k 23 Dec 1879 Kabul, gs abdomen
1589 Mehr Dil k 3 Sep 1879 Kabul Residency
1565 Mir Baz k 14 Dec 1879 Kabul, gs abdomen
1009 Nahir Sing sev w 14 Dec 1879 Kabul, gs cheeks
519 Nihala k 14 Dec 1879 Kabul, bursting of shell
1763 Rahim Dad dang w 14 Dec 1879 Kabul, gs chest, dow 15 Dec

Lance-Naiks
1352 Jangi k 3 Sep 1879 Kabul Residency
1358 Lehna sev w 14 Dec 1879 Kabul, gs leg

1173 Nand Sing sev w 14 Dec 1879 Kabul, gs hip
Turai sl w 13 Dec 1879 Kabul

Buglers
35 Abdullah k 3 Sep 1879 Kabul Residency
32 Dittu sev w 14 Dec 1879 Kabul, gs arm

Sepoys
2385 Abdulla k 14 Dec 1879 Kabul, gs chest
1807 Ajaib Shah k 3 Sep 1879 Kabul Residency
1934 Akbar Shah k 3 Sep 1879 Kabul Residency
1743 Akram Khan k 2 Jun 1879 on escort with rafts between Jellalabad & Dakka
2077 Alam Shah k 3 Sep 1879 Kabul Residency
1561 Amar Singh k 3 Sep 1879 Kabul Residency
Attar Singh sl w 14 Dec 1879 Kabul
Bahadur Sing sl w 14 Dec 1879 Kabul, gs thigh
1948 Baidulla k 3 Sep 1879 Kabul Residency
1989 Bhaggat Singh k 3 Sep 1879 Kabul Residency
Bir Sing sev w 14 Dec 1879 Kabul, gs knee
1779 Budh Sing sev w 14 Dec 1879 Kabul, gs chest
1704 Bur Sing sev w 14 Dec 1879 Kabul, gs nose
2200 Chanda Singh k 3 Sep 1879 Kabul Residency
1286 Devi Singh k 3 Sep 1879 Kabul Residency
2458 Didu k 14 Dec 1879 Kabul, gs thigh
2161 Duria Khan k 3 Sep 1879 Kabul Residency
1990 Esa Singh k 3 Sep 1879 Kabul Residency
1949 Fakir Muhamad sev w 14 Dec 1879 Kabul, gs chest, dow 15 Dec
654 Fateh Singh sev w 14 Dec 1879 Kabul, since d
1311 Fatteh Singh k 3 Sep 1879 Kabul Residency
1946 Gaja Singh k 3 Sep 1879 Kabul Residency
Ganda Sing sl w 14 Dec 1879 Kabul, gs arm
1549 Gobardhan k 3 Sep 1879 Kabul Residency
946 Gopal Sing sev w 14 Dec 1879 Kabul, gs hand
2058 Gowhur k 14 Dec 1879 Kabul, gs skull
2164 Gulab Shah sev w 14 Dec 1879 Kabul, gs finger
2211 Gulsher Khan sev w 14 Dec 1879 Kabul, gs thigh, awarded IOM 3rd Class (as Gul Shere)
1612 Gurdit Sing k 14 Dec 1879 Kabul, gs skull
1686 Gurdit Singh k 3 Sep 1879 Kabul Residency
2180 Gurdit Singh k 3 Sep 1879 Kabul Residency
2089 Hamzulla k 3 Sep 1879 Kabul Residency
2150 Hamzulla k 3 Sep 1879 Kabul Residency
Hardit Sing sev w 23 Dec 1879 Kabul, gs skull
2003 Harri Singh k 3 Sep 1879 Kabul Residency
1696 Hira Sing sev w 25 Apr 1880 Charasiah, gs chest
2146 Hira Singh k 3 Sep 1879 Kabul Residency
2852 Hukma sl w 25 Apr 1880 Charasiah, gs thigh
1557 Jai Singh k 3 Sep 1879 Kabul Residency
1860 Jetha Sing dang w 14 Dec 1879 Kabul, gs abdomen, dow 15 Dec
1908 Jodha sev w 14 Dec 1879 Kabul, gs,lost right arm
2342 Jowahir Sing k 25 Apr 1880 Charasiah, gs abdomen

2359 Jowala Sing sl w 25 Apr 1880 Charasiah, gs arm
Julleh Sing sev w 14 Dec 1879 Kabul, gs hip
Jurai sl w 13 Dec 1879 Kabul, gs side
1760 Kapura sl w 14 Dec 1879 Kabul, gs abdomen
508 Kharak Sing k 14 Dec 1879 Kabul, gs abdomen
915 Khoedad k 3 Sep 1879 Kabul Residency
2085 Labh Sing sev w 25 Apr 1880 Charasiah, gs spine
1963 Lal Beg sl w 25 Apr 1880 Charasiah, gs chest
1703 Lal Sing k 14 Dec 1879 Kabul, gs abdomen
1853 Mazum k 3 Sep 1879 Kabul Residency
2261 Mir Afzal sev w 25 Apr 1880 Charasiah, gs thigh
2513 Mir Aslam sev w 25 Apr 1880 Charasiah, gs chest
2081 Mir Baz Khan k 3 Sep 1879 Kabul Residency
2068 Mith Singh k 3 Sep 1879 Kabul Residency
2272 Musa Khan sev w 14 Dec 1879 Kabul, gs arm
2002 Narain Singh k 3 Sep 1879 Kabul Residency
2258 Narain Singh sl w 14 Dec 1879 Kabul, gs arm
1903 Nidhan Singh k 3 Sep 1879 Kabul Residency
2005 Oodm Singh k 3 Sep 1879 Kabul Residency
2544 Painda sl w 25 Apr 1880 Charasiah, gs shoulder
1389 Partab k 3 Sep 1879 Kabul Residency
2321 Phitha sl w 14 Dec 1879 Kabul, gs thigh
2214 Pundhari sl w 14 Dec 1879 Kabul, gs nose
1916 Ranju Singh k 3 Sep 1879 Kabul Residency
2063 Said Amir k 3 Sep 1879 Kabul Residency
2102 Shah Baz sl w 14 Dec 1879 Kabul, gs foot
1219 Shibba k 3 Sep 1879 Kabul Residency
1353 Sirsa k 3 Sep 1879 Kabul Residency
1107 Sonu k 3 Sep 1879 Kabul Residency
2409 Sonu sev w 14 Dec 1879 Kabul, gs forearm
2034 Suleman k 3 Sep 1879 Kabul Residency
1876 Tahil Sing k 3 Sep 1879 Kabul Residency
1538 Tota k 3 Sep 1879 Kabul Residency
Utter Sing sl w 14 Dec 1879 Kabul, contusion thigh
1519 Wariam Singh k 3 Sep 1879 Kabul Residency
2001 Wariam Singh k 3 Sep 1879 Kabul Residency
1259 Wazir Sing sl w 14 Dec 1879 Kabul, gs arm
1801 Yakub Khan k 3 Sep 1879 Kabul Residency
2154 Zaidulla k 3 Sep 1879 Kabul Residency

No 1 MOUNTAIN BATTERY, P F F

Captain

Kelso, John Andrew, RA cmdg k 2 Dec 1878 Peiwar Kotal, 'shot through the head while bringing his guns into action, just beyond the first stockade on the Spin Gawai Kotal' (D:3)

Gunners
362 Basawul Sing sev w 13 Dec 1878 Sapari Pass (D.6)
Hyder Shah sev w 23 Dec 1879 Kabul, gs back (D.33)
323 Sant Sing sev w 2 Dec 1878 Peiwar Kotal (D.3)

Driver
26 Kaim sl w 14 Oct 1879 Shutar Gardan, gs

No 2 MOUNTAIN BATTERY, P F F

Source D.33

Lieutenant
Montanaro, Charles Alfred dang w 19 Dec 1879 Kabul, gs chest, since dow

Havildar
Jowalla Sing sev w 14 Dec 1879 Kabul, gs leg

Naik
Pahilwan Sing sev w 14 Dec 1879 Kabul, gs thigh

Lance-Naik
Golam Mahomed sev w 14 Dec 1879 Kabul, gs buttock

Gunners
Abjulla dang w 14 Dec 1879 Kabul, gs chest
423 Bhola Sing k 14 Dec 1879 Kabul, gs chest
Ditta dang w 14 Dec 1879 Kabul, gs skull
402 Fazl Khan sl w 7 Jan 1879 Matun, sword cut left arm: sev w 14 Dec 1879 Kabul, gs leg (& D.9)
400 Mastan Sing sl w 25 Apr 1880 Charasiah, gs right wrist (D.39 & P/1537-11817)
Wassawa dang w 14 Dec 1879 Kabul, gs arm

Drivers
Heera sl w 12 Dec 1879 Sherpur, gs leg
29 Hyat Baksh k 14 Dec 1879 Kabul, gs thigh

No 4 MOUNTAIN BATTERY, P F F

Source D.34

Trumpet-Major
Imaum Bax sev w 18 Dec 1879 Jagdalak, gs left wrist

Trumpeter
Khushyal Sing sl w 19 Nov 1879 Jagdalak,gs penis

Gunner
Saidun Shah sl w 19 Dec 1879 Jagdalak, gs right side of neck

2nd SIKH INFANTRY, P F F

Sources D.36, D.51 &
P/1537-11502

Major
Slater, James Barry sev w 1 Sep 1880 Kandahar

Subadar
Gurbaj Sing sev w 27 Jul 1879 attack on Cpt Showers' escort at Dakan-Kach (D.32), awarded IOM 3rd Class as Subadar-Major

Havildars
Hasham Khan sev w 16 Aug 1880 Deh Khojah attchd 19th Bombay NI, gs,compound fracture little fingers (D.48 & P/1538-13867)
867 Terkhu sl w 1 Sep 1880 Kandahar, gs head
2021 Torabaz Khan sev w 19 Apr 1880 Ahmed Khel, gs leg

Lance-Naik
2184 Gulab Sing dang w 19 May 1879 attack on Cpt Wylie's escort at Haji-Kot (D.32)

Sepoys
2518 Amir Ali Khan dang w 19 Apr 1880 Ahmed Khel, gs abdomen
2214 Bahadur Sing sl w 1 Sep 1880 Kandahar, gs right leg
2644 Bhag Sing sl w 1 Sep 1880 Kandahar, gs left leg
3038 Bhola Sing sl w 19 Apr 1880 Ahmed Khel
2898 Das k 1 Sep 1880 Kandahar, gs chest
2968 Dasaunda sev w 1 Sep 1880 Kandahar, gs right leg
3125 Fateh Nur sl w 19 Apr 1880 Ahmed Khel, gs face
3086 Gopala mort w 19 May 1879 attack on Cpt Wylie's escort at Haji-Kot, dow 1 Jun (D.32)
3165 Gulab sev w 1 Sep 1880 Kandahar, gs right foot
3167 Hashim Ali sl w 1 Sep 1880 Kandahar, sword cut head
2694 Hira Sing sl w 1 Sep 1880 Kandahar, gs scalp, awarded IOM 3rd Class
2785 Hulasa sev w 1 Sep 1880 Kandahar, gs left arm
3115 Issar Sing sl w 1 Sep 1880 Kandahar, gs left buttock
3384 Issar Sing k 1 Sep 1880 Kandahar, gs neck
2210 Jai Sing sev w 1 Sep 1880 Kandahar, two sabre cuts left arm, awarded IOM 3rd Class
3102 Jewan Sing sl w 1 Sep 1880 Kandahar, gs right leg
2810 Jowahir Sing sl w 1 Sep 1880 Kandahar, sword cut left hand
3325 Jowaia k 19 Apr 1880 Ahmed Khel
2945 Khan Gul sl w 1 Sep 1880 Kandahar, gs left hand
3288 Kutabdin sev w 19 Apr 1880 Ahmed Khel, gs face
3257 Lehna sl w 1 Sep 1880 Kandahar, sabre cut left arm
3075 Makhmudin sev w 19 Apr 1880 Ahmed Khel, gs ankle
3285 Mehr sev w 1 Sep 1880 Kandahar, gs left thigh
3375 Mohar Sing dang w 1 Sep 1880 Kandahar, gs head, since d
3143 Musaddi sl w 1 Sep 1880 Kandahar, gs left hand
3166 Nanku sl w 1 Sep 1880 Kandahar, gs left leg
Nawab k 1 Sep 1880 Kandahar, gs abdomen

2851 Oulia Khan sev w 1 Sep 1880 Kandahar, gs ankle
2431 Partab Sing sev w 1 Sep 1880 Kandahar, gs right buttock, awarded IOM 3rd Class
3340 Piraga sev w 1 Sep 1880 Kandahar, gs left thigh
3053 Ram Sing sev w 19 Apr 1880 Ahmed Khel
3253 Regba sl w 1 Sep 1880 Kandahar, gs right leg
3283 Shah Mahomed sev w 19 Apr 1880 Ahmed Khel, gs thigh
2926 Shama sev w 1 Sep 1880 Kandahar, gs right arm
2783 Sohonu sl w 27 Jul 1879 attack on Cpt Showers' escort at Dakan-Kach (D.32)
3297 Sundar sl w 19 Apr 1880 Ahmed Khel, gs face

3rd SIKH INFANTRY, P F F

Sources D.21, D.30, D.33 & D.51

Major

Griffiths, Clement James sl w 2 Oct 1879 Shutar Gardan

Lieutenants

Cook, Walter sev w 11 Dec 1879 Arghandi, gs chest
Fasken, Edward James Nicols sev w 12 Dec 1879 Sherpur, gs thighs (see IOM GGO 425/1880)

Subadar

Syud Amir sev w 12 Dec 1879 Sherpur, gs jaw

Jemadars

Sahel Sing sev w 11 Dec 1879 Arghandi, gs thigh
Sher Mahomed sl w 14 Dec 1879 Kabul, gs back

Havildars

84 Azim Khan sev w 1 Sep 1880 Kandahar, gs
Fazul Jan k 27 Sep 1879 nr Karatiga, 'died gallantly, killing one of his opponents after he himself was wounded and before being finally overpowered' (D.20)
Herman Sing sl w 13 Dec 1879 Kabul, gs left shoulder

Naiks

Bhoota Sing sev w 10 Dec 1879 Paghman Valley, gs leg
116 Gunga Sing sev w 1 Sep 1880 Kandahar, sword cut
147 Mirbaz Khan sev w 18/19 Oct 1879 Shutar Gardan, gs
Narrain Singh sl w 2 Oct 1879 Shutar Gardan
Neaz Mahomed sev w 19 Dec 1879 Kabul, gs back
Said Gul sl w 10 Dec 1879 Paghman Valley, gs left shoulder
175 Sarkhu sev w 1 Sep 1880 Kandahar, gs

Bugler

Badawa Sing sev w 23 Dec 1879 Kabul, gs shoulder

Sepoys

Abdoola Khan sl w 0 Dec 1879 Paghman Valley, gs thigh
Anoke Sing sl w 19 Dec 1879 Kabul, gs foot

484 Atlai Khan sl w 14 Oct 1879 Shutar Gardan, gs
Babat Khan sev w 10 Dec 1879 Paghman Valley, gs back
856 Bahal Sing sl w 18/19 Oct 1879 Shutar Gardan, gs
Beer Singh sl w 2 Oct 1879 Shutar Gardan
Bhoop Sing k 12 Dec 1879 Sherpur, gs thigh
354 Burh Sing sl w 1 Sep 1880 Kandahar, round shell
Chattar Sing sev w 1 Sep 1880 Kandahar, gs
Chowdrie sl w 2 Oct 1879 Shutar Gardan
494 Dewan Sing dang w 14 Oct 1879 Shutar Gardan, gs
Fazl Din sl w 14 Dec 1879 Kabul, gs leg
Hyat Khan sl w 19 Dec 1879 Kabul, gs foot
Jewan Sing k 12 Dec 1879 Sherpur, gs head
Lehna Sing k 11 Dec 1879 Kabul, gs thigh
Nand Sing k 14 Dec 1879 Kabul, gs chest
Nehal Singh sev w 2 Oct 1879 Shutar Gardan
Nund Sing sev w 10 Dec 1879 Paghman Valley, gs foot
Nur Mahomed dang w 23 Dec 1879 Kabul, gs thigh, since d
Nuttha Sing sl w 14 Dec 1879 Kabul, gs thigh
203 Prem Sing sl w 1 Sep 1880 Kandahar, gs
Punjab Singh sl w 2 Oct 1879 Shutar Gardan (? = 232 Panjab Sing, awarded IOM 3rd Class)
Quari Sing sl w 19 Dec 1879 Kabul, gs thigh
Ram Ditta k 13 Dec 1879 Kabul, gs abdomen
Sahib Sing sl w 18/19 Oct 1879 Shutar Gardan, gs
913 Said Habib sl w 18/19 Oct 1879 Shutar Gardan, gs
Said Noor sev w 19 Dec 1879 Kabul, gs arm
Sudder Sing sev w 10 Dec 1879 Paghman Valley, gs arm
Sultan Ali k 12 Dec 1879 Kabul, gs chest
233 Teja Sing sev w 14 Oct 1879 Shutar Gardan, gs
Wazir Sing sl w 19 Dec 1879 Kabul, gs thigh

4th SIKH INFANTRY, P F F

The regiment suffered six casualties 5 Jan 1879 nr Tank (P/1534-6873)

Naik
Wazir Singh k

Sepoys
3351 Essur Singh sev w, gs chest
3570 Kalundar Khan very sev w, sword cuts head & both hands
3261 Nehalu sev w, gs thigh & pelvis
3415 Ram Dhan sev w, gs neck
2970 Sham Singh sev w, gs thigh

1st PUNJAB INFANTRY, P F F

Source D.32

Captain
Showers, Howe Frederick k 25 Mar 1880 by marauders on road between Chappar & Quetta (P/1535-8065)

Havildar
2696 Gulam Haidar sl w 24 Mar 1879 Baghao

Sepoys
3746 Bhagwan Sing k 9 Jan 1879 Arambi-Karez
3037 Bucha Khan sl w 24 Mar 1879 Baghao
3635 Gul Mahomed sl w 24 Mar 1879 Baghao, awarded IOM 3rd Class
3153 Kanh Sing dang w 24 Mar 1879 Baghao
2493 Maiah k 9 Jan 1879 Arambi-Karez
3796 Miri mort w 24 Mar 1879 Baghao, dow 19 Apr
3472 Ram Sing k 24 Mar 1879 Baghao
3704 Saiad Ahmed k 21 Mar 1879 Kandainah Pass, gs abdomen (& P/1371-4258)
2918 Zaman Shah k 24 Mar 1879 Baghao

2nd PUNJAB INFANTRY, P F F

Source D.32

Subadar
Jamal Khan sev w 2 Dec 1878 Peiwar Kotal, gs (see P/1537-12250 for wound pension)

Havildar
2163 Obab k 2 Dec 1878 Peiwar Kotal

Naik
2265 Tulsi sl w 2 Dec 1878 Peiwar Kotal

Sepoys
3498 Akbar Ali sl w 2 Dec 1878 Peiwar Kotal
2883 Bhaga k 2 Dec 1878 Peiwar Kotal
2927 Didu k 2 Dec 1878 Peiwar Kotal
3353 Dost Mahomed sl w 2 Dec 1878 Peiwar Kotal
3210 Gaibi sl w 2 Dec 1878 Peiwar Kotal
3554 Habib mort w 2 Dec 1878 Peiwar Kotal, dow 3 Dec
3522 Hakim Sing sl w 2 Dec 1878 Peiwar Kotal
3350 Hazrat Shah mort w 2 Dec 1878 Peiwar Kotal, dow 19 Dec
2464 Khaibat Shah sl w 2 Dec 1878 Peiwar Kotal
2994 Khawas Khan k 2 Dec 1878 Peiwar Kotal
2282 Mirzu sl w 2 Dec 1878 Peiwar Kotal
3127 Nadir sl w 2 Dec 1878 Peiwar Kotal
2992 Rur Sing k 2 Dec 1878 Peiwar Kotal
3518 Sarru Khan k 2 Dec 1878 Peiwar Kotal
3058 Sundar Sing sl w 2 Dec 1878 Peiwar Kotal

4th PUNJAB INFANTRY, P F F

Source P/1535-8361

Lieutenant
Renny, Thomas John O'Dwyer   sev w 14 Dec 1879 Zaimukht, bullet in head, dow 15 Dec Kohat (& P/1372-6654)

Havildar
Chara Sing   w 14 Dec 1879 Zaimukht, bullet thigh

Sepoy
Chanda Sing   w 14 Dec 1879 Zaimukht, bullet head, since d

5th PUNJAB INFANTRY, P F F

Sources D.24, D.32 & D.33

Captain
Young, Charles   sev w 6 Oct 1879 Charasiah, bullet left thigh

Subadar-Major
Aziz Khan Bahadur   mort w 28 Nov 1878 Peiwar, dow 5 Jan 1879

Subadar
Mirza Khan   sev w 28 Jul 1879 nr Gandiaur, gs (& P/1372-6242)

Jemadar
Khani Mulla   k 6 Oct 1879 Charasiah, bullet in face

Havildars
2483 Hurreef   sev w 14 Dec 1879 Kabul, gs leg
3145 Pasand Khan   sl w 28 Jul 1879 nr Gandiaur
2440 Sham Sing   sev w 13 Dec 1879 Kabul, gs,& sword cut face & head, awarded IOM 3rd Class, since dow

Lance-Havildar
1588 Panjaba   sev w 28 Jul 1879 nr Gandiaur

Naiks
1892 Chanda Sing   sev w 14 Dec 1879 Kabul, gs thigh
3371 Hassun   sev w 14 Dec 1879 Kabul, gs arm
2923 Rudhoo   sev w 14 Dec 1879 Kabul, gs abdomen, since d
3302 Sikandar Shah   k 28 Jul 1879 nr Gandiaur

Lance-Naiks
3083 Ahmed Khan   k 29 Dec 1878 Thal
3912 Jaffir   sl w 28 Jul 1879 nr Gandiaur
1378 Nathu   k 28 Jul 1879 nr Gandiaur

Buglers
Jai Ram   k 6 Oct 1879 Charasiah, bullet
3687 Samandar   sev w 28 Jul 1879 nr Gandiaur

Sepoys
3740 Aga Ram   sev w 14 Dec 1879 Kabul, gs thigh
3950 Asaf Khan   sev w 2 Dec 1878 Peiwar Kotal

3222 Assa Sing sl w 13 Dec 1879 Kabul, gs hand
1317 Awal Khan sev w 13 Dec 1879 Kabul, bayonet forehead
3598 Bahadur Sing sl w 28 Jul 1879 nr Gandiaur
4156 Buddu k 14 Dec 1879 Kabul
Chettoo Sing sev w 6 Oct 1879 Charasiah, bullet right arm
3843 Dewa Sing k 18 Dec 1879 Kabul
Ditta k 6 Oct 1879 Charasiah, bullet
3376 Durbaree sev w 17 Dec 1879 Kabul, gs leg
4201 Emambux sev w 14 Dec 1879 Kabul, gs forehead
3908 Fateh Khan sl w 28 Jul 1879 nr Gandiaur
2731 Ganga Sing sev w 28 Jul 1879 nr Gandiaur
Goorinditta dang w 6 Oct 1879 Charasiah, bullet, dow 7 Oct
3825 Gulam Mahomed sl w 28 Nov 1878 Peiwar
3303 Heera sev w 14 Dec 1879 Kabul, gs eye
4260 Issar Sing sev w 23 Dec 1879 Kabul, gs thigh
3203 Jang Khan sev w 2 Dec 1878 Peiwar Kotal
3711 Jowahir Sing sl w 28 Nov 1878 Peiwar
Jowalla Sing dang w 6 Oct 1879 Charasiah, bullet left leg
3774 Kaim Khan sev w 28 Nov 1878 Peiwar
3124 Kajir k 28 Jul 1879 nr Gandiaur
3485 Kantha sev w 14 Dec 1879 Kabul, gs leg
3778 Kassim sev w 14 Dec 1879 Kabul, gs abdomen, since d
3401 Kharak Sing sev w 2 Dec 1878 Peiwar Kotal
4024 Korban Ali sev w 13 Dec 1879 Kabul, gs thigh
3268 Kowda sev w 14 Dec 1879 Kabul, gs buttock
Labb Sing k 6 Oct 1879 Charasiah, bullet
4302 Lall Sing sev w 14 Dec 1879 Kabul, gs arm, since d
3560 Mahomed Ali sl w 11 Dec 1879 Kabul, gs eyelid
4126 Mahomed Yar k 11 Dec 1879 Arghandi, body not recovered
4129 Mahtab sev w 14 Dec 1879 Kabul, gs ankle
3948 Miah Sing sl w 28 Nov 1878 Peiwar
4050 Mir Khan sev w 28 Jul 1879 nr Gandiaur
3833 Nial Sing dang w 11 Dec 1879 Arghandi, gs leg
4136 Noor Khan sev w 14 Dec 1879 Kabul, gs arm
3256 Sahail Sing sev w 11 Dec 1879 Arghandi, gs leg, since d
3633 Saif Ali sev w 11 Dec 1879 Arghandi, gs finger
4292 Sham Sing sev w 23 Dec 1879 Kabul, gs hand
Sundar sev w 6 Oct 1879 Charasiah, bullet chest
3753 Taru sl w 2 Dec 1878 Peiwar Kotal
3795 Wassim sev w 11 Dec 1879 Arghandi, gs chest, since d
3897 Wazir Sing sl w 28 Jul 1879 nr Gandiaur

1st CENTRAL INDIA HORSE

Sources D.41 & D.51

Lieutenant

Chamberlain, Neville Francis Fitzgerald sl w 1 Sep 1880 Kandahar

Jemadar
Faim Khan very sev w 19 May 1880 Besud, left elbow joint cut through by knife

Daffadar
Lachman Dubeh sev w 1 Sep 1880 Kandahar, gs hip

Sowars
Ali Hussain sev w 1 Sep 1880 Kandahar, sword cut elbow
1090 Kadi Khan sev w 19 May 1880 Besud, bullet over liver
Kasi Sing sl w 1 Sep 1880 Kandahar, sword cut ear
Mujud Khan sl w 1 Sep 1880 Kandahar, sword cut hand
933 Nand Singh sev w 19 May 1880 Besud, right calf cut through with knife,very deep
Pardal Khan sev w 1 Sep 1880 Kandahar, gs shoulder

MHAIRWARA BATTALION

The following casualties were all suffered at Kam Dakka 22 Apr 1879 (D.32 & P/1534-7134)

Havildars
1858 Hamira k
1767 Lala k
529 Rosan Khan k
1983 Sabdar Ali sev w

Naik
1945 Rupa dang w

Sepoys
828 Bajja sev w
20 Bhao sev w
79 Bhima sev w
2148 Dudha sl w
1860 Enda sl w
2266 Karma sl w
2354 Lumba sev w
422 Rama sev w
1704 Suja sl w
550 Tila sev w

HYDERABAD CONTINGENT

Captains
Garrett, Annesley John w 8 May 1880 nr Kandahar, gs,arm broken (P/1537-11879)
Goad, Frederick Theophilus, Transport Dept very sev w 13 Dec 1878 Sapari Pass, dow 14 Dec (D.6 & D.32)

3rd BOMBAY LIGHT CAVALRY

Sources D.44, D.48 & D.51

Lieutenant
Owen, William Charles   k 27 Jul 1880 Maiwand, 'when charging the enemy'

Rissaldar
Kalka Parsad   w 16 Aug 1880 Deh Khojah

Ressaidar
Shaik Karim Baksh   k 1 Sep 1880 Kandahar

Jemadars
Byjoo Parsad   sl w 3 Aug 1880 siege of Kandahar
Hassan Ali Khan   w 16 Aug 1880 Deh Khojah
Shumboo Parsad   w 6 Aug 1880 Deh Khojah

Kot-Daffadars
589 Dowlut Rao Mohitay   k 27 Jul 1880 Maiwand
330 Gungadeen   w 27 Jul 1880 Maiwand
466 Wazeer Khan   k 27 Jul 1880 Maiwand

Daffadars
582 Dowlut Rao Gharkay   k 27 Jul 1880 Maiwand
Kalka Sing   sl w 20 Aug 1880 siege of Kandahar
507 Rajpal Sing   w 27 Jul 1880 Maiwand
440 Shaik Abdoola   w 16 Aug 1880 Deh Khojah
394 Shaik Mykoo   w 27 Jul 1880 Maiwand

Naiks
800 Buldeo Sing   k 27 Jul 1880 Maiwand
839 Buldeo Sing   k 27 Jul 1880 Maiwand
1084 Din Daial   w 27 Jul 1880 Maiwand
714 Eshwant Rao   w 27 Jul 1880 Maiwand
834 Seetaram   k 16 Aug 1880 Deh Khojah
805 Soobay Khan   w 27 Jul 1880 Maiwand

Sowars
1160 Antajee Kenjray   k 27 Jul 1880 Maiwand
872 Ashruff Khan   w 27 Jul 1880 Maiwand
1144 Bhikoo Sackpal   w 27 Jul 1880 Maiwand
1026 Bhugwan Sing   k 27 Jul 1880 Maiwand
833 Burmadeen   w 27 Jul 1880 Maiwand, awarded IOM 3rd Class
952 Dookchor Sing   w 27 Jul 1880 Maiwand
933 Dwarka Sing   k 27 Jul 1880 Maiwand
866 Emajee Mohitay   w 16 Aug 1880 Deh Khojah
1000 Fatteh Khan   k 16 Aug 1880 Deh Khojah
867 Goolab Sing   k 27 Jul 1880 Maiwand
1075 Humma Ootayker   w 27 Jul 1880 Maiwand
1140 Hummunt Rao Chowan   k 27 Jul 1880 Maiwand
1086 Hunmunt Rao   w 27 Jul 1880 Maiwand
920 Jagarnath   w 16 Aug 1880 Deh Khcjah
1108 Kaesar Sing   w 16 Aug 1880 Deh Khojah
1022 Kampta Pursad   w 27 Jul 1880 Maiwand

1059 Krishna Powar k 27 Jul 1880 Maiwand
921 Luximon Narayan w 16 Aug 1880 Deh Khojah
1138 Mahadoo Baber k 27 Jul 1880 Maiwand
840 Mahomed Bux k 27 Jul 1880 Maiwand
710 Mahomed Khan w 16 Aug 1880 Deh Khojah
1068 Mahomed Khan k 27 Jul 1880 Maiwand
1289 Mahomed Khan w 16 Aug 1880 Deh Khojah, dow 17 Aug
1201 Marotee Mallee k 27 Jul 1880 Maiwand
797 Mathoora Coonba k 16 Aug 1880 Deh Khojah
Monir Khan w 1 Sep 1880 Kandahar
803 Mutroo Sing k 27 Jul 1880 Maiwand
983 Noor Ali w 27 Jul 1880 Maiwand
754 Ragoobar Opadhia w 16 Aug 1880 Deh Khojah
927 Ramdut Tewari k 27 Jul 1880 Maiwand
1002 Ramparsad k 27 Jul 1880 Maiwand
1030 Ram Sing k 27 Jul 1880 Maiwand
1115 Sewdurson Sing k 27 Jul 1880 Maiwand
1122 Shaik Hoosain w 27 Jul 1880 Maiwand
1034 Shaik Jockoo k 16 Aug 1880 Deh Khojah
756 Shaik Kadir Bux k 27 Jul 1880 Maiwand
1058 Shaik Kassim k 27 Jul 1880 Maiwand
1044 Shaik Mustaffa w 16 Aug 1880 Deh Khojah
1175 Shaik Yasseen w 27 Jul 1880 Maiwand
1207 Shri Krishna k 27 Jul 1880 Maiwand
894 Sooraj Bullee k 27 Jul 1880 Maiwand
1151 Suckaram Powar k 27 Jul 1880 Maiwand
1093 Suckeram Nurray w 27 Jul 1880 Maiwand
1213 Sumber Sing w 27 Jul 1880 Maiwand
909 Thakoor Dayal k 27 Jul 1880 Maiwand
Tookaram Jamblay sl w 25 Aug 1880 siege of Kandahar

POONA HORSE

Sources D.48 &
P/1538-13867

Surgeon
Stewart, Alexander Kenneth sl w 16 Aug 1880 Deh Khojah. gs

Ressaidar
Goodfran Khan k 16 Aug 1880 Deh Khojah, gs

Sowars
479 Innait Russool Khan dang w 16 Aug 1880 Deh Khojah, gs, awarded IOM 3rd Class
445 Lal Sing sl w 3 Aug 1880 siege of Kandahar, gs
452 Mahomed Sharrif sl w 16 Aug 1880 Deh Khojah, gs
88 Nubbee Bux sl w 16 Aug 1880 Deh Khojah, gs
335 Reeyajatoolla Khan k 28 Jul 1880 nr Kokeran (? = Rugotoollah Khan in D.46)
406 Saiwaram sl w 12 Aug 1880 siege of Kandahar, bayonet
384 Shaik Abdool Latif dang w 16 Aug 1880 Deh Khojah, gs

3rd SIND HORSE

Sources D.14, D.32, D.44, D.48, P/1372-5463 & P/1538-13867

After Maiwand 'the Officer Commanding 3rd Sind Horse reports he is unable to give the regimental numbers of the men, as the Rolls in possession of the Pay Sowar were lost on the day of the action.'

Colonel
Malcolmson, John Henry Porter, cmdg   sl w 26 Feb 1879 Kushki-Nakhud; sev w 16 Aug 1880 Deh Khojah, gs

Major
Reynolds, William, 2-i-c   k 26 Feb 1879 Kushki-Nakhud

Lieutenant
Monteith, Arthur Mackworth   sl w 27 Jul 1880 Maiwand

Daffadars
Abdul Rahim Khan   w 27 Jul 1880 Maiwand
Mahomed Nubbee Khan   k 27 Jul 1880 Maiwand
Seedee Saley Mahomed   w 27 Jul 1880 Maiwand

Naiks
2 Dhull Sing   sev w 26 Feb 1879 Kushki-Nakhud, 'while following his Commanding Officer'
Fateh Mahomed Khan   k 26 Feb 1879 Kushki-Nakhud
Meer Hasan Ali   w 27 Jul 1880 Maiwand

Lance-Naiks
Goojur Sing   k 27 Jul 1880 Maiwand
733 Mardan Khan   dang w 26 Feb 1879 Kushki-Nakhud
374 Mehindad Khan   k 16 Aug 1880 Deh Khojah, sword
Rahim Khan   k 27 Jul 1880 Maiwand
127 Sher Mahomed Khan   sev w 12 Aug 1880 siege of Kandahar

Sowars
488 Akhbar Khan   mort w 26 Feb 1879 Kushki-Nakhud, dow 1 Aug
Aladad Khan   w 27 Jul 1880 Maiwand
1 Alimoodeen   w 16 Aug 1880 Deh Khojah
Bahadur Sing   k 27 Jul 1880 Maiwand
Basant Sing   k 27 Jul 1880 Maiwand
Bikram Sing   k 27 Jul 1880 Maiwand
Buddan Sing   k 27 Jul 1880 Maiwand
Dilda Khan   w 27 Jul 1880 Maiwand
Ewaz Khan (2)   k 27 Jul 1880 Maiwand
452 Gajadar   sl w 26 Feb 1879 Kushki-Nakhud
262 Gulab Khan   dang w 26 Feb 1879 Kushki-Nakhud
271 Ful Baz Khan   sev w 26 Feb 1879 Kushki-Nakhud
68 Harlal Sing   sl w 1 Sep 1880 Kandahar, sword
Humroodeen Khan   sev w 16 Aug 1880 Deh Khojah, gs
528 Huza Sing   w 25 Aug 1880 siege of Kandahar, stray gs, since dow

95 Jabar Khan sev w 26 Feb 1879 Kushki-Nakhud
Jowala Parsad k 27 Jul 1880 Maiwand
339 Juggernath Sing k 16 Aug 1880 Deh Khojah, gs
371 Khan Mahomed Khan sl w 26 Feb 1879 Kushki-Nakhud
Kumaroodeen Khan w 16 Aug 1880 Deh Khojah
Mahadeo Pershad k 26 Feb 1879 Kushki-Nakhud
Mahomed Ali Khan k 27 Jul 1880 Maiwand
41 Meer Akbar Ali k 16 Aug 1880 Deh Khojah, gs
314 Ramadhar k 16 Aug 1880 Deh Khojah, swcrd
Sahib Sing k 27 Jul 1880 Maiwand
67 Sarfaraz Khan sl w 26 Feb 1879 Kushki-Nakhud
Shah Mahomed Khan k 27 Jul 1880 Maiwand
Shaik Alimoodeen sl w 16 Aug 1880 Deh Khojah, gs
214 Shaikh Ahmed sl w 26 Feb 1879 Kushki-Nakhud
164 Shaikh Makdum Baksh sev w 26 Feb 1879 Kushki-Nakhud
Shaikh Ramzan k 26 Feb 1879 Kushki-Nakhud
369 Shewnath k 16 Aug 1880 Deh Khojah, gs
216 Suda Shaw k 16 Aug 1880 Deh Khojah, gs
Syud Imam Ali k 16 Apr 1880 Dabrai (P/1536-9901 & see IOM GGO 689/1880)
Tilok Sing k 26 Feb 1879 Kushki-Nakhud

No 2 Co BOMBAY SAPPERS & MINERS

Sources D.44, D.48 & P/1538-13867

Captain

Cruickshank, George Macdonald, RE k 16 Aug 1880 Deh Khojah, 'whilst leading his men in the most forward manner'

Lieutenant

Henn, Thomas Rice, RE k 27 Jul 1880 Maiwand

Sergeant

12023 Heaphy, E. D. RE k 27 Jul 1880 Maiwand

1st Corporal

8692 Ashman, J. RE k 27 Jul 1880 Maiwand

Subadar

Shaik Mahomed Hoossain w 27 Jul 1880 Maiwand

Jemadar

Mulloo dang w 16 Aug 1880 Deh Khojah, gs back

Havildar

223 Mohamed Khan k 27 Jul 1880 Maiwand

Naik

119 Sewram Wanjaree k 27 Jul 1880 Maiwand

Bugler

620 Shaik Abudoola k 27 Jul 1880 Maiwand

Hospital Assistant

498 Rungayeh k 16 Aug 1880 Deh Khojah

Privates

639 Abdoola Khan dang w 16 Aug 1880 Deh Khojah, gs back & right leg, awarded IOM 3rd Class
675 Amboojee k 27 Jul 1880 Maiwand
679 Balnac Yesnac k 27 Jul 1880 Maiwand
375 Bhyroo Neekum k 27 Jul 1880 Maiwand
681 Buyajee Mallu w 27 Jul 1880 Maiwand; sl w 16 Aug 1880 Deh Khojah, gs contusion neck
29 Chocknac k 27 Jul 1880 Maiwand
545 Curramet Khan sev w 16 Aug 1880 Deh Khojah, gs chest & left forearm
Gopal Ittoba k 16 Aug 1880 Deh Khojah
107 Govindrao Moray k 27 Jul 1880 Maiwand
435 Ittoo Dumoo k 27 Jul 1880 Maiwand
357 Jelloppa Purwaree sev w 16 Aug 1880 Deh Khojah, gs right leg
669 Jungoo Nursoo k 27 Jul 1880 Maiwand
317 Koostnac Luximonac w 27 Jul 1880 Maiwand
683 Lalla Dube w 27 Jul 1880 Maiwand
419 Mahomed Khan k 16 Aug 1880 Deh Khojah
666 Papudoo Maysoo w 27 Jul 1880 Maiwand
686 Posuttee Peerajee k 27 Jul 1880 Maiwand
6 Ramalall k 16 Aug 1880 Deh Khojah
670 Rama Powar k 27 Jul 1880 Maiwand
495 Ramjee Telakur k 27 Jul 1880 Maiwand
530 Rampursad Paniday sev w 16 Aug 1880 Deh Khojah, gs right shoulder
397 Sayed Mahomed w 27 Jul 1880 Maiwand; sev w 16 Aug 1880 Deh Khojah, gs left foot, awarded IOM 3rd Class
690 Sewoo Mullappa w 27 Jul 1880 Maiwand
2 Sewparsan Misser k 16 Aug 1880 Deh Khojah
627 Sewratan Sing k 27 Jul 1880 Maiwand
493 Shaik Abdool Gunee k 16 Aug 1880 Deh Khojah
161 Shaik Peer Bux k 27 Jul 1880 Maiwand
357 Zellapa Purwarree w 16 Aug 1880 Deh Khojah

1st BOMBAY NATIVE INFANTRY

Privates

801 Ameer Khan sl w 10 Aug siege of Kandahar, gs left hand
1556 Kalkaparsad Opadhia sev w 10 Aug 1880 siege of Kandahar, gs head (both D.48 & P/1538-13867)

The regiment suffered the following casualties at Maiwand 27 Jul 1880 (D.44)

Lieutenant-Colonel
Anderson, Horace Searle, cmdg   sev w (& see IOM GGOs 59 & 222/1881

Captain
Grant, James, offcg Wing Commander   w

Lieutenants
Hinde, Charles William, Adjutant   k
Whitby, Clement George, Wing Officer   k

Subadar-Major
Bhewa Pallow   k

Subadars
Hurree Purrub   k
Ragnac Mhadnac   k
Shaik Hoosain   k

Jemadars
Budun Sing   k
Ebrahim   w
Gungadeen Tumbolee   k
Ittoo Missal   w
Lalla Doolichund   k
Narayan Lode   k
Niyal Sing   w
Soobanah Manay   w

Colour-Havildars
365 Gunnac Mhadnac   k
488 Ragoo Thakoor   k
90 Thomas, Francis   k

Havildars
567 Bala Surung   k
279 Bhikajee Bhoolay   k
187 Budree Sing   k
16 Daisoo Sing   k
774 Ganpattee Sinday   k
239 Govind Golutkur   k
2 Gunda Sing   w, awarded IOM 3rd Class
312 Jagarnath Pandy   k
568 Kaitan Rozario   k
671 Kasum Khan   w
252 Ramjee Maiter   k
868 Remijio Sevilkur   k
304 Sewparsad   k
65 Shaik Rahiman   k

Naiks
528 Appa Wadaykur   k
908 Bakoo Sawunt   k
936 Balajeerao Chowan   k
934 Balkrishna Sulgowkur   k
858 Daveljee Baide   w
1355 Gopal Maiter   w
496 Govindrao Jadow   k
26 Kondajee Baider   k
461 Koondlick Joosee   k
618 Ootun Sing   k
629 Pancham Aheer   k
582 Prag Awasti   w
547 Ragnac Dhondnac   k
491 Ram Sawunt   k
819 Sewbadan Aheer   k
892 Shaik Abdool   k
1001 Shaik Eman   k
928 Shaikh Hassan   k
552 Shaik Osman   k
714 Suckaram Purrub   k

Drummers
253 Balnac Bhicknac   k
981 Rozario, Antoon   k
87 Shaik Oosman   k
83 Sucknac Doolumnac   k

Fifers
546 Ramnac Pandnac   k
89 Rozario, John   k

980 Shaik Oosman   k

Privates
899 Annac Narnac   k
680 Annuppa Chiptakur   k
1185 Anok Sing   k
769 Anunt Parsad   k
826 Appa Nagray   w
1020 Assoo Gowas   k
439 Babajee Bowkur   k
1552 Babajee Dewkur   k

768 Babajee Ghongay k
1093 Babajee Moray w
997 Babajee Sinday k
817 Babnac Bhagnac k
1018 Baboo Patkur k
804 Baboo Raylay k
400 Baboo Ringnaykur k
1358 Bahadur Sing k
588 Bahari Misser k
1344 Bajeerao Ghaj k
1321 Bala Nikum k
1133 Balajeerao Chowan k
1566 Balia Luximon k
988 Balnac Gonac k
649 Balookhatowkur k
1306 Bapoo Rawool k
1359 Basoo Passee k
1429 Bhagirat Sukal k
500 Bhagnac Gondnac w
346 Bhagnac Kootunnac k
969 Bhagojee Sinday k
1548 Bhagojee Sinday k
1380 Bhagoojee Jadow k
1104 Bhairoo Chicknay k
1308 Bhamnac Dhamnac k
757 Bhew Sawunt k
1293 Bhewa Salookay k
945 Bhicknac Gonnac k
1084 Bhicknac Prusnac k
1061 Bhicksett Settaway k
495 Bhikajee Jadow k
1096 Bhikajee Jadow k
480 Bhikari Lall Sukal k
1225 Bhikoo Malee k
713 Bhisajee Awlaygowkur k
1383 Bhojoo Gowra k
1428 Bhooda Sing k
932 Bhoor Sawunt k
767 Bhow Rao k
1291 Bhowanee Jadow k
1221 Bhowaniparsad Misser w
855 Bhowannac Iltnac k
177 Bhugwandeen Dichit w
1014 Bhugwunt Jadow k
1229 Bhugwunt Lall k
1431 Bisram w
76 Boodh Sing k
736 Buchnac Ramnac k
1170 Buchoo Sing k
1312 Buchram Jadow k
1187 Bucktawar Sing k
201 Buldeo Sing k
1360 Burma Tewari k
913 Chand Khan k
601 Chandi Pattack k
1424 Chooni Lall k
1564 Chundi Aheer k
1284 Dajee Sinday k
1054 Dani Pursad k
43 Dani Sing k
300 Davideen Aheer k
182 Davie Sing w
1559 Deen Sawunt k
406 De Sequera, Domingo k
531 Dewjee Maiter k
1016 Dewnac Sewnac k
834 Dhaknac Salnac k
512 Dhanoo Guduria k
806 Dharumnac Rainac k
741 Dhondee Rawooth k
1390 Dhondoo Sawunt k
1152 Dhurmajee Gowra w
551 Dhurmnac Balnac w
1247 Dilawar Khan w
295 Doorga Nawo k
1194 Dun Sing w
23 Durjan Pattack k
765 Essernac Girujnac k
480 Essoo Chowan k
1227 Essoo Khundalgay k
862 Essoo Satuno k
1085 Eswant Rao Sinday w
1146 Fateh Sing k
955 Fazul Khan k
1143 Fuzl Sindee k
211 Gaiadin Awasti k
1161 Gainoo Tawray k
1419 Ganpat Rao Chowan k
369 Gauri Sankar Lalla k
869 Gondnac Bicknac k
961 Gondnac Doolnac w
1131 Gonnac Kalnnac k
1314 Gonnac Tannac k
1116 Goolab Khan k
1560 Goolzar Khan w
747 Goona Ranim k
944 Goonnac Dhacknac k
1205 Goordut Sing w
1315 Gopal Salnee k
1369 Gopal Satum k
703 Gopal Sitt k
949 Gopala Chowan w

1320 Govind Kimsay w
911 Govind Maiter k
895 Govind Sawunt k
1199 Gunda Sing w
648 Gungadeen Nawo k
762 Gungadeen Dube k
1407 Gungajee Khopkur k
965 Gungaram Chowan k
744 Gungnac Bhicknac k
244 Gunnac Bhagnac w
1031 Gunnac Gondnac w
754 Gunnac Lucknac k
1385 Gunnoo Jadow k
1331 Gunnoo Kunsay k
1405 Gunnoojee Raiwalay k
1370 Gunputrao Moray k
1216 Hanooman Misser k
1076 Huray Khan k
902 Hurnac Lumnac k
829 Hurree Cuddum k
1404 Hurree Jadow k
1094 Hurree Pedneykur k
1000 Iltnac Gunnac k
1344 Ittoo Eswatilrao k
325 Jagarnath Tali k
1065 Jannoo Purwal k
379 Jarbundun Sing k
786 Jowahir Dube k
292 Jowahir Sing k
1244 Junnac Gondnac k
876 Kaider Sukal k
1367 Kairoo Gaicowar k
1248 Kalideen Gadario k
1270 Kalka Dube w
1556 Kalkaparsad Opadia w
670 Kanuppa k
950 Kaseeram Luckray w
1362 Kasidin Tewari k
1420 Katoo Chowan k
1339 Kessoo Garway k
1272 Khooshal Kachee k
1047 Kishna Ootaikur k
1423 Kisum Babur k
1086 Kondajee Talaykur k
1299 Koondlick Jadow k
1263 Kowra Misser k
1015 Krishna Gowra k
663 Krishnajee Baider w
321 Krishnajee Chiknay k
883 Lackhaie Guduria k
1090 Ladoo Gowra k
772 Ladoo Kailuskur k
1257 Ladoo Purrub k
8 Laina Sing k
890 Lalla Ramcharn k
46 Lalta Parsad Dube k
1044 Limbajee Baider k
1301 Lucknac Balnac k
939 Lucknac Iltnac k
1592 Luximon Hoosiana w
Luximon Hurree k
Luximon Parsad k
810 Luximon Pattack k
735 Luximon Sawunt k
Luximon Soopaikur w
593 Luximon Sukal w
1277 Luximon Warree k
1412 Mahadeo Korpay k
367 Mahadeo Tewari k
825 Mahadoo Advelkur k
1416 Mahadoo Bhoslay k
1145 Mahadoo Khatal k
694 Mahadoo Khawrulkur k
901 Mahadoo Khot w
1384 Mahadoo Sinday k
1264 Mahadoo Sawunt w
1121 Mahilall Sailar k
396 Mahis Sing w
Mahomed Beg w
1126 Mahomed Beg k
621 Maia Sing k
522 Mainnac Balnac k
44 Man Sing k
501 Man Sukal k
940 Mark, John w
675 Marroo k
964 Mhadnac Changnac k
1565 Mhadnac Sumnac k
1183 Mira Bux k
1253 Mookund Sawunt k
56 Mool Sing k
13 Moon Sing k
118 Motee Khan k
1357 Mugray Pasee w
1171 Nadar Baksh k
700 Nagoo Kainee w
878 Nagoo Wanjada k
1354 Namajee Parkalay w
1391 Narayen Chowan k
1274 Narayen Cuddum k
1220 Narayen Penduckur k
1334 Narayen Powar k
738 Narayen Salnee k
1026 Narayen Sinday k

976 Naroojee Lotunkur k
1136 Nasul Khan k
1182 Natha Sing k
1159 Nickloo Marano Manizes k
1177 Nika Sing k
1372 Nilloo Cuddum w
268 Niloo Dulnee k
607 Niyal Sing w
1005 Nursaya Coonbee k
999 Oomer Khan k
1233 Oorree Moriai k
1189 Ootum Sing k
1201 Ootum Sing w
Pandoo Bawajee k
1373 Pandoo Lokhunday k
1392 Pandoo Mahaduk k
994 Pandoo Salnee k
1332 Pandoorung Babajee k
1261 Patilbawajee Bhaye w
1210 Peera Dufta k
1053 Pinto, Jao Joze k
1523 Pragas Sing k
1271 Praj Sing k
1425 Punjnac Mularnac w
1207 Pursram Gagun k
1062 Rag Sawunt k
1057 Ragoo Chowan k
1567 Ragoo Nowala k
1231 Rajaram Misser w
Rajba Moray k
1349 Ram Maiter k
1069 Ram Sawunt k
906 Ram Sawuntoorawdaykur k
686 Rama k
1316 Rama Chipkur w
947 Rama Dhooree k
529 Rama Huttay k
617 Rama Jadow k
1091 Rama Kesurkur w
812 Rama Salnee k
1351 Ramchunder Tawria k
305 Ramchunder Tewari k
455 Ramdeen Coonbee k
793 Ramdhun Pandy k
196 Ramdeen Sing k
162 Ramjee Baider k
863 Ramjee Baider k
1322 Ramjee Jadow k
1151 Ramjee Massokur k
430 Ramjee Ootaykur k
1411 Ramjee Palaykur k
1223 Ramjee Powar k
971 Ramjee Raynay k
962 Ramoöjee Baider k
968 Ramnac Iltnac k
1346 Ramphul k
1557 Ramsarup k
51 Ranoojee Baider w
1049 Rowjee Gaicowar k
1414 Rowjee Jadow k
1275 Rowjee Suckpall k
1228 Rowjee Thawer k
1179 Ruthun Sing k
748 Rutnoo Jadow k
1059 Ruttun Sawunt k
879 Sadoo Achraykur k
794 Sadoo Chicknay k
1389 Sadoo Kamtaykur w
721 Sagoonnac Boburnac w
1002 Sakaram Baider k
1558 Sakaram Chowan k
972 Sakaram Lotunkur k
578 Sakoo Maiter k
752 Sakoojee Chowan k
1408 Sama Sivilkur k
581 Santa Sing k
459 Satsell Warree w
1305 Sedoo Phurtaray k
1399 Sewa Cooma k
519 Sewchurn Sing k
333 Sewdha Sing k
1222 Sewdin Pattack k
1032 Sewnac Bhornac k
903 Sewnac Essnac k
848 Sewnac Ruttunnac k
117 Sewnandan Pandy k
420 Sewnarain Sukal k
930 Shaik Abdool k
1251 Shaik Abdoola k
1142 Shaik Allabux k
799 Shaik Bhaggoo k
1029 Shaik Daiem k
1232 Shaik Ellahibux k
1117 Shaik Emambux k
1263 Shaik Haidar k
998 Shaik Hassan k
1219 Shaik Jamal k
1173 Shaik Kooda Bux k
1397 Shaik Mahomed Ali w
1113 Shaik Masoom k
662 Shaik Mohideen k
916 Shaik Sooltan k
643 Shumsoodeen k
708 Soma Garee k

1033 Sonnac Heernac k
985 Sonnac Sucknac k
1062 Sonnac Sumnac k
1101 Sonoo Tornay k
1064 Sooban Chunder Kur k
659 Soobaya k
102 Soojai Sing k
1115 Soojat Ali k
1226 Sooknac Lucknac k
125 Sooknandan Pandy k
516 Soonoo Kaslay k
1243 Soorujbulli Sing k
1123 Sownath Coonbee k
077 Subajee Rao Nalawray k
1022 Suckaram Dhoree k
780 Suckaram Gawo k
1278 Suckaram Ghatray k
1378 Suckaram Sawunt k
900 Suddoo Sailar w
1072 Sumbajee Baider k
1393 Sumbajee Rao Moray k
167 Sumbar Aheer k
1068 Sumboo Ranay k
1240 Sundar k
1200 Sundar Sing k
603 Sunkoor Coomar k
960 Sutwajee Baider k
492 Tanoo Suckpall k
1009 Tanoo Maiter k
887 Tawjeenaik Tawray k
1213 Thakurdin Dube w
596 Tilooka Sing k
894 Took Sawant k
742 Tookaram Pilundkur k
1371 Tookaram Powar k
1302 Tookaram Sailar k
563 Vishnoo Kindray k
1114 Vishnoo Sootar k
1075 Vittul Arrotta k
1245 Zahageer Khan k
216 Zam Aheer k
1255 Zunda Khan k

4th BOMBAY NATIVE INFANTRY

Privates

1164 Mhadnac Narasnack sl w 12 Aug 1880 siege of Kandahar, gs (P/1538-13867)

1987 Vittoo Purub, attchd 19th Bombay NI k 16 Aug 1880 Deh Khojah (D.48)

11th BOMBAY NATIVE INFANTRY

Private

2098 Sudoo Khan, attchd 19th Bombay NI k 16 Aug 1880 Deh Khojah (D.48)

14th BOMBAY NATIVE INFANTRY

Privates

2532 Diog Jakee, attchd 19th Bombay NI k 16 Aug 1880 Deh Khojah (D.48)

2514 Paskal Sirolkar, attchd 19th Bombay NI sl w 16 Aug 1880 Deh Khojah, gs left hand (D.48 & P/1538-13867)

16th BOMBAY NATIVE INFANTRY

The regiment suffered the following casualties at Kach
16 Aug 1880 (P/1538-13877)

Lieutenant
Seymour, Henry William   k

Naiks
Anandrao Soorwey   sl w, since d
Doorgapersad Dooby   sl w

Privates
Amboo Nyer   sl w
Arjoon Gaoker   sev w
Babajee Sonor   k
Luxoomunroo Salwee   sl w
Mahadewroo Soorwey   sl w
Ramjee Morey   k

17th BOMBAY NATIVE INFANTRY

Sources D.48 &
P/1538-13867

Privates, attchd 19th Bombay NI
1908 Bairam Sing   k 16 Aug 1880 Deh Khojah
2130 Balnac Dharamnac   dang w 12 Aug 1880 siege of Kandahar, gs fractured skull, since d
2067 Thakoor Durjee   k 16 Aug 1880 Deh Khojah

18th BOMBAY NATIVE INFANTRY

Sources D.48 &
P/1538-13867

Privates, attchd 19th Bombay NI
646 Babajee Shellar   mort w 8 Aug 1880 siege of Kandahar, gs buttock, since d
537 Haitoo Hajam   sl w 16 Aug 1880 Deh Khojah, gs contusion back
651 Ramjee Powar   k 16 Aug 1880 Deh Khojah
570 Randhir Sing   k 16 Aug 1880 Deh Khojah
569 Rughoober Sing   sev w 16 Aug 1880 Deh Khojah, gs compund fracture right leg
758 Tookaram Sewankar   k 16 Aug 1880 Deh Khojah

19th BOMBAY NATIVE INFANTRY

Sources D.48 &
P/1538-13867

Majors

Trench, Richard John Le Poer k 16 Aug 1880 Deh Khojah
Waudby, Sidney James k 16 Apr 1880 Dabrai (MR, Shadbolt & see IOM GGO 689/1880)

Lieutenant

Stayner, Francis Charles k 16 Aug 1880 Deh Khojah

Trench & Stayner = 'whilst leading their men in the most forward manner'

Subadar

Samuel, Abraham dang w 16 Aug 1880 Deh Khojah, gs,compound fracture humerus

Colour-Havildar

378 Sudashew Mheter sev w 16 Aug 1880 Deh Khojah, gs right knee joint

Havildars

464 Gun Mheter k 16 Aug 1880 Deh Khojah
541 Nubeeyar Khan dang w 16 Aug 1880 Deh Khojah, gs chest

Naiks

814 Krushnajee Sett k 16 Aug 1880 Deh Khojah
647 Rowjee Thakur sev w 16 Aug 1880 Deh Khojah, gs,compound fracture elbow

Lance-Naiks

781 Mahadoo Dewlee k 16 Aug 1880 Deh Khojah
522 Narayan Sing sl w 8 Aug 1880 siege of Kandahar, gs inner knee

Privates

Abdoola Khan k 16 Aug 1880 Deh Khojah
580 Ali Mahomed Khan sev w 16 Aug 1880 Deh Khojah, gs right arm
1115 Baldeo Ram sev w 8 Aug 1880 siege of Kandahar, gs right thigh
657 Bhewjee Bhagday sl w 16 Aug 1880 Deh Khojah, gs shoulder
681 Bhewjee Jadow sl w 16 Aug 1880 Deh Khojah, gs right middle finger
1106 Buktawar Gudurya sev w 16 Aug 1880 Deh Khojah, gs left middle finger
1108 Chandersekar Sukal k 16 Aug 1880 Deh Khojah
721 Dadoo Toomrey k 16 Aug 1880 Deh Khojah
799 Dewjee Suckpal k 16 Aug 1880 Deh Khojah
1120 Dwarka Sukal sev w 16 Aug 1880 Deh Khojah, gs scalp
Elahi Bux k 16 Apr 1880 Dabrai (P/1536-9901 & see IOM GGO 689/1880)
538 Gunnoojee Jugtab dang w 16 Aug 1880 Deh Khojah, gs chest, since d

763 Harbarao Nudum dang w 16 Aug 1880 Deh Khojah, gs,compound fracture lower jaw
149 Krishnajee Jadow sl w 16 Aug 1880 Deh Khojah, gs head
548 Moonalall Dube k 16 Aug 1880 Deh Khojah
929 Oosman Khan sev w 16 Aug 1880 Deh Khojah, gs chest
588 Raghoo Gotekar dang w 16 Aug 1880 Deh Khojah, gs,compound fracture left thigh
1171 Raghoo Sarmalkar sl w 16 Aug 1880 Deh Khojah, gs knee
842 Ramjee Jadow sev w 16 Aug 1880 Deh Khojah, gs lower jaw
761 Ramjee Sawant k 16 Aug 1880 Deh Khojah
963 Ramjee Sukpal sev w 16 Aug 1880 Deh Khojah, gs,compound fracture shoulder joint
1054 Runchor Kolee (2) sev w 12 Aug 1880 siege of Kandahar, gs left leg
797 Sewajeerao Bhoslay sl w 16 Aug 1880 Deh Khojah, gs contusion back
1102 Sewratan Ahir sev w 12 Aug 1880 siege of Kandahar, gs head
Sonnak Tannak k 16 Apr 1880 Dabrai (P/1536-9901 & see IOM GGO 689/1880)
819 Vittoo Koombhar k 16 Aug 1880 Deh Khojah
1001 Zilloojee Koombhar k 16 Aug 1880 Deh Khojah

23rd BOMBAY NATIVE INFANTRY

Private
348 Dwarka Sing, attchd 19th Bombay NI k 16 Aug 1880 Deh Khojah (D.48)

26th BOMBAY NATIVE INFANTRY

Private
1164 Mhadnac Narasnac, attchd 4th Bombay NI sl w 12 Aug 1880 siege of Kandahar (D.48)

28th BOMBAY NATIVE INFANTRY

Sources D.48 & P/1538-13867

Privates
369 Baboo Row k 2 Aug 1880 siege of Kandahar
704 Bhissa Rawool sl w 31 Jul 1880 siege of Kandahar, gs
915 Kondajee Sablay k 31 Jul 1880 siege of Kandahar, gs
613 Luximan Pavar w 28 Mar 1880 nr Panizai, arm & hip (P/1537-11401)

684 Tookaram Bhingaray sev w 31 Jul 1880 siege of Kandahar, gs
792 Tookaram Jadow w 28 Mar 1880 nr Panizai, eye (P/1537-11401)

All the following casualties were suffered at Deh Khojah 16 Aug 1880

Lieutenant-Colonels
Newport, William Henry k, 'whilst leading his men in the most forward manner'
Nimmo, Thomas Rose sev w, two gs

Colour-Havildars
1088 Shaik Ebram sl w, gs
810 Sham Sing sev w, gs

Havildar
81 Bhowanrow Moray k

Naiks
349 Gungadeen Lodh sev w, gs
146 Heera Sing sl w, gs
1005 Sewa Sing k
3073 Shaik Towkall sl w, gs
3025 Some Dhooree k

Lance-Naiks
509 Appa Mhadaysar sev w, gs
30 Dharam Sing k
3410 Gunnoo Scindia dang w, gs neck
16 Mahadow Ahir k
745 Raie Mehter very dang w, gs
544 Sewajee Dahew sev w, gs

Privates
780 Anunta Teli k
485 Atmajee Gowda k
784 Dam Mehter k
462 Dowjee Sellar sl w, gs
466 Dowjee Yadow sev w, gs
461 Dowlutjee Powar sl w, gs
366 Essoo Madow sl w, gs
830 Goolam Hyder k
487 Gopal Purub dang w, gs
669 Govind Singaray k
768 Gun Mehter k
779 Hunmunta Bhoslay k
68 Hunmuntrao Khopray k
763 Hunmuntrow Manay k
1180 Ishram Heerlaykar sev w, two gs
249 Ittoo Cuddum sl w, gs
975 Jowahir Chaubi k
524 Kessoo Manay k
183 Luximon Scinday k
872 Luximon Tambay sev w, gs
1315 Mookoond Londay k
653 Moosajee Samuel k
601 Namnac Bohirnac k
334 Pirthi Ahir k
180 Raghojeerow Dalvee k
761 Rama Mali k
879 Rama Piplay sev w, gs
753 Rama Sawunth k
715 Rayajee Kolee sl w, gs
510 Rowjee Mitbowkar k
655 Sewajee Soorway k
647 Shaik Bappoo dang w, gs, since d
772 Shaik Oomar k
599 Suckaram Ghoolay k
697 Suckoo Gowda k
916 Sunkur Rawoot sev w, gs
Surub Jeet k
53 Tannoo Kangnay dang w, two gs

29th BOMBAY NATIVE INFANTRY (2ND BELOOCH REGIMENT)

Private
2660 Mohamed Baksh sl w 1 Sep 1880 Kandahar, shell splinter (D.51)

30th BOMBAY NATIVE INFANTRY (JACOB'S RIFLES)

Privates
1688 Jai Ram sl w 27 Mar 1879 Saiad-Bud (D.32)
2005 Jamanally Shah sl w 12 Aug 1880 siege of Kandahar, gs (D.48 & P/1538-13867)
873 Jooma Khan sl w 15 Aug 1880 siege of Kandahar, gs (D.48 & P/1538-13867)
1311 Seo Ram sl w 27 Mar 1879 Saiad-Bud (D.32)
Shah Ballum sev w 12 Aug 1880 siege of Kandahar, gs (D.48 & P/1538-13867)

The regiment suffered the following casualties at Maiwand 27 Jul 1880 (D.44)

Major
Iredell, James Shrubb sev w

Captain
Smith, Hugh Frederick k

Lieutenants
Cole, Duncan k
Justice, William Napier k

Subadars
Dewjee Kopekur k
Krishnajee Bhagway k
Ramjee Katoo sev w

Jemadars
800 Mehtab Sing sev w, since dow
Moossa Khan k
845 Ragojee Bhoslay sl w
328 Ramzan Khan sl w

Havildar-Major
Brindaban k see IOM GGO 356/1882

Pay Havildars
Daveedeen k
Dhunnee Sing k

AW K

Imam Bux k
Sew Govind Patack k

Quarter Master Havildar
173 Futteh Chund k see IOM GGO 356/1882

Havildars
Fateh Deen k
705 Gungaram k
Sohel Sing k
Sooruj Buccus k
1243 Zurreek Khan k

Naiks
Buchoo Lall k
1157 Chandi Ahir k
917 Doorga Parsad k
Gaia Pursaud k
1027 Imaun Ali Khan k
1200 Kallay Khan k
1097 Krishnajee Row Chowan k
1136 Maher Khan k
978 Maljee Kurjowkur k
1438 Panjab Sing k
1116 Shere Khan k
819 Urjoon Sing k

Lance-Naik
1374 Sew Mangal Sukal sl w

Buglers
971 Beelooch Khan k
1733 Faiz Mahomed k
1760 Feroze Ali sl w
1222 Innaum Bax k
1396 Jooma Khan sev w
Noor Khan k
Sudda Sing k see IOM GGO 356/1882

Privates
1564 Abdool Akum k
1489 Abdoola sl w
1565 Abdool Russool k
1963 Ahmed Ali k
1725 Ali Bux sl w
1538 Alla Bux (1) k
Alla Bux (2) k
2013 Alla Ditta k
2014 Alladeen sl w
1199 Allum Khan k
Ameer Bux k
Anoop Sing k
1840 Arub Khan k
1478 Babajee Mooray k
Babajee Rao Mooray k
1788 Badri Dube k
1871 Badri Misser k
1831 Baharat Sing k
Baijnath k
1704 Balloojee Kudum k
1973 Beer Sing k
Bhala Sing k
Bhoajee Indoolkur k
1698 Bhola Khan k
1933 Bhoota sev w
1654 Bhowani Parsad k
1884 Bhyroo Sing k
1171 Bhyru Misser k
1978 Birroo Khan k
Bissasar Misser k

1901 Bomba Sing sl w
1750 Bood Surrun k
Boola Khan k
1824 Buchoo Lall k
1957 Bucka Mahomed k
Buldeo k
1608 Bulla Sing k
1204 Chondi Khan sl w
Choolla Khan k
1668 Chundee Passee k
753 Davee Deen k
1919 Deen Mahomed (1) k
Deen Mahomed (2) k
1342 Dial Sing k
Dongur Sing k
1825 Doolia Sing sev w
1299 Doongur Sukal k
Doorga Sing k
1815 Doosa Sing sev w
1475 Dowlut Rao Sinday k
Dulleep Sing k
Esram Rao Chowan k
Faiz Mahomed k
1999 Futteh Deen k
Gaia Deen k
Geanoo Meanday k
1746 Gojee Deen sev w
Gokool Chund k
1219 Gool Mahomed k
1537 Goolam Mahomed k <u>see</u> IOM GGO 356/1882
851 Goolam Nio sev w
Goolam Russool k
2019 Goora Sing k
1724 Goormuk Sing sev w
1690 Gopal Rao Jadoo k
Gopal Sing k
1480 Govind Mohitay k
1692 Govind Row Mooray k
Govind Suckpall k
Gumoo Suckall k
1694 Gumwajee Mohitay k
Gunga Ram k
1728 Gunput Meekum k
Habiboola Khan k
Hajee Khan k
1655 Harnam Sing sl w
1635 Harpal Tewari k
1572 Hassan Khan k
1037 Heera Sing k
1910 Hoolam Sing k
893 Hunmunta Chowan k
1993 Hurnam Sing k
1444 Imaun Bux (1) k
Imaun Bux (2) k
Imaun Bux (3) k
1955 Imaun Deen (1) k
Imaun Deen (2) k
1738 Isree Parsad k
1790 Isree Rair k
1687 Ittoojee Rao Chowan k
1736 Jagonath sev w
Jan Mahomed k
1830 Jogoal Kissoor k
1526 Jooman Khan k
Jowaher Khan k
1863 Jowaher Sing k
1749 Jowahir Sing k
Juffur Khan k
1722 Jyran sev w
Kalka Sing k
1193 Kallay Khan k
Kalleedeen k
1983 Kair Sing k
953 Kan Sing k
1595 Kanoojee Bhaie k
1593 Khooda Bux (1) k
Khooda Bux (2) k
Khooda Bux (3) k
1916 Kirpal Sing k
1130 Koodiar Khan k
1671 Kowra Khan (1) sl w
Kowra Khan (2) k
1510 Kunda Khan k
1067 Lall Bux k
Lall Chund k
1479 Luximon Powar k
1940 Mahomed Ali (1) k
Mahomed Ali (2) k
1270 Mahomed Bux (1) k
1609 Mahomed Bux (2) k
1764 Mahomed Bux (3) k
Mahomed Khan (1) k
Mahomed Khan (2) k
1703 Madoo Rao Chowan k
1576 Mahomed Saffi k
Mahomed Shah k
1053 Meer Khan (1) k
1925 Meer Khan (2) k
Meer Khan (3) k
Meera Bux k
1811 Mehm Bun sl w
2029 Mehtab Khan k
Mela Ram k

1547 Miza sev w
1310 Mohabut Khan k
1787 Mohun Sing k
2039 Moola Khan k
Mudday Khan k
1912 Mussooda Sing (1) k
Mussooda Sing (2) k
Mustan Sing k
2045 Nadar Khan k
1823 Nadur Ali k
Nagoo Bhaye k
Narrain Dass k
Narrien Khan k
1640 Nawab Khan k
1980 Neeka Sing k
1876 Nehal Bux k
Nekbur Khan k
1506 Nizamoodeen k
2007 Nizamoodeen k
Nizamudin k
1597 Noojee Rao Mooray k
2051 Noor Deen k
1626 Nubbee Sher Khan dang w
Nunda Ram k
1662 Pahelwan Khan k (<u>but</u> returned from captivity in Sep 1881 P/1725-20929)
1994 Pakoor Sing k
1917 Partab Sing k
1825 Peer Bux k
1617 Prem Sing sev w
Priam Dube k
1835 Ram Bux dang w
Ram Deen k
1717 Ram Kisson k
1278 Ram Parsad k
Ramjee Bhaie k
Ramjee Bhoye k
973 Ramjee Cuddum k
1696 Ramjee Kudum k
1781 Rooda Khan k
1902 Rooda Khan k
Rookun Deen k
Rowjee Gag k
Saefah Shah k
Sahibdad Khan k
1645 Sankar Parsad k
1964 Sawun Khan k
1799 Sewraj k
Shaik Mehtab k
Sham Sing k
Shere Jung k
Soobai k
Sooltan Mahomed k
Soomur Khan k
1279 Sooraj Bullee (1) dang w
Sooraj Bullee (2) k
Sowlea Khan k
1612 Suckoojee Suckpall k
Surfoodeen k
2043 Surfraz Khan k
1794 Surjoo k
2010 Syud Ali sl w
1881 Toolsee Dass k
Toolsee Ram k
Ulloo Khan k
2037 Urjoon Sing k
1961 Wahab Deen k
1571 Waheed Bux k
1636 Wulayet Hoosein k
Wuzzeer Khan k

4th MADRAS NATIVE INFANTRY

The regiment suffered three casualties at Fort Battye 26 Mar 1880 (P/1537-11180)

Havildar
Ghous Khan   k, gs

Sepoys
Mahomed Ameen   k, gs
Mahomed Khan   sl w, gs

CIVILIANS

Gordon, Rev George Maxwell, Church Missionary Society   k 16 Aug 1880 Deh Khojah, 'whilst attending the men under a heavy fire' (D.48)

Jenkyns, William, Bengal Civil Service   k 3 Sep 1879 Kabul Residency

Wood, O. B., Bengal Police   Local Lieutenant, Transport Service k 1 May 1880 Chapri (MR)

GALLANTRY AWARDS

VICTORIA CROSS

ADAMS, Rev James William, Bengal Chaplain

During the action at Killa Kazi on the 11th December 1879, some men of the 9th Lancers having fallen, with their horses, into a wide and deep 'nullah' or ditch, and the enemy being close upon them, the Rev J.W.Adams rushed into the water (which filled the ditch), dragged the horses from off the men, upon whom they were lying, and extricated them, he being at the time under a heavy fire and up to his waist in water. At this time the Afghans were pressing on very rapidly, the leading men getting within a few yards of Mr Adams, who, having let go his horse in order to render more effectual assistance, had eventually to escape on foot.
LG 26 Aug 1881

ASHFORD, Private Thomas, 2nd Btn HM 7th Fusiliers

CHASE, Lieutenant William St Lucien, 28th Bombay Native Infantry

For conspicuous gallantry on the occasion of the sortie from Kandahar on the 16th August 1880 against the village of Deh Khoja, in having rescued and carried for a distance of over 200 yards, under the fire of the enemy, a wounded soldier, Private Massey of the Royal Fusiliers, who had taken shelter in a block-house. Several times they were compelled to rest, but they persevered in bringing him to a place of safety. Private Ashford rendered Lieut. Chase every assistance, and remained with him throughout.
LG 7 Oct 1881

COLLIS, Gunner James, C/B Royal Horse Artillery

For conspicuous bravery during the retreat from Maiwand to Kandahar on the 28th July 1880, when the officer commanding the battery was endeavouring to bring in a limber, with wounded men, under a cross-fire, in running forward and drawing the enemy's fire on himself, thus taking off their attention from the limber.
LG 17 May 1881

COOK, Major John, 5th Gurkha Regiment

For a signal act of valour at the action of the Peiwar Kotal on the 2nd December 1878, in having, during a very heavy fire, charged out of the entrenchments with such impetuosity that the enemy broke and fled. When perceiving at the close of the melee the danger of Major Galbraith, Assistant Adjutant-General, Kurram Column Field Force, who was in personal conflict with an Afghan soldier, Capt.Cook distracted his attention to himself, and aiming a sword-cut, which the Douranee avoided, sprang upon him and, grasping his throat, grappled with him. They both fell to the ground. The Douranee, a most powerful man, still endeavouring

to use his rifle, seized Capt.Cook's arm in his teeth, until the struggle was ended by the man being shot through the head.
LG 18 Mar 1879

CREAGH, Captain Garrett O'Moore, Mhairwara Battalion

On the 21st April 1879 Capt.Creagh was detached from Daka, with two companies of his battalion, to protect the village of Kam Daka on the Cabul River against a threatened incursion of the Mohmands, and reached that place the same night. On the following morning the detachment (150 men) was attacked by the Mohmands in overwhelming numbers (about 1,500); and the inhabitants of the Kam Daka having themselves taken part with the enemy, Capt.Creagh found himself under the necessity of retiring from the village. He took up a position in a cemetery not far off, which he made as defensible as circumstances would admit of, and this position he held against all the efforts of the enemy, repeatedly repulsing them with the bayonet until three o'clock in the afternoon, when he was relieved by a detachment sent for the purpose from Daka. The enemy were then finally repulsed and, being charged by a troop of the 10th Bengal Lancers, under the command of Capt.D.M.Strong, were routed and broken, and great numbers of them driven into the river. The Commander-in-Chief in India has expressed his opinion that but for the coolness, determination, and gallantry of the highest order, and the admirable conduct which Capt.Creagh displayed on this occasion, the detachment under his command would, in all probability, have been cut off and destroyed.
LG 18 Nov 1879

DICK-CUNYNGHAM, Lieutenant William Henry, HM 92nd Highlanders

For the conspicuous gallantry and bravery displayed by him on the 13th December 1879 at the attack on the Sherpur Pass in Afghanistan, in having exposed himself to the full fire of the enemy, and by his example and encouragement rallied the men, who, having been beaten back, were at the moment wavering at the top of the hill.
LG 18 Oct 1881

HAMILTON, Lieutenant Walter Richard Pollock, Guides Cavalry

For conspicuous gallantry during the action at Futtehabad on the 2nd April 1879, in leading on the Guides Cavalry in a charge against very superior numbers of the enemy, and particularly at a critical moment, when his commanding officer (Major Wigram Battye) fell. Lieut.Hamilton - then the only officer left with the regiment - assumed command and cheered on his men to avenge Major Battye's death. In this charge Lieut.Hamilton, seeing Sowar Dowlut Ram down and attacked by three of the enemy whilst entangled with his horse (which had been killed), rushed to the rescue and, followed by a few of his men, cut down all three and saved the life of Sowar Dowlut Ram.
LG 7 Oct 1879

HAMMOND, Captain Arthur George, Guides Infantry

For conspicuous coolness and gallantry at the action on the Asmai Heights near Kabul on the 14th December 1879, in defending the top of the hill, with a rifle and fixed bayonet, against large numbers of the enemy, while the 72nd Highlanders and Guides were retiring; and again, on the retreat down the hill, in stopping to assist in carrying away a wounded sepoy, the enemy being not 60 yards off, firing heavily all the time.
LG 18 Oct 1881

HART, Lieutenant Reginald Clare, Royal Engineers

For his gallant conduct in risking his own life to save the life of a private soldier. The Lieutenant-General commanding the 2nd Division, Peshawar Field Force, reports that when on convoy duty with that force on the 31st January 1879, Liet.Hart of the Royal Engineers took the initiative in running some 1,200 yards to the rescue of a wounded sowar of the 13th Bengal Lancers in a river bed exposed to the fire of the enemy, of unknown strength, from both flanks, and also from a party in the river bed. Lieut. Hart reached the wounded sowar, drove off the enemy, and brought him under cover with the aid of some soldiers who accompanied him on the way.
LG 10 Jun 1879

LEACH, Captain Edward Pemberton, Royal Engineers

For having in action with the Shinwaris near Maidanak, Afghanistan, on the 17th March 1879, when covering the retirement of the Survey Escort, who were carrying Lieut.Barclay, 45th Sikhs, mortally wounded, behaved with the utmost gallantry in charging, with some men of the 45th Sikhs, a very much larger number of the enemy. In this encounter Capt.Leach killed two or three of the enemy himself and received a severe wound from an Afghan knife in the left arm. Capt.Leach's determination and gallantry in this affair, in attacking and driving back the enemy from the last position, saved the whole party from annihilation.
LG 9 Dec 1879

MULLANE, Sergeant Patrick, Royal Horse Artillery

For conspicuous bravery during the action of Maiwand on the 27th July 1880, in endeavouring to save the life of Driver Pickwell Istead. This non-commissioned officer, when the battery to which he belonged was on the point of retiring, and the enemy were within ten or fifteen yards, unhesitatingly ran back about two yards and picked up Driver Istead, placed him on the limber, where, unfortunately, he died almost immediately. Again, during the retreat, Sergt.Mullane volunteered to procure water for the wounded, and succeeded in doing so by going into one of the villages in which so many men lost their lives.
LG 17 May 1881

SARTORIUS, Captain Euston Henry, HM 59th Regiment

For conspicuous bravery during the action at Shahjui on the 24th October 1879, in leading a party of five or six men of the 59th Regt against a body of the enemy, of unknown strength, occupying an almost inaccessible position on the top of a precipitous hill. The nature of the ground made any sort of regular formation impossible, and Capt.Sartorius had to bear the first brunt of the attack from the whole body of the enemy, who fell upon him and his men as they gained the top of the precipitous pathway; but the gallant and determined bearing of this officer, emulated as it was by his men, led to the most perfect success, and the surviving occupants of the hill top, seven in number, were all killed. In this encounter Capt.Sartorius was wounded by sword-cuts in both hands, and one of his men was killed.
LG 16 May 1881

SELLAR, Lance-Corporal George, HM 72nd Highlanders

For conspicuous gallantry displayed by him at the assault on the Asmai Heights round Kabul on the 14th December 1879, in having in a marked manner led the attack, under a heavy fire, and, dashing on in front of the party up a slope, engaged in a desparate conflict with an Afghan who sprang out to meet him. In this encounter L-Corpl.Sellar was severely wounded.
LG 18 Oct 1881

VOUSDEN, Captain William John, 5th Punjab Cavalry,PFF

For the exceptional gallantry displayed by him on the 14th December 1879 on the Koh Asmai Heights near Kabul, in charging, with a small party, into the centre of the line of the retreating Kohistani Force, by whom they were greatly outnumbered, and who did their utmost to close round them. After rapidly charging through and through the enemy, backwards and forwards, several times, they swept off round the opposite side of the village and joined the rest of the troops.
LG 18 Oct 1881

WHITE, Major George Stuart, HM 92nd Highlanders

For conspicuous bravery during the engagement at Charasiah on the 6th October 1879 when, finding that the artillery and rifle fire failed to dislodge the enemy from a fortified hill which it was necessary to capture, Major White led an attack on it in person. Advancing with two companies of his regiment, and climbing from one steep ledge to another, he came upon a body of the enemy strongly posted and outnumbering his force by about eight to one. His men being much exhausted and immediate action being necessary, Major White took a rifle and, going on by himself, shot the leader of the enemy. This act so intimidated the rest that they fled round the side of the hill, and the position was won. Again, on the 1st September 1880, at the Battle of Kandahar,

Major White, in leading the final charge under a heavy fire from the enemy, who held a strong position and were supported by two guns, rode straight up to within a few yards of them and, seeing the guns, dashed forward and secured one, immediately after which the enemy retired.
LG 3 Jun 1881

DISTINGUISHED CONDUCT MEDAL

Recipients are named in the recommendations submitted to the Queen (Public Record Office: **WO 146/1**) and in Royal Artillery Regimental Order 26/Aug 1881 - for full details see Major P.E. Abbott's definitive Recipients of the Distinguished Conduct Medal 1855-1909 (London,1975). Although there are normally no citations other than the name of the action, some information can be gleaned from the published despatches and this is given below.

Battle, Edward
927 Pte, 66th Regt   Maiwand 27 Jul 1880

Bishop, James
3426 Dvr, E/B RHA   Maiwand and retreat 27-28 Jul 1880

Bonar, Daniel
1489 Pte, 72nd Hldrs   Peiwar Kotal 2 Dec 1878

Burridge, Thomas
4194 Sgt, E/B RHA   Maiwand and retreat 27-28 Jul 1880

Clayton, William
1163 Pte, 66th Regt   Maiwand 27 Jul 1880

Clunas, James
1582 Lce-Corp, 72nd Hldrs   Kabul Dec 1879

Cox, William
1768 Sgt, 72nd Hldrs   Peiwar Kotal 2 Dec 1878, also 'greatly distinguished at Takht-i-Shah 12 Dec 1879 and on the following day again brought himself to notice by his coolness and judgment when escorting the wounded from the Bala Hissar hill to Sherpur' (D.33)

Dennis, John
1163 Pte, 92nd Hldrs   Kandahar 1 Sep 1880, 'behaved with distinguished gallantry' (D.51)

Druce, Francis
1565 Lce-Corp, 9th Lcrs   Killa Kazi nr Kabul 11 Dec 1879, 'conspicuous for gallantry and coolness' (D.33)

England, Henry
548 Troop Sgt-Maj, 9th Lcrs   Killa Kazi nr Kabul 11 Dec 1879

Finn, Harry
1356 QM Sgt, 9th Lcrs   Killa Kazi nr Kabul 11 Dec 1879, 'conspicuous for gallantry and coolness' (D.33)

Gillon, Patrick
58B/1007 Pte, 72nd Hldrs   Kabul Dec 1879

Gordon, Thomas
1951 Corp, 72nd Hldrs   Kandahar 1 Sep 1880, 'having been very conspicuous during the advance on the village of Gandi Mullah Sahibdad' (D.51)

Gray, David
1506 Pte, 92nd Hldrs   Kandahar 1 Sep 1880, 'remarked for gallantry and forwardness during the capture of Ayub Khan's camp' (D.51)

Greer, William
Sgt (promoted to 2nd Lt 30 Apr 1879), 72nd Hldrs   Peiwar Kotal 2 Dec 1878

Grieve, Peter
8159 Pte, 92nd Hldrs   Kandahar 1 Sep 1880, 'remarked for gallantry and forwardness during the capture of Ayub Khan's camp' (D.51)

Hallett, Eli
627 Pte, 2/7th Fus   Maiwand and retreat 27-28 Jul 1880

Hamilton, John
1088 Sgt, 1/25th Regt   defence of convoy between Pezwan and Jagdalak 29 Jun 1880

Harbart, William George
1108 Pte, 2/7th Fus   Maiwand and retreat 27-28 Jul 1880

Harsent, Samuel William
1374 Pte, 9th Lcrs   Killa Kazi nr Kabul 11 Dec 1879, 'conspicuous for gallantry and coolness' (D.33)

Heath, William
1475 Corp, 67th Regt   Doaba 10 Nov 1879

Jacobs, George
514 Col-Sgt, 72nd Hldrs   Kabul Dec 1879; bar for Kandahar 1 Sep 1880, 'having been very conspicuous during the advance on the village of Gandi Mullah Sahibdad' (D.51)

Jones, Herbert James
4345 Tmptr, E/B RHA   Maiwand and retreat 27-28 Jul 1880

Kidgell, Charles
1675 Pte, 66th Regt   Maiwand 27 Jul 1880   (MR = George)

Lauder, Robert Renwick
1569 Col-Sgt, 72nd Hldrs   Charasiah 6 Oct 1879; bar for Kandahar 1 Sep 1880, 'having been very conspicuous during the advance on the village of Gandi Mullah Sahibdad' (D.51)

Long, Alfred
1706 Pte, 9th Lcrs   Killa Kazi nr Kabul 11 Dec 1879

Longworth, Jonathan
32B/104 Pte, 1/12th Regt   Besud 19 May 1880, 'a desperate hand to hand fight in which three Afghans were killed' (D.41)

Lougheed, Henry
949 Pte, 9th Lcrs   Killa Kazi nr Kabul 11 Dec 1879, 'conspicuous for gallantry and coolness' (D.33)

Lovell, Frederick
B.1503 Sgt, 66th Regt   Maiwand 27 Jul 1880

Lumsden, Thomas
1124 Col-Sgt, 72nd Hldrs   Peiwar Kotal 2 Dec 1878

McAnary, Richard
1789 Pte, 72nd Hldrs   Charasiah 6 Oct 1879

MacDonald, William
1415 Col-Sgt, 72nd Hldrs   Takht-i-Shah nr Kabul 12 Dec 1879, 'greatly distinguished by the cool and intelligent manner in which he superintended the construction of a breastwork under a very heavy fire' (D.33)

McGillivray, William
1539 Corp, 92nd Hldrs   Kandahar 1 Sep 1880, 'remarked for gallantry and forwardness during the capture of Ayub Khan's camp' (D.51)

McGlynn, John Joseph
362 Tmptr, C/2 RA   Deh Khojah 16 Aug 1880

McIlveen, Robert
1544 Sgt, 72nd Hldrs   Peiwar Kotal 21 Dec 1878, also 'greatly distinguished at Takht-i-Shah 12 Dec 1879' (D.33)

McIntosh, John
B.249 Pte, 92nd Hldrs   Kandahar 1 Sep 1880, 'remarked for gallantry and forwardness during the capture of Ayub Khan's camp' (D.51)

McKay, Edward
B.694 Lce-Corp, 92nd Hldrs   Asmai Heights nr Kabul 14 Dec 1879, 'distinguished by great personal gallantry on this occasion' (D.33)

McLaren, John
1844 Sgt, 92nd Hldrs   Asmai Heights nr Kabul 14 Dec 1879, 'distinguished by great personal gallantry on this occasion' (D.33)

McMahon, Michael
58B/800 Pte, 72nd Hldrs   Charasiah 6 Oct 1879, 'This young soldier, by his courage and coolness, closely followed by a few Goorkhas, was to a great extent instrumental in taking the extremely strong position on our left flank. His intrepidity was specially remarked by Captain Cook, VC, 5th Gurkhas, and I purpose addressing to the Military Secretary a recommendation that he may be granted the decoration of the Victoria Cross.' (D.22)

Martin, John
Lce-Corp, 66th Regt   Maiwand 27 Jul 1880   (B.76 or 1504)

Munro, John
4192 QM Sgt, E/B RHA   Maiwand and retreat 27-28 Jul 1880

Openshaw, James
55 Pte, 1/5th Fus   Besud 19 May 1880, 'a desperate hand to hand fight ensued, in which three Afghans were killed' (D.41)

Paton, William
4198 Sgt-Maj, E/B RHA   Maiwand and retreat 27-28 Jul 1880

Payne, William
4266 actg Bmdr, E/B RHA   Maiwand and retreat 27-28 Jul 1880

Pike, James
1628 Pte, 66th Regt   Girishk 14 Jul 1880

Pitchford, Samuel
1707 Lce-Corp, 2/7th Fus   Maiwand and retreat 27-28 Jul 1880

Regan, Denis
49B/893 Pte, 2/7th Fus   Deh Khojah 16 Aug 1880

Rhodes, Henry
55 Corp, 2/7th Fus   Deh Khojah 16 Aug 1880

Roddick, James
1767 Drm, 92nd Hldrs   Kandahar 1 Sep 1880, 'behaved with distinguished gallantry' (D.51)

Ross, Henry
2522 Pte, 2/7th Fus   Maiwand and retreat 27-28 Jul 1880

Salmond, Alexander
1497 Sgt, 72nd Hldrs   Peiwar Kotal 2 Dec 1878

Spittle, Henry
722 Troop Sgt-Maj, 9th Lcrs   Killa Kazi nr Kabul 11 Dec 1879, 'conspicuous for gallantry and coolness' (D.33) - kia 13 Dec

Taylor, Robert
2132 Pte, 2/7th Fus   Deh Khojah 16 Aug 1880

Thorogood, Frederick
4336 Corp, E/B RHA   Maiwand and retreat 27-28 Jul 1880

Tighe, Thomas
4278 Gnr, E/B RHA   Maiwand and retreat 27-28 Jul 1880

Waterstone, John
1309 Pte, 72nd Hldrs   Charasiah 6 Oct 1879

Wheeler, George
1938 Col-Sgt, 67th Regt   Doaba 10 Nov 1879

Williams, Frederick
B.1396 Lce-Corp, 66th Regt   Maiwand 27 Jul 1880

Woods, John
2027 Col-Sgt, 1/5th Fus   Besud 19 May 1880, 'a desperate hand to hand fight ensued, in which three Afghans were killed ... as soon as the conflict in the courtyard had ended Col-Sergeant Woods with dashing gallantry rushed up the debris and disappeared into the tower, closely followed by Captain Kilgour, and there these two found and slew five desperate men at bay. A finer display of courage cannot well be imagined.' (D.41)

Woolley, Michael
40B/89 Corp, 67th Regt   Doaba 10 Nov 1879

Young, Robert
705 Troop (later Regtl) Sgt-Maj, 9th Lcrs   Killa Kazi nr Kabul 11 Dec 1879, 'by whose gallantry and exertions Lt-Col Cleland's life was saved' (D.33)

Regimental list

E/B RHA	8 Maiwand
C/2 RA	1 Deh Khojah
9th Lcrs	8 Kabul
1/5th Fus	2 Besud
2/7th Fus	4 Maiwand 3 Deh Khojah
1/12th Regt	1 Besud
1/25th Regt	1 Pazwan-Jagdalak
66th Regt	1 Girishk 6 Maiwand
67th Regt	3 Kabul
72nd Hldrs	6 Peiwar Kotal 4 Charasiah 4 Kabul 1 Kandahar + 2 bars
92nd Hldrs	2 Kabul 6 Kandahar
	61 + 2 bars

Numerical abstract

Peiwar Kotal 2 Dec 1878	6
Charasiah 6 Oct 1879	4
Operations around Kabul Dec 1879	17
Besud 19 May 1880	3
Pazwan-Jagdalak convoy 9 Jun 1880	1
Girishk 14 Jul 1880	1
Maiwand and retreat 27-28 Jul 1880	18
Deh Khojah 16 Aug 1880	4
Kandahar 1 Sep 1880	7 + 2 bars

INDIAN ORDER OF MERIT

GGO 33/10 Jan 1879
Admiited to 3rd Class
Lance-Naik Sheea Sing, 29th (Punjab) Bengal NI
For gallantry in action with the enemy at the capture of the Peiwar Kotal on the 2nd December 1878.

GGO 89/24 Jan 1879
Admitted to 3rd Class

29th (Punjab) Bengal NI
Subadar-Major Juggut Singh
Havildar Nutha Sing
For conspicuous gallantry in action at the assault of the Spin Gawai Kotal on the 2nd December 1878.
Havildar Goormukh Singh
Sepoy Heeram Singh
For conspicuous gallantry in carrying Lieutenant A J F Reid out of a heavy fire, when wounded, in the action of the 28th November 1878 at the Turai Glen near the Peiwar Kotal.

5th Gurkha Regt
Subadar Rugobir Nuggerkoti
For conspicuous gallantry in action at the attack on the Spin Gawai Kotal on the 2nd December 1878, in leading his company with great determination, though wounded.
Havildar Jaggat Sing Rana
Bugler Soorbir Damai
Sepoy Kishnbiar Nuggurkoti
Sepoy Hushtbir Khuttrie
For conspicuous gallantry in checking the advance of the enemy in action at the Mangiar Pass on the 13th December 1878.
Havildar Pursoo Khuttrie
For conspicuous gallantry in the operations on the Peiwar Kotal on the 2nd December 1878, when he protected the life of Major Fitzhugh, and again on the 13th December 1878, in defending the baggage attacked in the Mangiar defile.
Naik Wazir Sing Adkary
For conspicuous gallantry in leading the charge at the storming of the Spin Gawai Kotal on the 2nd December 1878.
Sepoy Munraj Poon
For conspicuous gallantry in being the first to enter the breastwork of the enemy at the storming of the Spin Gawai Kotal on the 2nd December 1878.

GGO 106/31 Jan 1879
Admitted to 3rd Class
Kot-Daffadar Jhandah Sing, 5th Punjab Cav,PFF
For conspicuous gallantry in heading the charge of his troop against

a force many times its number and under a heavy fire in the fight against the Mangals on the 7th January 1879.

GGO 164/21 Feb 1879
Admitted to 3rd Class
14th Bengal NI
Havildar Dewah Sing
Sepoy Heerah Sing
For conspicuous gallantry in action on the 21st November 1878 in the attack on Ali Musjid and in assisting Captain J G Maclean, when wounded, out of a heavy fire.
Havildar Maun Sing
Sepoy Gour Khan
For conspicuous gallantry in action on the 21st November 1878 in the attack on Ali Musjid.
Sepoy Utter Sing
Sepoy Dan Sing
Sepoy Boodh Sing
For conspicuous gallantry in action on the 21st November 1878 in the attack on Ali Musjid and in volunteering, when under a continuous and heavy fire, to bring back the body of Major H H Birch, who had been killed.

GGO 230/13 Mar 1879
Admitted to 3rd Class
27th (Punjab) Bengal NI
Subadar Deo
Sepoy Ummer Sing
For conspicuous gallantry in action on the 21st November 1878 at Ali Musjid, in assisting Lieutenant T O Fitzgerald, when he was wounded, and placing him under cover.
Jemadar Ram Sing
Havildar Dyal Sing
For conspicuous gallantry in action on the 21st November 1878 at Ali Musjid, in carrying Sepoy Jowahir Singh, when wounded, out of a heavy fire.
Havildar Goordit Sing
Sepoy Goordit Sing
Sepoy Asa Sing
For conspicuous gallantry in action on the 21st November 1878 at Ali Musjid, in advancing to occupy a 'sanga' close to the enemy's position.
Sepoy Luchman Dass
For conspicuous gallantry in action on the 21st November 1878 at Ali Musjid, in carrying Sepoy Nuthoo, when wounded, under a very heavy fire, to a place of safety.

GGO 271/28 Mar 1879
Admitted to 3rd Class
Sepoy Hussan Khan, 24th (Punjab) Bengal NI
For conspicuous gallantry on the 27th January 1879 in the Bazar Valley, in coming to the assistance of Lieutenant B E Spragge, 51st Regiment, when suddenly attacked by a party of Afridis.

GGO 299/11 Apr 1879
Promoted to 2nd Class
Ressaidar Salim Khan, 1st Punjab Cav,PFF
For conspicuous gallantry in attacking an Afghan fanatic single-handed at Camp Kandahar on the 6th February 1879.

GGO 365/2 May 1879
Admitted to 3rd Class
Hospital Assistant 2nd Class Shunkur Dass, attchd 5th Gurkha Regt
For conspicuous gallantry on the 13th December 1878, when the regiment was attacked in the Supri Defile.

GGO 366/2 May 1879
Admitted to 3rd Class
Sowar Kishen Sing, 4th Punjab Cav,PFF
For conspicuous gallantry during the attack made on the Sulemain Kheyl Village in the Gomal Valley on the 5th January 1879.

GGO 532/14 Jun 1879
Promoted to 1st Class
Subadar Fyztulub Khan, 1st Punjab Inf,PFF
In consideration of the excellent arrangements made by him when in command of a detachment of his regiment at Fort Abdoola (near Gulistan Karez, Afghanistan), by which two determined attacks by Kakozai and Atchakazai raiders were successfully repulsed on the nightof the 9th January 1879.

P/1372 Nos 6433-38 - He was also chosen to receive a sword offered by Mir Imdad Ali, CSI, for presentation to the native officer or soldier who had distinguished himself most in the 'late' Afghan War.

GGO 533/14 Jun 1879
Corps of Guides
Promoted to 2nd Class
Rissaldar Prem Sing
Admitted to 3rd Class
Daffadar Nand Singh
Sowar Jewan Singh
Sowar Kardoo Singh
Sowar Dewan Singh
Sowar Yakub Simgh

For conspicuous gallantry in action against the Khugiani tribes near Fatteabad on the 2nd April 1879.

GGO 583/27 Jun 1879
1st Punjab Inf,PFF
Promoted to 1st Class
Subadar-Major Pyabb 'Sirdar Bahadur'
Admitted to 3rd Class
Jemadar Mir Butt
Naik Peer Mahomed
Sepoy Gool Mahomed 3635
Sepoy Heera Sing
For conspicuous gallantry in action with the enemy at Baghao on the 24th March 1879.

GGO 605/4 Jul 1879
Admitted to 3rd Class
45th (Rattray's Sikhs) Bengal NI
Sepoy Lall Singh
Sepoy Nund Singh
For conspicuous gallantry on the 7th March 1879 near Maidaneck, when on escort duty with a survey party.

Mhairwara Btn
Hospital Assistant Syud Noor Khan
Naik Gopa (2nd)
Sepoy Madari
For conspicuous gallantry in action at Kam Dakka on the 22nd April 1879.

GGO 736/1 Aug 1879 and **GGO 798/22 Aug 1879**
Admitted to 3rd Class
24th (Punjab) Bengal NI
Havildar Ahmed Khan
Sepoy Kapur Singh

45th (Rattray's Sikhs) Bengal NI
Naik Hakim
Sepoy Theraj Singh

For conspicuous gallantry in action in the Choora Valley on the 31st January 1879.

GGO 797/22 Aug 1879
Admitted to 3rd Class
Store Lascar Chukun Singh, E-4th Royal Artillery
For conspicuous gallantry in having, when unarmed, opposed and disarmed a fanatic who rushed into the camp at Kandahar on the 5th February 1879.

GGO 1260/26 Dec 1879
Promoted to 2nd Class
5th Gurkha Regt
Sepoy Kissen Beer Nuggerkoti
Admitted to 3rd Class
Subadar Hurree Dewa Jaiesie
Bugler Choonee Damai

5th Punjab Inf,PFF
Subadar Budh Sing

23rd (Punjab) Bengal NI
Jemadar Boor Sing
Havildar Goordial Sing
Naik Ootum Sing
Sepoy Jhunda Sing
Sepoy Hurditt Sing
Sepoy Boota Sing
Sepoy Chunda Sing
Sepoy Gunda Sing

For conspicuous gallantry in action at Charasia on the 6th October 1879.

GGO 20/2 Jan 1880
Admitted to 3rd Class
Jemadar Gunesa Sing, 3rd Sikh Inf,PFF
For conspicuous gallantry in leading his company up a steep hill under a very heavy fire from the enemy and capturing with his own hands one of their standards at Camp Shuturgurdan on the 2nd October 1879.

GGO 117/20 Feb 1880
Admitted to 3rd Class
Jemadar Fuzl Achmud, 29th (Punjab) Bengal NI
For conspicuous gallantry in charging the enemy single-handed during the assault on Zawa in the Zaimukht Country, on the 13th December 1879.

GGO 131/27 Feb 1880
Admitted to 3rd Class
14th Bengal Lancers
Jemadar Gopal Sing (since dead of his wounds)
Daffadar Kanhiya Lal
For conspicuous gallantry in the Churdeh Valley on the 11th December 1879.

GGO 132/27 Feb 1880
Admitted to 3rd Class
Sowar Bhagwan Sing, 10th Bengal Lancers

For gallant conduct on the 15th December 1879 whilst carrying the mail from Pezwan to Jagdalak.

GGO 133/27 Feb 1880
Admitted to 3rd Class
Sowar Zeadeh Khan, 18th Bengal Cav
For conspicuous gallantry in attacking single-handed a party of marauders between Mandoria and Chapri in the Kuram Valley on the 20th November 1879, and compelling them to abandon their plunder and disperse.

GGO 150/5 Mar 1880
Admitted to 3rd Class
Ressaidar Bahawaklin Khan, 11th Bengal Lancers
For conspicuous gallantry at the storming of a fortified 'serai' near Kabul on the 13th December 1879.

GGO 152/5 Mar 1880
Admitted to 3rd Class
21st (Punjab) Bengal NI
Recruit Sher Khan
Recruit Fateh Khan
For conspicuous gallantry in action at the Sarkai Kotal on the 14th October 1879.

GGO 190/19 Mar 1880
Promoted to 2nd Class
Rissaldar Mir Alam Khan, 1st Punjab Cav,PFF
For conspicuous gallantry in the action fought at Saiad-But in Shorawak on the 27th March 1879.

GGO 233/16 Apr 1880
Admitted to 3rd Class
Sowar Zaidulla, Guides Cav,PFF
For conspicuous gallantry in action at Kabul on the 13th December 1879.

GGO 251/23 Apr 1880
Promoted to 1st Class
5th Gurkha Regt
Naik Kishenbir Nagarkoti (1212)
For conspicuous gallantry in action at Kabul on the 12th December 1879.

Promoted to 2nd Class
5th Punjab Cav,PFF
Kot-Daffadar Shadil Khan (40)

For conspicuous gallantry in action at Kabul on the 14th December 1879.

5th Punjab Inf,PFF
Subadar Juma Khan
For conspicuous gallantry in action at Kabul on the 23rd December 1879.

GGO 252/23 Apr 1880
Admitted to 3rd Class

28th (Punjab) Bengal NI
Havildar Shahgood Khan 732
Sepoy Akbar Khan 1669
For conspicuous gallantry on the 19th December 1879 in carrying, at great personal risk, important despatches from Latabad to Jagdalak, through a country at the time wholly in possession of the enemy.

23rd (Punjab) Bengal NI
Subadar Mehtab Sing
Havildar Gulab Sing 64
For conspicuous gallantry in action at Latabad on the 16th December 1879.

No 2 (Derajat) Mtn Bty,PFF
Subadar Nuzzur Khan
Havildar Kootub Deeb 336
Naik Alumshere 298
Driver-Naik Fuzl 5

5th Punjab Cav,PFF
Rissaldar Amir Ali Shah
Daffadar Kesar Sing 183
Trumpeter Shah Alum 17
Sowar Bussawa Sing 1371
Sowar Nutha Sing 1444
Sowar Hidayutullah 1487
Sowar Maiah Sing 1678
Sowar Oottum Sing 1681
Sowar Harsa Sing 1756
Sowar Zeeaoodeen 1863

28th (Punjab) Bengal NI
Sepoy Rahim Khan 1013

Guides Inf,PFF
Havildar-Major Uttur Sing 967
Havildar Jugbir 366
Havildar Jowalla Sing 447
Havildar Jewund Sing 1057
Havildar Ommrah
Naik Hazir 1440
Sepoy Dillia 1214
Sepoy Lehnu

Sepoy Chunder Bir 1278
Sepoy Mahomed Shuffi 1374
Sepoy Wurriam Sing 1796
Sepoy Gule Shere 2211

5th Punjab Inf,PFF
Subadar Baz Gul
Havildar Sham Sing (since dead of his wounds)
Naik Surwan Sing 3482
Sepoy Man Sing 3483
Sepoy Akram 3568
Sepoy Niamat 3689
Sepoy Umra 4084

5th Gurkha Regt
Havildar Kurm Sing Negi 593
Sepoy Dummer Sing 1771

For conspicuous gallantry in action at Kabul and in the vicinity between the 10th and the 23rd December 1879.

GGO 294/14 May 1880
Admitted to 3rd Class
Jemadar Hazrat Shah, 2nd Punjab Cav,PFF
For conspicuous gallantry in the action fought at Shahjui on the 24th October 1879, on which occasion, during the charge, he cut down one of the leaders of the enemy and was chiefly instrumental in killing their Chief, Sahibjan, whom he was the first to attack.

GGO 336/4 Jun 1880
Admitted to 3rd Class

Ressaidar Mansur Khan, 2nd Punjab Cav,PFF
For conspicuous gallantry in action at Shahjui on the 24th October 1879, in rescuing Sowar Ommar Buksh of the same regiment, whose horse had fallen on him, and one of whose assailants he killed. Also for gallant conduct in the subsequent charge of the regiment on the same occasion.

Lance-Daffadar Gujar Sing 1534, 2nd Punjab Cav,PFF
For conspicuous gallantry in the charge of the regiment at Shahjui on the 24th October 1879, in aiding Ressaidar Lahrasaf Khan and Sowar Sawan Sing of the same corps when attacked by superior numbers of the enemy, several of whom he cut down and killed.

GGO 390/2 Jul 1880
Admitted to 3rd Class
Havildar Davi Sing, 4th Sikh Inf,PFF
For conspicuous gallantry in action at Gumal on the 6th April 1880, on which occasion, with a detachment of eighteen men, he attacked and drove off a large body of Waziri raiders and saved the village from destruction.

GGO 391/2 Jul 1880
Admitted to 3rd Class
Corps of Guides,PFF
Duffadar Mahomed Yunus 73
Sepoy Izzat 1815
For conspicuous gallantry in action near Charasia on the 25th April 1880.

GGO 425/23 Jul 1880
3rd Sikh Inf,PFF

Promoted to 2nd Class
Jemadar Ganesha Sing
Naik Sham Sing 52
For conspicuous gallantry in action at Mir Karez on the 10th December 1879, on which occasion they were most forward in the attack on the enemy's position and set a brilliant example to the men of the regiment.

Admitted to 3rd Class
Havildar Gurdit Sing 5
For conspicuous gallantry in action near Kabul on the 14th December 1879, on which occasion, when a detachment of the regiment was retiring from the Conical Hill near the Aliabad Kotal, he ran back under a heavy fire and rescued a wounded man, who would otherwise have been killed by the enemy.

Havildar Saiad Gul 134
For conspicuous gallantry in action at Mir Karez on the 10th December 1879 when, with Jemadar Ganesha Sing and Naick Sham Sing, he was very forward in the attack on the enemy's position, setting the men a brilliant example and receiving a severe wound in hand-to-hand conflict with the Afghans.

Sepoy Panjab Sing 232
For conspicuous gallantry in action at the Takht-i-Shah Hill near Kabul on the 12th December 1879, in proceeding, under a heavy fire, to the assistance of Lieutenant E J N Fasken, who was severely wounded, remaining with him and eventually carrying him out of fire.

Hospital Assistant 2nd Class Nehal Chand
For conspicuous gallantry in action at the Takht-i-Shah Hill near Kabul on the 12th December 1879, in twice proceeding, under a heavy fire, to the assistance of Lieutenant E J N Fasken, who was severely wounded.

GGO 426/23 Jul 1880
Admitted to 3rd Class
Private Lall Mir Khan 148, 29th Bombay NI
For conspicuous gallantry in action at Kaj-Boz near Kelat-i-Ghilzai on the 2nd May 1880, on which occasion he was very forward in the storming of the position taken up by the enemy, several of whom were killed.

GGO 443/30 Jul 1880
Admitted to 3rd Class
Hospital Assistant 2nd Class Haidar Khan, attchd Corps of Guides,PFF
For conspicuous gallantry in action at Charasiah on the 25th April 1880, on which occasion he continued, under a heavy fire, passing across the open from group to group of the skirmishers so as to ensure no wounded man remaining long without assistance. In the performance of this duty he himself fell severely wounded.

GGO 533/17 Sep 1880
1st Punjab Cav,PFF
Admitted to 3rd Class
Daffadar Gholam Jelani 668
For conspicuous gallantry in action at Patkao Shana on the 1st July 1880, in singly engaging and killing two of the enemy, armed with swords and rifles, himself receiving a severe wound in the encounter.

Daffadar Chait Sing 1472
For conspicuous gallantry in action at Patkao Shana on the 1st July 1880, on which occasion he killed three of the enemy, one of them being a deserter.

Lance-Daffadar Mowaz Khan 1422
For conspicuous gallantry in action at Ahmed Khel on the 19th April 1880, on which occasion, observing that two ghazis, armed with guns and tulwars, had taken post in a nullah, he dismounted and, holding his horse with one hand, engaged both of them, killing one in a hand-to hand fight.

Sowar Bootah Sing 1255
For conspicuous gallantry in action at Arzu on the 23rd April 1880, in singly engaging and cutting down in a hand-to-hand fight two of the enemy.

Sowar Jowahir Sing 1588
For conspicuous gallantry in action at Ahmed Khel on the 19th April 1880, on which occasion he dismounted and attacked two of the enemy who had taken post in a nullah, killing one in a hand-to-hand encounter.

Sowar Fazl Khan 1807
For conspicuous gallantry in action at Patkao Shana on the 1st July 1880, on which occasion he attacked and killed in succession three of the enemy, himself receiving two wounds in the encounter with the third.

GGO 563/1 Oct 1880
19th Bengal Lancers
Admitted to 3rd Class
Jemadar Mahomed Khan 603
For conspicuous gallantry in action at Ahmad Khel on the 19th April 1880, in defending his commanding officer, Colonel P S

Yorke, from the attacks of the ghazis by whom he was assailed; also for conspicuous gallantry in action at Patkao Shana on the 1st July 1880.

Kot-Daffadar Hubboob Sing 238
For conspicuous gallantry in action at Ahmad Khel on the 19th April 1880, in charging with a few men a superior number of the enemy who had suddenly attacked the flank of the squadron to which he belonged; also in rescuing Jemadar Gulab Sing, who was wounded, dismounted and surrounded by the enemy.

Kot-Daffadar Hookum Sing 738
For conspicuous gallantry in action at Patkao Shana on the 1st July 1880, in charging singly five of the enemy and killing two of them.

Daffadar Hurdit Sing 197
For conspicuous gallantry in action at Ahmad Khel on the 19th April 1880, on which occasion he, although already severely wounded, engaged and cut down two of the enemy who were attacking Sowar Boota Sing.

Daffadar Nowrung Sing 830
For conspicuous gallantry in action at Patkao Shana on the 1st July 1880, on which occasion he was very forward and killed several of the enemy.

Daffadar Alum Ali Shah 931
For conspicuous gallantry in action at Ahmad Khel on the 19th April 1880, in rescuing Duffadar Hookum Sing, who was badly wounded and surrounded by ghazis.

Daffadar Mahomed Ishak 1130
For conspicuous gallantry in action at Ahmad Khel on the 19th April 1880, in charging three of the enemy who were attacking Sowar Saidal, 19th Bengal Lancers, killing two of them and saving the sowar's life; also in action at Patkao Shana on the 1st July 188., on which occasion he dismounted and singly attacked seven or eight of the enemy, who had taken post behind some rocks, and killed four or five of them.

Lance-Daffadar Kair Sing 1091
For conspicuous gallantry in action at Ahmad Khel on the 19th April 1880, in saving the life of Ressaidar Gunda Sing, 19th Bengal Lancers, when the latter was attacked by two of the enemy; also, on the same occasion, in singly charging a group of eight or ten ghazis and killing two of them.

Lance-Daffadar Surdar Sing 1185
For conspicuous gallantry in action at Ahmad Khel on the 19th April 1880, in charging, with Kot-Duffadar Hubboob Sing, a superior number of the enemy who had suddenly attacked the flank of the squadron to which be belonged, and killing two of them.

Sowar Kushal Sing 915
For conspicuous gallantry in action at Ahmad Khel on the 19th

April 1880, in rescuing Kot-Duffadar Kurram Sing, 19th Bengal Lancers, who was severely wounded and nearly overcome in a conflict with two ghazis.

Sowar Ram Sing 1047
For conspicuous gallantry in action at Ahmad Khel on the 19th April 1880, in charging three of the enemy's horsemen who were rushing on Surgeon W R Murphy, killing one of them and saving that officer's life.

Sowar Gulab Sing 1071
For conspicuous gallantry in action at Ahmad Khel on the 19th April 1880, in dismounting and leading an attack, under a heavy fire, on a number of the enemy who had posted themselves in a ditch, killing more than one of them and setting an excellent example to the other men with him.

Sowar Utter Sing 1126
For conspicuous gallantry in action at Ahmad Khel on the 19th April 1880, on which occasion, although wounded in two places, he charged two ghazis, killed one of them, and saved the life of Duffadar Narain Sing, whom they had beset.

Sowar Kait Ram 1223
For conspicuous gallantry in action at Ahmad Khel on the 19th April 1880, in charging, with Kot-Duffadar Hubboob Sing, a superior number of the enemy who had suddenly attacked the flank of the squadron to which he belonged, and killing two of them in personal conflict.

Sowar Kan Jan Khan 1396
For conspicuous gallantry in action at Ahmad Khel on the 19th April 1880, in dismounting and attacking a number of the enemy posted in a deep ditch, jumping into the ditch among them, cutting down two of them and saving the life of Sowar Gulab Sing, himself receiving a wound in the conflict.

GGO 638/19 Nov 1880
Promoted to 2nd Class
Subadar Dewa Sing, 23rd Bengal NI (Pioneers)
For conspicuous gallantry in action near Kandahar on the 1st September 1880, on which occasion he led the way in a charge on one of the enemy's sangas, which he was the first to enter, and in which two guns were captured.

GGO 639/19 Nov 1880
Admitted to 3rd Class, for conspicuous gallantry in action near Kandahar on the 1st September 1880:-

3rd Punjab Cav,PFF

Daffadar Burkut Ally 1134
In charging, during the pursuit of the enemy, three ghazis, armed with rifles and fixed bayonets, who were attacking

Lance-Duffadar Maiboob Ally Khan of the same regiment, killing one of them and saving the Lance-Duffadar's life.

23rd Bengal NI (Pioneers)

Sepoy Chatar Sing 1735
In leaping across a wet ditch in the face of some forty of the enemy, and bayonetting one of them.

Sepoy Gunda Sing 2024
In bayonetting two of the enemy in a charge on one of their sangas, in which he was particularly forward, and saving the life of Subadar Dewa Sing, whom these men had attacked.

24th Bengal NI

Naik Dhurm Sing 104
Naik Soobah Sing 1123
During the advance on the enemy's position, two of the mules carrying the reserve ammunition having been shot down, these non-commissioned officers, with great coolness, under a heavy fire of artillery and musketry, unloaded the mules carrying the entrenching tools, transferred the ammunition to them, and distributed the entrenching tools on other mules.

Sepoy Maroof Shah 1765
In descending from a dandi in which, being wounded, he was being conveyed from the field, and killing two out of four ghazis who had rushed on him and the kahars who were carrying him.

2nd Gurkha Regt

Naik Gopal Borah 420
In leading the way during the advance against the gardens and orchards held by the enemy, and setting a most praiseworthy example to the men.

Rifleman Mungal Joyser 584
In attacking, with two other men of the regiment, a number of ghazis who had posted themselves in a court-yard in the village of Sahibdad, killing some and driving the others out, himself receiving a severe wound in the conflict.

Rifleman Wuzeer Sing Nagarkoti 901
In attacking, with the aid of two other men of the regiment, a number of ghazis who had taken up a position in a court-yard in the village of Sahibdad, killing some and driving the rest out, and himself receiving two wounds in the encounter.

Rifleman Inderbeer Lama 1123
In leading the way in a charge on the Afghan position, on which occasion he was the first to reach one of the enemy's guns, which was captured. Also in singly attacking and bayonetting two ghazis who had posted themselves behind a rock.

Rifleman Moneyram Lohar 1124
In springing forward and bayonetting a ghazi who had suddenly assailed and was on the point of cutting down Subadar Moteeram Thappa of the same regiment, thereby saving the Subadar's life.

Rifleman Ticcaram Kwas 1138
in leading the way during the advance against the gardens and orchards held by the enemy, and setting an excellent example to his comrades.

Rifleman Bisram Thappa 1319
In singly attacking a number of ghazis posted in a court-yard in the village of Sahibdad, on which occasion he received a very severe wound.

Rifleman Mukkereah Rana 1360
In attacking, with two other men of the regiment, a number of ghazis posted in a court-yard in the village of Sahibdad, some of whom were killed and the rest driven out, he himself receiving a wound in the encounter.

2nd Sikh Inf,PFF

Subadar-Major Gurbaj Sing
In gallantly leading and encouraging the men during the advance on the enemy's position, and charging a band of ghazis under a hot fire.

Jemadar Ala Sing
In leading a charge on a band of ghazis who had made a stand, cutting down one of them and showing a splendid example to the men.

Naik Davie Sing 1802
In leading the way in a charge on a strong band of ghazis.

Sepoy Jai Sing 2210
In singly attacking several ghazis and killing two of them, himself receiving a severe wound in the encounter.

Sepoy Pertab Sing 2431
Sepoy Hira Sing
These men exhibited great coolness and intrepidity under a very hot fire from the enemy. They were both severely wounded while prominently in front during the advance on the Afghan position.

Sepoy Hakim 2967
In joining Naick Davie Sing in a charge on a strong band of ghazis, one of whom he killed.

GGO 689/17 Dec 1880

3rd Class

The undermentioned men, who were killed with the late Major S J Waudby in the defence of the post of Dabrai on the 16th April 1880, would, if they had lived, have been admitted to the 3rd Class:-

3rd Sind Horse

Sowar Syud Imman Ali

19th Bombay NI

Private Elahi Bux
Private Sounak Tannack

The widows of these men will be allowed to draw the usual Order of Merit pension for three years from the 16th April 1880, in addition to the ordinary pension allowed by regulations.

GGO 20/7 Jan 1881

Admitted to 3rd Class

29th Bombay NI

Naik Rahim Khan

For conspicuous gallantry in endeavouring, at great personal risk, in August 1880, to convey a message from Khelat-i-Ghilzai to the garrison of Kandahar, then closely besieged by Sirdar Mahomed Ayub Khan. In carrying out this duty he was taken prisoner by the enemy.

Private Lall Mahomed

For conspicuous gallantry in August 1880 in conveying, at great personal risk, a letter from General Primrose at Kandahar to the officer commanding at Chaman, the intervening country being entirely in the hands of the enemy, who had intercepted and put to death several messengers previously despatched on the same errand.

GGO 58/4 Feb 1881

Admitted to 3rd Class

Poona Horse

Lance-Naik Mahomed Seedick Khan 359

Lance-Naik Innait Russul Khan 479

For conspicuous gallantry in action at Deh Khojah near Kandahar on the 16th August 1880, on which occasion they charged down a street of the village in order to clear the way for the late Brigadier-General Brooke (whose orderlies they were) and a small party of the 7th Fusiliers, who were at the time surrounded by the enemy. In cutting their way through the enemy, Innait Russul Khan received four severe wounds, and his comrade's horse was badly wounded.

GGO 59/4 Feb 1881

Ressaidar Dhowkul Sing, 3rd Bombay Lt Cav

Promoted to 2nd Class

For conspicuous gallantry in action near the Helmand on the 14th July 1880, in riding up under a heavy fire and rescuing a sowar of the 3rd Sind Horse, whose horse had fallen with him near the enemy's guns.

Promoted to 1st Class

For conspicuous gallantry during the retreat from Maiwand on the 27th July 1880 (on which occasion he was instrumental in saving the life of Lieutenant-Colonel H S Anderson, 1st Bombay Native Infantry, who was severely wounded), and in the attack on the village of Deh Khojah near Kandahar on the 16th August 1880.

GGO 60/4 Feb 1881
Admitted to 3rd Class

3rd Bombay Lt Cav
Naik Rughbur Misser 813
For conspicuous gallantry and coolness during the retreat from Maiwand on the 27th July 1880.

Poona Horse
Daffadar Hamudoollah Khan
Daffadar Aktar Nowaz Khan
Naik Mahomed Esack Khan
Lance-Naik Goolshair Khan
Sowar Ameer Khan
Sowar Shaik Hoossain
Sowar Baboo Rao Khanwalkar
For conspicuous gallantry in action near the banks of the Argandab on the 28th July 1880, when serving with the detachment sent out under the command of the late Brigadier-General Brooke to help in to Kandahar the remnants of Brigadier-General Burrows' force, then retreating from Maiwand.

3rd Sind Horse
Ressaidar Shaik Jamal
Kot-Daffadar Abdoolla Khan 240
Daffadar Sarfaraz Khan 361
Lance-Naik Bishun Sing 378
Lance-Naik Jaimul Sing 502
Trumpeter Soonder Sing 266
Sowar Beer Sing 142
Sowar Lena Sing 229
Sowar Jowala Sing 255
For conspicuous gallantry during the retreat from Maiwand on the 27th July 1880, in keeping off parties of the enemy's cavalry who were in pursuit, and saving the lives of many wounded and exhausted men.

No 2 Co Bombay Sappers & Miners
Lance-Naik Shaik Abdoolla 71
Private Abdoolla Khan 639
Private Saiad Mahomed 397
For conspicuous gallantry in the attack on Deh Khojah near Kandahar on the 16th August 1880, in endeavouring to rescue the late Captain G M Cruickshank, RE, on that officer falling severely wounded. In doing this Saiad Mahomed and Abdoolla Khan were themselves wounded, the latter severely in three places.

GGO 136/4 Mar 1881
Admitted to 3rd Class
19th Bengal Lancers
Ressaidar Jowahir Sing

For conspicuous gallantry in action at Ahmed Khel on the 19th April 1880, on which occasion, at the head of three dismounted men, who dashed through some fifteen or twenty of the enemy, who were resisting the passage of a nullah, killing two of them with his own hand and himself receiving a wound in the encounter.

Trumpet-Major Mangal Sing
For conspicuous gallantry in action at Ahmed Khel on the 19th April 1880, in singly charging a superior number of the enemy's cavalry.

GGO 222/4 Mar 1881
Admitted to 3rd Class
1st Bombay NI
Havildar Ganda Sing 2
Private Bhagwan Sing 1057
For conspicuous gallantry and devotion in and after the battle of Maiwand on the 27th July 1880, on which occasion they saved the life of Lieutenant-Colonel H S Anderson, carrying him off the field on his falling severely wounded at the close of the action.

GGO 438/5 Aug 1881
Admitted to 3rd Class
Sowar Sirbuland Khan, 1st Punjab Cav,PFF
For conspicuous gallantry in action at Patkao Shana in the Logar Valley on the 1st July 1880, on which occasion he singly charged three of the enemy, armed with guns, killing two of them and himself receiving a severe gun-shot wound from the third.

GGO 478/26 Aug 1881
Admitted to 3rd Class
Sowar Burma Deen 853, 3rd Bombay Lt Cav
For conspicuous gallantry in action at Maiwand on the 27th July 1880, in having, under a heavy fire, when Brigadier-General Burrows' horse was killed under him, promptly dismounted and given his own horse to the Brigadier-General, though he was himself at the time badly wounded.

GGO 59/3 Feb 1882
Admitted to 3rd Class
Woordie-Major Shaik Amir Ali, 3rd Sind Horse

1stly, for exhibiting great coolness and presence of mind before the enemy during the retreat from Maiwand on the 27th July 1880;

2ndly for his energy and gallantry at the attack on Deh Khoja near Kandahar on the 16th August 1880; and

3rdly for gallantry displayed at the battle of Mazra, Kandahar, on the 1st September 1880.

GGO 356/23 Jun 1882
Admitted to 3rd Class
30th Bombay NI
Subadar-Major Hyder Khan
Havilda (now Jemadar) Heera Sing
Naik Suddu Sing
Bugler Chuddo Beg
For conspicuous gallantry and coolness during the retreat from Maiwand on the 27th July 1880.

The undermentioned men who were killed in that action would, if they had lived, have been admitted to the 3rd Class:
Havildar-Major Brindaban
Quartermaster-Havildar Futteychund
Private Goolam Mahomed
Bugler Suddu Sing
The widows of Private Goolam Mahomed and Bugler Suddu Sing and, as a special case, the daughter of Havildar-Major Brindaban will be allowed to draw the usual Order of Merit pension for three years from the 27th July 1880.

GGO 432/10 Jun 1887
Admitted to 3rd Class
Sowar (now Kot-Daffadar) Mazr Ali, 1st Bengal Cav
For conspicuous gallantry in action at Bhagwana in the Chardeh Valley, near Kabul, on the 11th December 1879, when employed as orderly to Lieutenant-General Sir F S Roberts, KCB, VC, Commanding the Forces in Northern Afghanistan, on which occasion, at great personal risk, after his horse had been shot under him, he seized the Malik of Bhagwana, who had treacherously attempted the life of the Lieutenant-General.

Alphabetical list

General Order/Year
Abdoolla Khan 240 Kot-Daffadar, 3rd Sind Horse 60/1881
Abdoolla Khan 639 Private, No 2 Co Bombay S & M 60/1881
Ahmed Khan Havildar, 24th Bengal NI 736/1879
Akbar Khan 1669 Sepoy, 28th Bengal NI 252/1880
Akram 3568 Sepoy, 5th Punjab Inf,PFF 252/1880
Aktar Nowaz Khan Daffadar, Poona Horse 60/1881
Ala Sing Jemadar, 2nd Sikh Inf,PFF 639/1880
Alum Ali Shah 931 Daffadar, 19th Bengal Lcrs 563/1880
Alumshere 298 Naik, No 2 Mtn Bty,PFF 252/1880
Ameer Khan Sowar, Poona Horse 60/1881

Amir Ali Shah Rissaldar, 5th Punjab Cav,PFF 252/1880
Asa Sing Sepoy, 27th Bengal NI 230/1879

Baboo Rao Khanwalkar Sowar, Poona Horse 60/1881
Bahawaklin Khan Ressaidar, 11th Bengal Lcrs 150/1880
Baz Gul Subadar, 5th Punjab Inf,PFF 252/1880
Beer Sing 142 Sowar, 3rd Sind Horse 60/1881
Bhagwan Sing Sowar, 10th Bengal Lcrs 132/1880
Bhagwan Sing 1057 Private, 1st Bombay NI 222/1881
Bishun Sing 378 Lance-Naik, 3rd Sind Horse 60/1881
Bisram Thappa 1319 Rifleman, 2nd Gurkha Regt 639/1880
Boodh Sing Sepoy, 14th Bengal NI 164/1879
Boor Sing Jemadar, 23rd Bengal NI 1260/1879
Boota Sing Sepoy, 23rd Bengal NI 1260/1879
Bootah Sing 1255 Sowar, 1st Punjab Cav,PFF 533/1880
Brindaban Havildar-Major, 30th Bombay NI see 356/1882
Budh Sing Subadar, 5th Punjab Inf,PFF 1260/1879
Burkut Ally 1134 Daffadar, 3rd Punjab Cav,PFF 639/1880
Burma Deen 853 Sowar, 3rd Bombay Lt Cav 478/1881
Bussawa Sing 1371 Sowar, 5th Punjab Cav,PFF 252/1880

Chait Sing 1472 Daffadar, 1st Punjab Cav,PFF 533/1880
Chatar Sing 1735 Sepoy, 23rd Bengal NI 639/1880
Choonee Damai Bugler, 5th Gurkha Regt 1260/1879
Chuddo Beg Bugler, 30th Bombay NI 356/1882
Chukun Sing Store Lascar, E/4 Royal Artillery 797/1879
Chunda Sing Sepoy, 23rd Bengal NI 1260/1879
Chunder Bir 1278 Sepoy, Guides Inf,PFF 252/1880

Dan Sing Sepoy, 14th Bengal NI 164/1879
Davi Sing Havildar, 4th Sikh Inf,PFF 390/1880
Davie Sing 1802 Naik, 2nd Sikh Inf,PFF 639/1880
Deo Subadar, 27th Bengal NI 230/1879
Dewa Sing Subadar, 23rd Bengal NI 638/1880 (2nd Class)
Dewah Sing Havildar, 14th Bengal NI 164/1879
Dewan Sing Sowar, Guides Cav,PFF 533/1879
Dhowkul Sing Ressaidar, 3rd Bombay Lt Cav 59/1881 (2nd & 1st Class)
Dhurm Sing 104 Naik, 24th Bengal NI 639/1880
Dillia 1214 Sepoy, Guides Inf,PFF 252/1880
Dummer Sing 1771 Sepoy, 5th Gurkha Regt 252/1880
Dyal Sing Havildar, 27th Bengal NI 230/1879

Elahi Bux Private, 19th Bombay NI see 689/1880

Fateh Khan Recruit, 21st Bengal NI 152/1880
Fazl Khan 1807 Sowar, 1st Punjab Cav,PFF 533/1880
Futteychund QM Havildar, 30th Bombay NI see 356/1882
Fuzl 5 Driver-Naik, No 2 Mtn Bty,PFF 252/1880
Fuzl Achmud Jemadar, 29th Bengal NI 117/1880
Fyztulub Khan Subadar, 1st Punjab Inf,PFF 532/1879 (1st Class)

Ganda Sing 2 Havildar, 1st Bombay NI 222/1881
Ganesha Sing Jemadar, 3rd Sikh Inf,PFF 425/1880 (2nd Class)
Gholam Jelani 668 Daffadar, 1st Punjab Cav,PFF 533/1880
Gool Mahomed 3635 Sepoy, 1st Punjab Inf,PFF 583/1879

Goolam Mahomed   Private, 30th Bombay NI   see 356/1882
Goolshair Khan   Lance-Naik, Poona Horse   60/1881
Goordial Sing   Havildar, 23rd Bengal NI   1260/1879
Goordit Sing   Havildar, 27th Bengal NI   230/1879
Goordit Sing   Sepoy, 27th Bengal NI   230/1879
Goormukh Singh   Havildar, 29th Bengal NI   89/1879
Gopa (2nd)   Naik, Mhairwara Btn   605/1879
Gopal Borah   420 Naik, 2nd Gurkha Regt   639/1880
Gopal Sing   Jemadar, 14th Bengal Lcrs   131/1880
Gour Khan   Sepoy, 14th Bengal NI   164/1879
Gujar Sing   1534 Lance-Daffadar, 2nd Punjab Cav,PFF   336/1880
Gul Shere   2211 Sepoy, Guides Inf,PFF   252/1880
Gulab Sing   64 Havildar, 23rd Bengal NI   252/1880
Gulab Sing   1071 Sowar, 19th Bengal Lcrs   563/1880
Gunda Sing   Sepoy, 23rd Bengal NI   1260/1879
Gunda Sing   2024 Sepoy, 23rd Bengal NI   639/1880
Gunesa Sing   Jemadar, 3rd Sikh Inf,PFF   20/1880
Gurbaj Sing   Subadar-Major, 2nd Sikh Inf,PFF   639/1880
Gurdit Sing   5 Havildar, 3rd Sikh Inf,PFF   425/1880

Haidar Khan   Hospital Asst, Corps of Guides,PFF   443/1880
Hakim   Naik, 45th Bengal NI   736/1879
Hakim   2967 Sepoy, 2nd Sikh Inf,PFF   639/1880
Hamudoollah Khan   Daffadar, Poona Horse   60/1881
Harsa Sing   1756 Sowar, 5th Punjab Cav,PFF   252/1880
Hazir   1440 Naik, Guides Inf,PFF   252/1880
Hazrat Shah   Jemadar, 2nd Punjab Cav,PFF   294/1880
Heera Sing   Sepoy, 1st Punjab Inf,PFF   583/1879
Heera Sing   Havildar (now Jemadar), 30th Bombay NI   356/1882
Heerah Sing   Sepoy, 14th Bengal NI   164/1879
Heeram Singh   Sepoy, 29th Bengal NI   89/1879
Hidayutullah   1487 Sowar, 5th Punjab Cav,PFF   252/1880
Hira Sing   Sepoy, 2nd Sikh Inf,PFF   639/1880
Hookum Sing   738 Kot-Daffadar, 19th Bengal Lcrs   563/1880
Hubboob Sing   238 Kot-Daffadar, 19th Bengal Lcrs   563/1880
Hurdit Sing   197 Daffadar, 19th Bengal Lcrs   563/1880
Hurditt Sing   Sepoy, 23rd Bengal NI   1260/1879
Hurree Dewa Jaiesie   Subadar, 5th Gurkha Regt   1260/1879
Hushtbir Khuttrie   Sepoy, 5th Gurkha Regt   89/1879
Hussan Khan   Sepoy, 24th Bengal NI   271/1879
Hyder Khan   Subadar-Major, 30th Bombay NI   356/1882

Inderbeer Lama   1123 Rifleman, 2nd Gurkha Regt   639/1880
Innait Russul Khan   479 Lance-Naik, Poona Horse   58/1881
Izzat   1815 Sepoy, Guides Inf,PFF   391/1880

Jaggat Sing Rana   Havildar, 5th Gurkha Regt   89/1879
Jai Sing   2210 Sepoy, 2nd Sikh Inf,PFF   639/1880
Jaimul Sing   502 Lance Naik, 3rd Sind Horse   60/1881
Jewan Singh   Sowar, Guides Cav,PFF   533/1879
Jewund Sing   1057 Havildar, Guides Inf,PFF   252/1880
Jhandah Sing   Kot-Daffadar, 5th Punjab Cav,PFF   106/1879
Jhunda Sing   Sepoy, 23rd Bengal NI   1260/1879
Jowahir Sing   Ressaidar, 19th Bengal Lcrs   136/1881

Jowahir Sing 1588 Sowar, 1st Punjab Cav,PFF 533/1880
Jowala Sing 255 Sowar, 3rd Sind Horse 60/1881
Jowalla Sing 447 Havildar, Guides Inf,PFF 252/1880
Jugbir 366 Havildar, Guides Inf,PFF 252/1880
Juggut Singh Subadar-Major, 29th Bengal NI 89/1879
Juma Khan Subadar, 5th Punjab Inf,PFF 251/1880 (2nd Class)

Kair Sing 1091 Lance-Daffadar, 19th Bengal Lcrs 563/1880
Kait Ram 1223 Sowar, 19th Bengal Lcrs 563/1880
Kanhiya Lal Daffadar, 14th Bengal Lcrs 131/1880
Kan Jan Khan 1396 Sowar, 19th Bengal Lcrs 563/1880
Kapur Singh Sepoy, 24th Bengal NI 736/1879
Kardoo Singh Sowar, Guides Cav,PFF 533/1879
Kesar Sing 183 Daffadar, 5th Punjab Cav,PFF 252/1880
Kishenbir Nagarkoti Sepoy, 5th Gurkhas 89/1879, 1260/1879 (2nd Class) Naik 251/1880 (1st Class)
Kishen Sing Sowar, 4th Punjab Cav,PFF 366/1879
Kootub Deen 336 Havildar, No 2 Mtn Bty,PFF 252/1880
Kurm Sing Negi 593 Havildar, 5th Gurkha Regt 252/1880
Kushal Sing 915 Sowar, 19th Bengal Lcrs 563/1880

Lall Mahomed Private, 29th Bombay NI 20/1881
Lall Mir Khan 148 Private, 29th Bombay NI 426/1880
Lall Singh Sepoy, 45th Bengal NI 605/1879
Lehnu Sepoy, Guides Inf,PFF 252/1880
Lena Sing 229 Sowar, 3rd Sind Horse 60/1881
Luchman Dass Sepoy, 27th Bengal NI 230/1879

Madari Sepoy, Mhairwara Btn 605/1879
Mahomed Esack Khan Naik, Poona Horse 60/1881
Mahomed Ishak 1130 Daffadar, 19th Bengal Lcrs 563/1880
Mahomed Khan 603 Jemadar, 19th Bengal Lcrs 563/1880
Mahomed Seedick Khan 359 Lance-Naik, Poona Horse 58/1881
Mahomed Shuffi 1374 Sepoy, Guides Inf,PFF 252/1880
Mahomed Yunus 73 Daffadar, Guides Cav 391/1880
Maiah Sing 1678 Sowar, 5th Punjab Cav,PFF 252/1880
Man Sing 3483 Sepoy, 5th Punjab Inf,PFF 252/1880
Mangal Sing Trumpet-Major, 19th Bengal Lcrs 136/1881
Mansur Khan Ressaidar, 2nd Punjab Cav,PFF 336/1880
Maroof Shah 1765 Sepoy, 24th Bengal NI 639/1880
Maun Sing Havildar, 14th Bengal NI 164/1879
Mazr Ali Sowar (now Kot-Daffadar), 1st Bengal Cav 432/1887
Mehtab Sing Subadar, 23rd Bengal NI 252/1880
Mir Alam Khan Rissaldar, 1st Punjab Cav,PFF 190/1880 (2nd Class)
Mir Butt Jemadar, 1st Punjab Inf,PFF 583/1879
Moneyram Lohar 1124 Rifleman, 2nd Gurkha Regt 639/1880
Mowaz Khan 1422 Lance-Daffadar, 1st Punjab Cav,PFF 533/1880
Mukkereah Rana 1360 Rifleman, 2nd Gurkha Regt 639/1880
Mungal Joyser 584 Rifleman, 2nd Gurkha Regt 639/1880
Munraj Poon Sepoy, 5th Gurkha Regt 89/1879

Nand Singh Daffadar, Guides Cav,PFF 533/1879
Nehal Chand Hospital Asst, 3rd Sikh Inf,PFF 425/1880
Niamat 3689 Sepoy, 5th Punjab Inf,PFF 252/1880

Nowrung Sing 830 Daffadar, 19th Bengal Lcrs 563/1880
Nund Singh Sepoy, 45th Bengal NI 605/1879
Nutha Sing Havildar, 29th Bengal NI 89/1879
Nutha Sing 1444 Sowar, 5th Punjab Cav,PFF 252/1880
Nuzzur Khan Subadar, No 2 Mtn Bty,PFF 252/1880

Oomrah Havildar, Guides Inf,PFF 252/1880
Oottum Sing 1681 Sowar, 5th Punjab Cav,PFF 252/1880
Ootum Sing Naik, 23rd Bengal NI 1260/1879

Panjab Sing 232 Sepoy, 3rd Sikh Inf,PFF 425/1880
Peer Mahomed Naik, 1st Punjab Inf,PFF 583/1879
Pertab Sing 2431 Sepoy, 2nd Sikh Inf,PFF 639/1880
Prem Sing Rissaldar, Guides Cav,PFF 533/1879 (2nd Class)
Pursoo Khuttrie Havildar, 5th Gurkha Regt 89/1879
Pyabb Subadar-Major, 1st Punjab Inf,PFF 583/1879 (1st Class)

Rahim Khan 1013 Sepoy, 28th Bengal NI 252/1880
Rahim Khan Naik, 29th Bombay NI 20/1881
Ram Sing 1047 Sowar, 19th Bengal Lcrs 563/1880
Ram Sing Jemadar, 27th Bengal NI 230/1879
Rughbur Misser 813 Naik, 3rd Bombay Lt Cav 60/1881
Rugobir Nuggerkoti Subadar, 5th Gurkha Regt 89/1879

Saiad Gul 134 Havildar, 3rd Sikh Inf,PFF 425/1880
Saiad Mahomed 397 Private, No 2 Co Bombay S & M 60/1881
Salim Khan Ressaidar, 1st Punjab Cav,PFF 299/1879 (2nd Class)
Sarfaraz Khan 361 Daffadar, 3rd Sind Horse 60/1881
Shadil Khan Kot-Daffadar, 5th Punjab Cav,PFF 251/1880 (2nd Class)
Shah Alum 17 Trumpeter, 5th Punjab Cav,PFF 252/1880
Shahgood Khan 732 Havildar, 28th Bengal NI 252/1880
Shaik Abdoolla 71 Lance-Naik, No 2 Co Bombay S & M 60/1881
Shaik Amir Ali Woordie-Major, 3rd Sind Horse 59/1882
Shaik Hoossain Sowar, Poona Horse 60/1881
Shaik Jamal Ressaidar, 3rd Sind Horse 60/1881
Sham Sing 2440 Havildar, 5th Punjab Inf,PFF 252/1880
Sham Sing 52 Naik, 3rd Sikh Inf,PFF 425/1880 (2nd Class)
Sheea Sing Lance-Naik, 29th Bengal NI 33/1879
Sher Khan Recruit, 21st Bengal NI 152/1880
Shunkur Dass Hospital Asst, 5th Gurkha Regt 365/1879
Sirbuland Khan Sowar, 1st Punjab Cav,PFF 438/1881
Soobah Sing 1123 Naik, 24th Bengal NI 639/1880
Soonder Sing 266 Trumpeter, 3rd Sind Horse 60/1881
Soorbir Damai Bugler, 5th Gurkha Regt 89/1879
Sounak Tannak Private, 19th Bombay NI see 689/1880
Suddu Sing Naik, 30th Bombay NI 356/1882
Suddu Sing Bugler, 30th Bombay NI 356/1882
Surdar Sing 1185 Lance-Daffadar, 19th Bengal Lcrs 563/1880
Surwan Sing 3482 Naik, 5th Punjab Inf,PFF 252/1880
Syud Imman Ali Sowar, 3rd Sind Horse see 689/1880
Syud Noor Khan Hospital Asst, Mhairwara Btn 605/1879

Theraj Sing Sepoy, 45th Bengal NI 736/1879
Ticcaram Kwas 1138 Rifleman, 2nd Gurkha Regt 639/1880

Ummer Sing   Sepoy, 27th Bengal NI   230/1879
Umra   4084 Sepoy, 5th Punjab Inf,PFF   252/1880
Utter Sing   1126 Sowar, 19th Bengal Lcrs   563/1880
Utter Sing   Sepoy, 14th Bengal NI   164/1879
Uttur Sing   967 Havildar-Major, Guides Inf,PFF   252/1880

Wazir Sing Adkary   Naik, 5th Gurkha Regt   89/1879
Wurriam Sing   1796 Sepoy, Guides Inf,PFF   252/1880
Wuzeer Sing Nagarkoti   901 Rifleman, 2nd Gurkha Regt   639/1880

Yakub Singh   Sowar, Guides Cav,PFF   533/1879

Zeadeh Khan   Sowar, 18th Bengal Cav   133/1880
Zeeaoodeen   1863 Sowar, 5th Punjab Cav,PFF   252/1880
Zaidulla   Sowar, Guides Cav,PFF   233/1880

R e g i m e n t a l   l i s t

attchd E/4 Royal Artillery   797/1879

1st Bengal Cavalry   432/1887
10th Bengal Lancers   132/1880
11th Bengal Lancers   150/1880
14th Bengal Lancers   131/1880
18th Bengal Cavalry   133/1880
19th Bengal Lancers   563/1880, 136/1881

14th Bengal NI   164/1879
21st (Punjab) Bengal NI   152/1880
23rd (Punjab) Bengal NI   1260/1879, 252/1880, 638/1880, 639/1880
24th (Punjab) Bengal NI   271/1879, 736/1879, 639/1880
27th (Punjab) Bengal NI   230/1879
28th (Punjab) Bengal NI   33/1879, 89/1879, 117/1880
45th (Rattray's Sikhs) Bengal NI   605/1879, 736/1879

2nd Gurkha Regt   639/1880
5th Gurkha Regt   89/1879, 365/1879, 1260/1879, 252/1880, 252/1880

Punjab Frontier Force
1st Punjab Cavalry   299/1879, 190/1880, 533/1880, 438/1881
2nd Punjab Cavalry   294/1880, 356/1880
3rd Punjab Cavalry   639/1880
4th Punjab Cavalry   366/1879
5th Punjab Cavalry   106/1879, 252/1880, 252/1880
Corps of Guides   533/1879, 233/1880, 252/1880, 391/1880, 443/1880
No 2 Mountain Battery   252/1880
2nd Sikh Infantry   639/1880
3rd Sikh Infantry   20/1880, 425/1880
4th Sikh Infantry   390/188
1st Punjab Infantry   532/1879, 583/1879
5th Punjab Infantry   1260/1879, 251/1880, 252/1880

Mhairwara Btn   605/1879

3rd Bombay Light Cavalry   59/1881, 60/1881, 478/1881
Poona Horse   58/1881, 60/1881
3rd Sind Horse   689/1880, 61/1881, 59/1882
No 2 Co Bombay S & M   60/1881
1st Bombay NI   222/1881
19th Bombay NI   689/1880
29th Bombay NI   426/1880, 20/1881
30th Bombay NI   356/1882

Numerical abstract

	3rd Class	2nd Class	1st Class
attchd E/4 Royal Artillery	1		
1st Bengal Cavalry	1		
10th Bengal Lancers	1		
11th Bengal Lancers	1		
14th Bengal Lancers	2		
18th Bengal Cavalry	1		
19th Bengal Lancers	16		
14th Bengal NI	7		
21st (Punjab) Bengal NI	2		
23rd (Punjab) Bengal NI	12	1	
24th (Punjab) Bengal NI	6		
27th (Punjab) Bengal NI	8		
28th (Punjab) Bengal NI	3		
29th (Punjab) Bengal NI	6		
45th Bengal NI	4		
2nd Gurkha Regt	8		
5th Gurkha Regt	12+1*	1*	1*
1st Punjab Cavalry	8	1	
2nd Punjab Cavalry	3		
3rd Punjab Cavalry	1		
4th Punjab Cavalry	1		
5th Punjab Cavalry	11	1	
Corps of Guides	21	1	
No 2 Mountain Battery	4		
2nd Sikh Infantry	7		
3rd Sikh Infantry	5	2	
4th Sikh Infantry	1		
1st Punjab Infantry	4		2
5th Punjab Infantry	8	1	
Mhairwara Btn	3		
3rd Bombay Light Cavalry	2	1*	1*
Poona Horse	9		
3rd Sind Horse	10+1**		
No 2 Co Bombay S & M	3		
1st Bombay NI	2		
19th Bombay NI	2**		
29th Bombay NI	3		
30th Bombay NI	5+3**		

* = same man
** = next-of-kin

NOTES

NOTES

NOTES

NOTES